Thinking and Learning
through Children's Literature

Thinking and Learning through Children's Literature

Miriam G. Martinez, Junko Yokota,
and Charles Temple

ROWMAN & LITTLEFIELD
Lanham • Boulder • New York • London

Published by Rowman & Littlefield
A wholly owned subsidiary of The Rowman & Littlefield Publishing Group, Inc.
4501 Forbes Boulevard, Suite 200, Lanham, Maryland 20706
www.rowman.com

Unit A, Whitacre Mews, 26-34 Stannary Street, London SE11 4AB, United Kingdom

British Library Cataloguing in Publication Information Available

Library of Congress Cataloging-in-Publication Data Available

ISBN 978-1-4758-2150-5 (cloth : alk. paper)
ISBN 978-1-4758-2151-2 (pbk. : alk. paper)
ISBN 978-1-4758-2152-9 (electronic)

∞™ The paper used in this publication meets the minimum requirements of American National Standard for Information Sciences—Permanence of Paper for Printed Library Materials, ANSI/NISO Z39.48-1992.

Printed in the United States of America

Contents

Preface   xiii
Acknowledgments   xv

1   Children and Reading   1
    Goals of Twenty-first Century Reading   2
        Making Personal Connections to Texts 2
        Reading Deeply to Understand 2
        Reading Critically 4
        Reading to Recognize Craft and Structure 4
        Making Connections across Texts 5
    Literary Reading   6
        A Model of Literary Meaning Making 6
            Being Out and Stepping In, 7
            Being In and Moving Through, 8
            Being In and Stepping Out, 9
            Stepping Out and Objectifying the Experience, 9
            Leaving the Envisionment and Going Beyond, 10
    Research on Children's Literary Meaning Making   11
    Literary Meaning Making in Diverse Kinds of Texts   13
    Diverse Perspectives on Literary Meaning Making   13
        Developmental Perspective on Children's Literary
            Meaning Making 13
        Social Perspective on Children's Literary Meaning Making 16
            Literature Discussion, 16
            Evolution of Response, 16
        Cultural Perspective on Reader Response 17
        Textual Perspective on Children's Literary Meaning Making 21
    Recommended Books for Young Readers   22
    References   26
    Resources   28
    Want to Know More?   29

2   How Literature Works   31
    Fiction   32

How Fiction Works: Literary Elements *32*
   Setting, 32
   Plot, 33
   Character, 33
   Theme, 35
   Style, 35
Subgenres of Fiction *36*
   Traditional Literature, 36
   Contemporary Realistic Fiction, 37
   Historical Fiction, 37
   Fantasy, 40
   Science Fiction, 42
Formats of Fiction   42
  Picture Books *42*
   Development of Literary Elements in Picture Books, 43
   Peritext, 43
   Tools of the Illustrator, 44
  Chapter Books *47*
  Graphic Novels *49*
  Digital Books *49*
Nonfiction   51
  How Nonfiction Works *51*
   Structure, 52
   Style, 52
   Organizational and Support Tools, 53
   Graphic and Visual Features, 53
  Subgenres of Nonfiction 54
Poetry   54
  How Poetry Works *55*
  Categories of Poetry *55*
Conclusion   56
Recommended Books   57
  Picture Books *57*
  Chapter-length Fiction *60*
  Nonfiction *61*
  Poetry *62*
References   62
Resources   64
Want to Know More?   64

Looking Closely at a Picture Book: *Freedom in Congo Square*   67

3 Inviting Children into Literature: Classroom Libraries, Read-Alouds,
and Storytelling   79
  The Literature-rich Classroom   79

The Classroom Library *80*
   Designing the Classroom Library Center, 80
   Stocking the Classroom Library, 83
Assessing Individual Student Interests *89*
Creating a Classroom Context That Promotes Reading *90*
Author Visits *93*
Reading Aloud to Children   94
   Research on Read-aloud Programs *94*
   When to Read Aloud *95*
   Selecting Books for Read-alouds *96*
   Preparing to Read Aloud *96*
   Introducing the Story *97*
   Reading the Story *98*
   After Reading *98*
Stories and Storytelling   99
   Storytelling: The Tenacious Art *99*
   Common Story Types: Personal Tales to Tall Tales *99*
      Personal Stories, 100
      Family Stories, 100
      Friend-of-a-Friend Stories, 100
      Scary Stories, 100
      Jokes and Riddles, 100
      Folktales, 101
      Myths, 101
      Legends, 101
      Tall Tales, 101
   Learning Stories to Tell *101*
      Practicing the Story, 102
Conclusion   103
Recommended Books   104
Books for Storytelling   107
References   108
Resources   110
Want to Know More?   110

4 Let's Talk about Literature   113
Exploring Settings   113
   The Historical Setting *113*
      Questions about the Historical Setting, 114
   The Geographical Setting *114*
      Questions about the Geographical Setting, 115
   The Social Setting, Wide View *115*
      Questions about the Social Setting, Wide View, 116
   The Social Setting, Close Up *117*
      Questions about the Social Setting, Close Up, 118

Getting to Know Characters 118
  Through Their Actions *119*
    Questions about Actions, 119
  Through Their "People" and Their Relations with Others *119*
    Questions about the Character's "People", 119
  Through Their Sense of Themselves *120*
  Through the Roles They Play in the Story *121*
  As the Author Describes the Characters *123*
  Characters Who Remind Us of Other Characters *124*

Exploring Plots 124
  Teaching Story Structure *126*
  Kinds of Plots *127*
    Bildungsroman or Coming-of-Age Stories, 127
    Journey Stories, 128
    Stories within Stories, 129
    Moralistic or Didactic Tales, 129

Exploring Themes 131
  Finding a Theme in a Statement from the Work *132*
  Finding the Theme in Actions in the Work *133*
  Finding the Theme in an Image in the Work *133*
  Questions about Themes *133*
    Draw a Picture of an Important Moment, 133
    Find the Most Important Paragraph, 133
    Role Play the Author, 134

Adopting a Point of View 134
  First-person Narration *134*
  Third-person Narration *135*
  Third-person Omniscient Narration *135*
  Taking the Role of the Implied Reader *136*

Reading for the Plot 137
  The Directed Reading Activity: Story Elements *137*
  The Directed Reading-thinking Activity: Predictions *139*
  Terms in Advance: Another Way to Encourage Prediction *140*
  Close Reading *140*
    Five Close Readings, 140

Encouraging Responses to Literature 141
  Shared Inquiry Discussion *143*
  Corners *144*
  Discussion Web *145*
  Academic Controversy *145*
  Value Line *147*
  "Save the Last Word for Me" *148*

Dramatizing a Story 148
  Immerse Students in Story *149*
  Choose Critical Moments *149*

Segment the Situation *149*
Dramatize the Scene *149*
Side Coach *149*
Invite Reflection *149*
Writing in Response to Fictional Work 150
English Language Learners' Responses to Literature *151*
Dual-entry Diaries *151*
Creative Writing Prompts *152*
Writing to Dramatic Roles, 152
Exploring Poetry 153
Sharing Poetry *153*
Performing Poetry *154*
Voices in Unison, 154
Poems in Two Parts, 155
Poems in Rounds, 156
Teaching Aspects of Poetry *157*
Calling out Features of Poetry in Daily or
Weekly Readings 157
Nonfiction 159
Helping Children Negotiate Nonfiction *161*
Following the Scripts of Contemporary Nonfiction *161*
Question-and-Answer Books, 161
Other Patterns for Presenting Information, 162
Instructional Strategies for Use with Nonfiction *163*
Preparing the Text, 163
As You Read the Text Together, 163
After Reading the Book, 164
Recommended Books 165
References 169
Resources 170

5   Literary and Content Units 173
Literary Units 174
The Power of Literary Units *174*
Planning and Organizing Literary Units *175*
Developing Different Types of Literary Units *176*
Genre Units, 176
Author/Illustrator Units, 178
Units Focused on Literary Elements and Devices, 181
Units Focused on Visual Devices, 181
Thematic Units, 181
Organizing Literary Units *182*
Selecting Unit Books, 182
Unit Structure, 183
Unit Activities, 184

Literature across the Curriculum   186
    The Need for Children's Literature in the Content Areas *187*
    Literature-based Content Units *187*
    Planning and Organizing Literature-based Content Units *187*
      Determining Unit Goals, 190
      Selecting Unit Books, 191
      Unit Structure, 192
Looking Beyond   194
Recommended Books   195
References   201
Resources   203
Want to Know More?   203

Index   205
About the Authors   213

Preface

Literature can move readers in many ways. When we see our lives reflected in stories, the stories affirm who we are. Or they open our eyes to the possibilities of who we might become—or even who we do not want to become. Books reveal new worlds and ideas and can inspire us to take action. And, of course, books can simply offer good reads that make us laugh or pull us deep into worlds of mystery or suspense. Just as literature can influence our lives as adult readers, so too can it impact the lives of children.

The teacher is well placed to ensure that literature touches children's lives in these many ways. But if these possibilities are to become realities, several things must happen. First, the teacher must be a committed reader of children's literature. Given that approximately six thousand children's books are published each year, continually reading and seeking out new books to put into children's hands is a teacher's calling. Second, the teacher must understand how children's literature "works." That knowledge includes understanding different genres of literature and the devices and structures used by authors and illustrators to shape their works. Teachers must know how to create motivating classrooms that put literature front and center in children's daily experiences. Finally, teachers must have the skills and techniques to organize and guide children's experiences with books. We wrote this book to help teachers create literature-rich classrooms that set children on a pathway to become lifelong readers of literature.

Acknowledgments

With many thanks to our old friend and editor, Sue Canavan, and also with gratitude to Virginia Lanigan and Aurora Martinez for early encouragement.

With appreciation to William Teale, the Friends of the Center for Teaching through Children's Books, and the International Board on Books for Young People and International Youth Library communities for all they have taught us.

CHAPTER 1

Children and Reading

When [Joseph] and Blink were immersed in a book together . . . sometimes a strange feeling would come over them as they'd race through the pages, and the words would dissolve, and they'd find themselves deep inside Oz, or Narnia, or the Andes, or Africa, where everything was real and vivid and alive.

—*The Marvels* by Brian Selznick (2015, 405)

Teachers delight when they see their students become engrossed in books like the characters in Brian Selznick's *The Marvels*, and it isn't difficult to spot those students. They are the ones who pull out a book to read as soon as they get to school and keep the book on their desk, ready to read, once their work is done. They are the ones who seek out recommendations for new books to read and clamor to visit the library to find new books. Yet too many twenty-first century students seem resistant to the power of books. Even those who read widely sometimes read shallowly. Perhaps they choose to read only books in the same series rather than seeking out more challenging books. Still others are "wired" to a computer or tablet or smartphone, choosing such devices over books. Other students simply choose to read as little as possible.

How can this situation be turned around? How do we engage students in reading not only in the digital world, but also in reading the rich array of fiction, nonfiction, and poetry that is available (in print and digital formats) for today's children and youth? How do we guide students in making connections across the varied texts they read? How do we ensure that they read not only widely but also deeply, thinking about the ideas and issues explored in texts? And perhaps the most important question is this: how do we motivate students to *want* to read widely, thoughtfully, and critically?

In this book, we seek to address these questions. We begin in chapter 1 by considering what it means to be a reader in the twenty-first century and reviewing what research reveals about how children think about and respond to literature. Because it is important that teachers have a deep knowledge of how literature "works," chapter 2 focuses on what is distinctive about the different genres and formats of literature. This information can position teachers to better guide their students' transactions with literature and help their students also learn about the inner workings of literature. In chapter 3 we explore ways of creating literature-rich classrooms by establishing high quality library centers and by making read-alouds and storytelling integral components of the instructional program. Chapter 4 highlights a range of instructional strategies including discussion, drama, and writing that helps children to read closely and think deeply about the literature they read. Chapter 5 focuses on the organization of both literary and content units.

▪ GOALS OF TWENTY-FIRST CENTURY READING

The twenty-first century demands that readers be proficient and critical readers of texts from different genres—fiction, nonfiction, and poetry. What are our goals in preparing children to meet the reading demands of this century? We believe that children must learn to (1) make personal connections to texts; (2) read deeply to understand, (3) read critically, (4) read with an eye toward the craft and structure of texts, and (5) make connections across texts.

Making Personal Connections to Texts

When readers read literature, their personal memories, feelings, and thought associations may be evoked by the text—regardless of whether the author anticipated those reactions. When we look at readers' personal responses during an encounter with a piece of literature, we are viewing reading as a transaction. This perspective on reading is also known as *reader response theory*, a theory first articulated by Louise Rosenblatt (1938, 1978). To understand this perspective on the reading process, you might find it helpful to reflect on your own reading experiences. Think of a story that has really engaged you and try to describe what that experience was like. Perhaps you became so wrapped up in the book that you flew from page to page to discover how the twists and turns of the story would unfold, and even though it was 3:00 a.m., you simply could not stop reading. Perhaps it was a book in which a character's plight moved you to tears because it was so like situations you have faced. This kind of engagement with a text clearly signals a motivated and involved reader who is making personal connections, and it is this kind of engagement that we want to encourage in the classroom.

Reading Deeply to Understand

Although readers do connect their own experiences to texts, this is not to say that the text is unimportant. Quite the contrary! In fact, Rosenblatt describes the text as the blueprint that guides readers as they construct literary meaning, drawing on both their own experiences and the text itself.

The importance of the text is reflected in educational standards such as the Common Core State Standards (National Governors Association Center for Best Practices and Council of Chief State Officers, 2010), an initiative that details what learners should know in the English language arts by the end of each grade level in the United States. These standards call on readers from kindergarten forward to identify key ideas and details in texts and to integrate knowledge and ideas. In a work of nonfiction, this means that readers must to be able to explain main ideas and how details from the text support those ideas or interpret material conveyed visually and connect it to textual information. In fiction, this might mean that a reader is able to determine the central problem a character faces and analyze why the character responds to events in particular ways—and to support their thinking using evidence from the text. To think further about what this might mean, take a look at the following excerpt from Beatrix Potter's *The Tale of Peter Rabbit* (1902):

> Mr. McGregor was on his hands and knees planting out young cabbages, but he jumped up and ran after Peter, waving a rake and calling out "Stop thief!"
>
> Peter was most dreadfully frightened; he rushed all over the garden, for he had forgotten the way back to the gate.
>
> He lost one shoe among the cabbages, and the other amongst the potatoes. After losing them, he ran on four legs and went faster. So that I think he might have got away altogether if he had not unfortunately run into a gooseberry net and got caught by the large buttons on his jacket. It was a blue jacket with brass buttons, quite new.
>
> Peter gave himself up for lost and shed big tears; but his sobs were overheard by some friendly sparrows who flew to him in great excitement and implored him to exert himself.
>
> Mr. McGregor came up with a sieve which he intended to pop on the top of Peter, but Peter wriggled out just in time.

To demonstrate understanding of this passage, students might be expected to respond to questions like the following with evidence from the passage:

- What problem does Peter face?
- How is Peter almost caught by Mr. McGregor?
- What does the author mean when she writes "his sobs were overheard by some friendly sparrows who flew to him in great excitement and implored him to exert himself"?
- How does Peter manage to escape from Mr. McGregor?

Understanding the written text is the foundation to reading comprehension, but it is also important to recognize that writers do not include everything in texts. This statement may seem strange at first, but if every detail were included in a text, there would be more information than a reader wants or needs. So texts have "holes" or "gaps" that require readers to make inferences (Iser, 1978). Oftentimes some of the most critical information in a text must be inferred, so filling the gaps in text can involve "deep reading." This is certainly the case in Christopher Paul Curtis's *The Watsons Go to Birmingham—1963* (1995), a story about a family caught up in the horror of the Birmingham church bombing in 1963 in which four young girls were killed. The characters in the book are impacted in different ways by their experiences in Birmingham. However, the author does not explicitly tell readers how the characters have changed as a result of these events; rather they must draw on textual details to make these key inferences. One young reader did just this when she observed that Byron, the older brother in the story, "was much wiser" at the end of the story. When asked why she believed this, the reader supported her position by talking about Byron's immature high jinks in the early part of the book and the way in which, at the end of the story, he reached out to help his little brother, who had been deeply traumatized by the events in Birmingham. This reader had drawn together textual details throughout the book to come up with an insightful inference about one of the major characters in *The Watsons Go to Birmingham—1963*.

Readers of nonfiction and poetry must also engage in deep reading, making critical inferences based on supporting text information. For example, in her nonfiction work *The Lincolns: A Scrapbook Look at Abraham and Mary* (Fleming, 2008), author Candace Fleming uses a scrapbook format to explore the lives of Abraham and Mary and the complex intertwining of their lives. The author invites readers to draw their own conclusions about these two remarkable figures by synthesizing the rich assortment of facts, anecdotes, images, and quotes that fill the pages of her biography.

Perhaps poetry by its very nature is the genre most likely to demand deep thinking. Although poetry written for children varies widely, the language of poetry is concise and often relies on imagery and metaphor to convey meaning. Certainly readers of poetry make connections to their own experiences, but they must also attend closely to textual clues as they reflect on the meanings that emerge from a poem.

Reading Critically

The twenty-first century also demands that children learn to engage in critical reading. When children come together to talk about a text and share their own interpretations, supporting them with reasons, they are engaged in critical reading. Also, if they examine stories from different perspectives, they are reading and thinking critically. For example, critical readers might read a text and question a set of ideas about society—such as the roles of men and women, black and white, or rich and poor. A book like Anthony Browne's *Voices in the Park* (2001) encourages readers to do just this. In this picture book, the author presents a visit to the park from the perspectives of four characters—a prosperous and condescending woman, her timid son, an impoverished (and likely unemployed) man, and his cheerful daughter. *Voices in the Park* can launch thought-provoking discussions about issues related to social class.

Critical reading also involves questioning an author's purpose. In *Teach a Donkey to Fish* (Smith, 2009) by Scott Smith, Libby wants a new backpack, so her friend Goppy teaches her the rewards of honest work and financial independence. It so happens that Goppy is an elephant whose hat and backpack both sport American flags. Libby is a donkey that wears a peace symbol around her neck and prefers asking for handouts rather than working. Attention to text and illustration details reveals that the author is advocating a conservative political agenda.

Reading to Recognize Craft and Structure

We also want children to learn to attend to the craft and structure of texts. Attention to these facets of text can impact both the reader's comprehension and appreciation of

What Do *You* Think?
What Is the Balance between Analyzing Literature and Enjoying Literature?

In high school and college, today's students are expected to read deeply and engage in higher level thinking in response to literature. Some educators argue that if students are to successfully meet these demands, they must engage in literary analysis beginning in elementary school. This will help ensure that students not only learn to read deeply, but also meet grade level reading expectations.

Others argue that before engaging children in analysis, we must first work to ensure that they develop a love of reading. Without developing this love of reading, children will not choose to read as a way of life.

What do *you* think? How do we find a balance between helping children learn to analyze literature and helping them to develop a habit of reading for pleasure?

texts. For example, a reader who first examines the table of contents before beginning to read a new informational book may be able to gather important clues about the way in which the author has organized information about the topic. This can, in turn, provide the reader with a framework for understanding what is read. Grasping structure can also facilitate a reader's understanding of a complex work of fiction such as Pam Muñoz Ryan's *Echo* (2015) in which the author weaves together a prologue and four plot strands, one set in 1933 in Germany, the second in 1935 in Pennsylvania, the third in 1942 in Southern California, and the final one in 1951 in New York City. A reader who recognizes this structure is in a better position to consciously follow each strand and seek connections among them. Attending to craft might also involve considering how sounds and imagery are used to convey meaning or how characters change and the way such changes affect the development of events.

Attention to craft can deepen a reader's appreciation of a literary work. In *Where the Wild Things Are* (Sendak, 1963), Maurice Sendak tells the story of a child who is punished by being sent to his room. There he travels to "where the wild things are" to become the king of all Wild Things. Sendak effectively builds tension in the picture book by manipulating the size of the borders surrounding the illustrations. As tension builds, the borders become smaller and smaller until Max and the Wild Things join together in a wild rumpus, at which point all borders disappear and the illustrations completely fill the double-page spreads. Awareness of Sendak's remarkable visual crafting adds a new dimension of appreciation to the reading experience.

Echo (Scholastic)

Making Connections across Texts

Yet another important goal for the twenty-first century is helping children learn to make connections across texts when they read. Bringing knowledge of other texts to the reading of particular books and reading a story in light of other stories is called *intertextuality* (Cairney, 1992). Making these kinds of connections can enrich and deepen the reading experience. This process of using knowledge of one text to make meaning of another is something mature readers do, and children can also be encouraged to read one story in light of another. For example, teachers might engage children in reading a variety of books representing a particular genre in order to discover the distinctive features of the genre. Another way to encourage intertextuality is by introducing children to various books written by the same author.

Increasingly, children's authors write stories that "lean on" other stories and hence encourage children to make connections across texts. For example, part of the delight children find in Jon Scieszka's *The Stinky Cheese Man and Other Fairly Stupid Tales* (1992) can be explained with reference to intertextuality. The book is a collection of folktale spin-offs: the title story, "The Stinky Cheese Man," is a spin-off of "The Gingerbread Man"; "The Princess and the Bowling Ball" is a spin-off of "The Princess and the Pea"; and "Jack's Bean Problem" is clearly related to "Jack and the Beanstalk." Children who know the original tales are the ones who delight the most in Scieszka's book.

■ LITERARY READING

Making these twenty-first century goals a reality in the classroom is challenging, but we believe that teachers who understand the nature of literary reading will be in a good position to succeed. To help you develop insights into the reading process, we next explore Judith Langer's (2010) model of literary reading.

A Model of Literary Meaning Making

Judith Langer uses the term *envisionment building* to describe literary meaning making. According to Langer, envisionment is what a reader understands about a text—whether that text is a work of fiction, nonfiction, or poetry. As readers move through texts, their understanding grows and sometimes even changes dramatically. For example, one preservice teacher reported that she initially envisioned Rebecca Stead's *When You Reach Me* (2009) as a mystery set in the 1970s in New York City. Yet as she read further, she began to reenvision the book as a work of science fiction about time travel, an envisionment that she found more consistent with the textual details that emerged in the book.

According to Langer, in creating their envisionments, readers may assume any one of five different stances (or different relationships with a text) as they read:

- Being out and stepping in: readers make their initial contact with a book.
- Being in and moving through: readers build a personal envisionment.
- Being in and stepping out: readers reflect on the way(s) in which a book relates to their own life or the lives of others.
- Stepping out and objectifying the experience: readers reflect on the story as a crafted object.

- Leaving the envisionment and going beyond: readers draw on the knowledge or insights from a richly developed envisionment to use in new or unrelated situations.

Being Out and Stepping In

Readers assume the stance of being out and stepping in as they make their initial contact with a book. They may try to get information to determine the genre of the text they are about to read. This is an important first step because an understanding of genre influences the way readers approach a text (Galda and Liang, 2003). Readers often start this process before reading the first page as they read the title and look at the cover illustration. Some readers choose to read information on the dust jacket or book cover. If a reader determines that the text is a work of fiction, then perhaps she will seek further information about the book's subgenre (e.g., fantasy, historical fiction), setting, characters, and story line in order to begin building an envisionment. In picture books readers often find important story clues related to genre and literary elements on the cover, endpapers, or title page of the book.

The process continues as one begins reading the story. First chapters are often particularly rich in story clues, for this is typically where readers make their initial acquaintance of characters, are introduced to the setting, and discover other basic story information. For example, a reader picking up Louis Sachar's *Holes* (1998) might first note that the dust jacket shows a scene of what appears to be a crater-pocked surface of a distant planet. Then, in the first chapter, the reader makes a number of important discoveries: The story is set not in space, but at Camp Green Lake, a place described as a wasteland in Texas. Camp Green Lake is run not by a camp director, but by a warden, and the campers at Camp Green Lake spend their time digging holes, not playing tennis or riding horses. At this point, the reader is likely to have more questions than answers and consequently may still feel very much "outside" the story. In fact, at the beginning of chapter 2, the narrator poses the very question the reader may be asking at this point: why would anyone go to Camp Green Lake? The reader soon discovers the answer: Camp Green Lake isn't a summer camp at all. It is a juvenile detention center. And with that information revealed, the reader is likely to enter into the world of *Holes*.

Don't Miss . . .
Fiction with First Chapters That Are Rich with Story Clues

Flora and Ulysses: The Illuminated Adventures by Kate DiCamillo

The Higher Power of Lucky by Susan Patron

Splendors and Glooms by Laura Amy Schlitz

One Came Home by Amy Timberlake

Or perhaps a reader has picked up a work of nonfiction. One way in which a reader might try to step into the work is by studying the book's table of contents or flipping through to look to look at the visuals. For example, a reader of *Sugar Changed the World* (Aronson and Budhos, 2010) who attends to the subtitle of the book (*A Story of Magic, Spice, Slavery, Freedom, and Science*) is likely to anticipate that the book is going to be a historical account. This expectation might be confirmed for the reader who flips through the book and sees that it contains various early maps of different parts of the world—a map from AD 1100 and another from AD 700. Reproductions of art from earlier centuries provide more hints that Marc Aronson and Marina Budhos's book is historical in nature.

Depending upon readers' background experiences, it may be more or less difficult for them to step into particular story worlds. Deborah Ellis's *My Name Is Parvana* (2012), a story set in present-day Afghanistan, serves as a helpful example. In the initial pages of the book, readers meet a protagonist wearing a chador who refuses to speak whether spoken to in Dari, Pashtu, or Uzbek. Mainstream American children who read the book may need support and guidance in stepping into this story world. By contrast, immigrant and refugee children from Afghanistan or surrounding regions may readily connect with Ellis's story world.

Try This
Using First Chapters to Invite Readers into a Story

First chapters (and accompanying front matter such as maps and prologues) often offer readers important information about a story's setting, characters, conflict, genre, and narrative structure. Read aloud the first chapter of a book such as Karen Cushman's *The Midwife's Apprentice* and invite the children to talk about the clues the first chapter offers related to the book's genre and literary elements. Invite the students to use these clues to make predictions about the story.

Being In and Moving Through

When readers are "in and moving through" an envisionment, they become absorbed in the book, using text information and their own store of experiences and knowledge to build their envisionment. This can be a complicated process, especially in more complex works. Clare Vanderpool's Newbery Award book *Moon over Manifest* (2010) is such a book. It consists of two narrative strands—one set in 1918 and one in 1936; readers must weave together these distinct story strands. The major strand, set during the Great Depression, features young Abilene who struggles to understand why her father has sent her to live in the town of his youth while he travels the country seeking work. Only through the stories of Miss Sadie—stories featuring events from 1918—does Abilene come to understand how the events of her father's youth led him to send his beloved daughter away.

Moving through a story world (or other types of texts) also involves connecting pieces of the story—filling in the many gaps that occur naturally in texts. Perhaps poetry with its compact use of language requires even more gap filling than other genres of literature. To fill these gaps, readers must draw on textual clues as well as their personal experiences and knowledge about the world.

In fictional works, character and plot—the building blocks of narratives—are especially important elements to focus on as readers move through story worlds. Readers must be actively involved in determining the intentions of story characters and in understanding how characters shape the story line and in turn are shaped by it (Lukens, Smith, and Coffel, 2012). In recent decades, stories written for children have increasingly featured rich, complex characters (Nikolajeva, 2002), and for these stories in particular character becomes an especially crucial conduit for moving through story worlds. Understanding characters' desires, feelings, and beliefs is central to literary reading (Emery, 1996). The centrality of understanding character is apparent in reading a book such as Patricia Reilly Giff's *Pictures of Hollis Woods* (2002). Initially, readers are likely to be drawn into this book by Hollis Woods, a tough foster child who is a "mountain of trouble" for all the foster families with whom she is placed. However, readers soon discover that beneath a calloused exterior, there is a child who longs to be part of a family. Readers are likely to find themselves pulled through the pages of this book as they seek to understand the seeming contradictions of Hollis Woods's character and to find out if she will let herself be reunited with the family she loves.

Being In and Stepping Out

When readers are in an envisionment and step out, they use the text as a basis for reflecting on their own lives, on the lives of others, or even on the human experience. This happened in one classroom when students read Thanhhà Lai's *Listen, Slowly* (2015). This is the story of Mai, a young American girl of Vietnamese descent who reluctantly travels with her grandmother to Vietnam. The book sparked a discussion among the readers about their own interest in trying to connect with their cultural roots (just as the character Mai in *Listen, Slowly* eventually does). Lai's book became the impetus for these students to step out of their envisionment and reflect on their lives.

Even young children can consider how texts relate to their own lives. For example, when a teacher shares a picture book biography such as Jen Johnson's *Seeds of Change* (2010) about the environmentalist Wangari who worked to transform her native Kenya, the class might explore the environmental problems in their own community and how they might help to alleviate some of them. Books dealing with social issues may be especially likely to engender this type of discussion.

Don't Miss . . .
Picture Books That Explore Issues of Social Justice

Separate Is Never Equal: Sylvia Mendez and Her Family's Fight for Desegregation by Duncan Tonatiuh

Si, Si, Puede!/Yes, We Can! Janitor Strike in L.A. by Diana Cohn, illustrated by Francisco Delgado

Henry and the Kite Dragon by Bruce E. Hall, illustrated by William Low

My Name Is Yoon by Helen Recorvits, illustrated by Gabi Swiatkowska

The Composition by Antonio Skármata, illustrated by Alfonso Ruano

---

Stepping Out and Objectifying the Experience

Langer's next stance, stepping out and objectifying the experience, is one in which readers distance themselves from the text world and talk about the work as a crafted

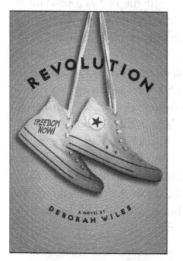

My Name Is Yoon
(Farrar, Straus, Giroux/Macmillan)

Revolution (Scholastic)

object, about other texts the book reminds them of, or about their own responses to the story. When a reader of Deborah Wiles's *Revolution* (2014) remarked on the author's use of period memorabilia throughout the book—memorabilia including song lyrics, photographs, and excerpts from newspapers—to bring to life the 1960s setting against which this story of the civil rights movement plays out, she was reflecting on author craft.

Leaving the Envisionment and Going Beyond

In Langer's final stance, leaving the envisionment and going beyond, readers draw on the knowledge or insights from a richly developed envisionment to use in new or unrelated situations. Langer explains that this stance "is generative in that we apply critical aspects of one richly developed envisionment toward the creation of a new envisionment-building experience. This happens when a composer might call upon aspects of a poem in the creation of a symphony" (2010, 21). This is just what happened in Ms. Sharp's fifth-grade class. When her students read Deborah Wiles's *Love, Ruby Lavender* (2001), they loved the humor in the book. In their literature circle discussions, they decided that exaggeration was one device Wiles used to create humor. After mining the book for examples of exaggeration, some of the students tried their own hand at humorous writing using this technique. These fifth graders were going beyond their envisionment to apply their insights into Wiles's craft to their own writing.

Technology Tip

Create a PowerPoint presentation of children responding to a story. Take digital pictures of them discussing or writing their responses. Write their responses as captions in the presentation. Group the pictures of the children's responses by Langer's stances: those that are examples of the student being out and stepping in, being in and moving through, and so on. The completed presentation can be used with children to talk about the different ways that readers think about and respond to literature, or it can be used instructionally with your peers.

▪ RESEARCH ON CHILDREN'S LITERARY MEANING MAKING

Earlier in this chapter, we discussed goals for reading in the twenty-first century and also examined what Judith Langer's envisionment building theory reveals about the complexity of the reading process. So what does this mean for those who work with children? Is it reasonable to expect that we can achieve these goals? Can children really assume all the stances identified in Langer's envisionment building theory? In light of what researchers have learned about children's literary meaning making, we believe the answer to these questions is yes. In this section, we share some of these research findings. Though much of the research has focused on children's responses to fictional works of literature, we focus on other types of texts as well.

The earliest studies of younger children's literary responses yielded a somewhat narrow view of their meaning making, suggesting that young children's text-centered responses occurred primarily at literal levels (Applebee, 1978). However, more recent research has revealed a very different view! There is ample evidence that children's engagement with text is active and dynamic. In particular, the work of Lawrence Sipe (2008) has revealed the potential complexity of children's literary meaning making. Analyzing the responses of children ages five through eight (kindergarten through second grade), Sipe found that almost 75 percent of their responses were analytical in nature. In describing these analytical responses, Sipe stated that they included responses in which the children "discussed the structure and meaning of the verbal text, the illustration sequence; the ways in which the verbal text and pictures related to each other; conventional visual semiotic codes; and the traditional elements of narrative . . . as well as narrative techniques" (2008, 85). These young children worked to understand the key elements of narratives including character and plot. They not only worked to understand external facets of character, but also the more important internal facets such as feelings, thoughts, and motivations. Sipe's subjects also assumed a structural perspective on stories as they stepped back from particular stories to talk about elements found across stories (e.g., the common use of elements occurring in "threes" in fairy tales, such as three wishes). The children's analytical responses also included thematic and quasi-thematic statements about stories.

In addition to analytical thinking, Sipe's subjects shared intertextual responses during storytime. That is, instead of talking only about the story being read, the children talked about how the target text related to other texts. Sipe argued that intertextual thinking seemed to serve the children in a variety of ways—in making predictions, interpreting character feelings and motivations, and drawing conclusions about sets of stories. Although we have highlighted Sipe's research, it is important to note that the work of many other researchers also points to the impressive literary meaning making in which children (both younger and older) engage (e.g., Galda, 1982; Hancock, 1993; Lehr, 1988; Lysaker, 2006; McGuire, Belfatti, and Ghiso, 2008; Pantaleo, 2008; Short, 1992). The impressive analytical and intertextual thinking of which children are capable suggests that we can indeed work with students to achieve rigorous goals.

Children also respond to the ways in which an author has crafted a work of literature, what Langer described as stepping out of the story to objectify the experience. This is just what Marcia, a fifth grader, did when discussing Sharon Creech's *Chasing*

Redbird (1997) with her classmates: "Sharon Creech made this book interesting because it has a lot of mysteries and you want to read more to find out." Although response to craft appears to be less frequent than other types of response, children seem especially likely to respond to the crafting of literature when teachers direct attention toward the artistry of literature (Bloem and Manna, 1999; Pantaleo, 2014; Sipe 2008). When Ms. Sharp invited her fifth graders to talk about the crafting of *Love, Ruby Lavender*, the students talked at length about techniques the author used to reveal character relationships:

> *Ms. Sharp:* Deborah Wiles didn't just say that Miss Eula and Ruby Lavender are close. What did she do instead of telling us that they are close?
> *Henry:* They are close because they do a lot of things together, risk-taking things together like when Miss Eula and Ruby kidnapped the chickens.
> *Pedro:* And when Eula said that she was going to Hawaii but she said she'd be back, Ruby started crying because Miss Eula was like her best friend. She liked to hang out with her, and they understood each other.
> *Ms. Sharp:* So she didn't have to say, "They were close." She has shown us. And she described them getting into the scrap with the chickens.
> *Pedro:* Oh, like it says they were partners.
> *Sandy:* And they write letters to each other. And Ruby said something like you're the best partner or something.
> *Ms. Sharp:* So they expressed those feelings with each other.

In describing children's literary meaning making, it is important to note that children also make personal connections to texts. That is, they build bridges between their personal experiences and the literature they read, making what Marilyn Cochran-Smith (1984) has called life-to-text connections. For example, children might talk about their own pets after listening to a story about a child and her pet. Numerous researchers described the personal associations children make when reading literature (e.g., Hickman, 1981; Short, 1992; Sipe, 1998). Children also become personally involved with story characters as they vicariously step into character roles and make judgments about how they would feel if they were in a character's situation (Hancock, 1993; Wollman-Bonilla and Werchadlo, 1995). This is, in effect, one way in which children make inferences about the characters they meet in stories.

Researchers have also found that children do what Langer termed "stepping out of stories" to reflect on how the stories relate to their own lives or the lives of others. For example, William McGinley and George Kamberelis (1996) found that third and fourth graders attempted to understand and negotiate social relationships and significant social problems through literature. The children in their investigation used literature as a lens through which they could better understand their own personal experiences and the community in which they lived. Sometimes children make these text-to-life connections long after hearing a story, as they play or work in situations that are well removed from storybook reading. In *Wally's Stories: Conversations in the Kindergarten* (Paley, 1981), author and kindergarten teacher Vivian Paley includes many examples of text-to-life connections. In one instance, a kindergartner told her about going to another child's house, only to find that the child would not let him in. A classmate proposed a literature-inspired solution: going down the chimney of the house. A second classmate suggested caution (also inspired by "The Three Little Pigs"): going down the chimney just might result in getting boiled. It is evident that the story experience does not always end for children when the reading is finished; a story can become a lens through which children attempt to understand their world.

■ LITERARY MEANING MAKING IN DIVERSE KINDS OF TEXTS

In much of the research that we have discussed, the children were responding to fiction, and perhaps this is because fiction has played such a central role in classrooms in the past. Yet in recent years this has changed. The Common Core standards, for example, call for the wide reading of nonfiction, a call echoed by many educators and scholars (e.g., Colman, 2007; Duke, 2000). Researchers have described children's meaning making in the context of nonfiction. Mary Heller (2006), observing the talk of first graders as they met in a book club to discuss informational books, found that her participants shared both aesthetic and efferent responses to these books. Many of their aesthetic responses were expressed nonverbally through body language, facial expressions, and laughter. In sharing verbal responses to the informational books, the children told personal and fictional narratives and "talk[ed] facts" (365). That is, they retold, shared intertextual connections, and posed questions. Celia Oyler and Anne Barry (1996) have also described the intertextual connections first graders make while discussing nonfiction, connections that include other books, songs, films, and television shows, as well as personal life stories.

Cathy Tower (2002) described the responses of young children to non-narrative informational picture books. As the children participated in discussions, they identified and described objects and events, connected information to their own lives, and drew conclusions based on information in the books as well as their own knowledge of the world. In particular, the children relied extensively on the illustrations in informational books as they worked together to construct meaning. Tower concluded that the children in her study "responded to the texts they heard in ways that indicate that they were attuned to particular characteristics of those texts that marked genre and purpose" (79).

■ DIVERSE PERSPECTIVES ON LITERARY MEANING MAKING

We can gain further insight into the way that children read and respond to literature by looking at their literary meaning making from four additional perspectives: developmental, social, cultural, and textual (Beach, 1993). See Table 1.1 for a definition of each perspective.

Developmental Perspective on Children's Literary Meaning Making

Educators who assume a developmental perspective realize that children in different stages of cognitive, moral, and social development think about the world in very

Table 1.1   Four Perspectives on Reader Response

Perspective	Definition
Developmental	A perspective that recognizes that children in different stages of cognitive, moral, and social development respond to literature differently
Social	A perspective that recognizes that a reader's literary transaction can be shaped by the responses of other readers
Cultural	A perspective that recognizes that readers' cultural values, attitudes, and assumptions shape their transactions with texts
Textual	A perspective that recognizes that readers' responses are influenced by their knowledge of narrative conventions, literary elements, genre conventions, and other aspects of a text

different ways, and these differences are reflected in the ways they respond to literature. Arthur Applebee (1978) and Janet Hickman (1981) conducted extensive studies of the ways in which children's thinking about literature changes across age levels. Applebee interviewed six year olds and nine year olds about stories and asked thirteen year olds and seventeen year olds to write about literature. Hickman obtained her data by spending a full semester observing and recording children's spontaneous responses to literature in three combined-grade classrooms: kindergarten/first, second/third, and fourth/fifth. Both researchers found distinctive differences in the ways children of different ages respond to literature.

Applebee found that when the six year olds in his study were invited to talk about a favorite story, they did so by retelling the plot in great detail. However, nine year olds responded to the same invitation by briefly summarizing the story. Only the thirteen and seventeen year olds in Applebee's study, with their more sophisticated cognitive abilities, analyzed the structures of stories and made generalizations about their meanings.

Hickman found that the children she observed spontaneously expressed their ideas, feelings, and understanding about stories in many different forms, not just by talking and writing. The children responded to literature through movement—by clapping, smiling, and even kissing book covers. Their literature-based artwork, writing, and dramatic presentations were also vehicles for expressing their thinking about stories. The younger children in Hickman's study were especially likely to rely on nonverbal ways of expressing their responses. Hickman found other differences in the responses of the younger (kindergarten/first graders) and older (fourth/fifth graders) children in her study. These differences are summarized in Table 1.2. However, the responses of the second and third graders were harder to characterize. Sometimes they responded much as the kindergartners and first graders did; at other times, their responses were more sophisticated, like those of the fourth and fifth graders. What set the second and third graders apart was their concern with becoming independent readers. They spent long periods of time reading and had much to say about the conventions of print.

Hickman, like Applebee, found that younger children were likely to become caught up in the action of stories. However, Hickman found that the kindergartners and first graders could also reduce stories to "lessons" when invited to interpret the meaning of a story. For example, one first grader offered the following thematic

Table 1.2   Characteristic Responses of Children in Hickman's Study

Responses of Kindergartners and First Graders	*Responses of Fourth and Fifth Graders*
Relied on their bodies to express responses as they imitated movements in stories, acted out story elements to explain them, and incorporated story elements in their dramatic play	Expressed strong feelings for and against particular selections
"Collected" story elements in pictures rather than trying to present a cohesive story line through their artwork	Demonstrated extensive knowledge of story conventions and story structure in their literature-based writing, artwork, and skits
Spent time browsing in their independent contacts with books—that is, they picked up a book, briefly flipped through its pages, and then moved on to the next book	Sustained their attention for long periods of time in their independent contacts with books
Were concerned with sorting out what was happening in stories and frequently used a retelling strategy when answering questions about stories	Had less need to focus on literal meanings in their verbal responses
Made personal statements loosely tied to the story	Often revealed connections between their own experiences and an interpreted story meaning
Expressed a concern with the reality of stories by talking about whether stories were "true" or "possible"	Relied on literary terminology in discussing the reality of stories
Could reduce stories to "lessons" when invited to interpret their meaning	Expressed understanding of stories using disembedded thematic statements
Expressed more interest in stories than in the authors of stories	Clearly recognized the role of author as the creator of a story

statement for "The Little Red Hen": "When someone already baked a cake and you haven't helped, they're probably just gonna say no." This child expressed the story's lesson in the context of the story situation. By contrast, the fourth and fifth graders in Hickman's study expressed their thematic understandings by using more abstract statements not tied directly to the content of a story.

Although the work of both Applebee and Hickman helps to explain the developmental differences in children's responses, Hickman's work, which was done in a classroom setting, also demonstrates how important it is to watch children closely if you want to understand how they interact with literature. Just asking children questions about stories doesn't give a complete picture: it might tell you about their story comprehension but not necessarily about what they are thinking, feeling, and wondering. To learn about those things, it is important to observe students throughout the day—watching their body movements; seeing how they express their ideas about stories through art, writing, and drama; and listening to their spontaneously expressed ideas during storybook reading and literature discussion.

As the research described in this section suggests, children of different ages respond to literature in different (although equally interesting) ways. Therefore it is important for teachers to become attuned to how children of different ages think about literature. Yet it is also important to realize that children of the same ages may exhibit individual styles of response (Galda, 1982; Hancock, 1993). For example, Lawrence Sipe (1998) characterized one of the first graders in his study as a child whose specialties in discussing stories were logical reasoning and close analysis. By contrast, second grader Charles typically expressed his response through performance, whereas first grader Krissy frequently invented alternatives to the plots of stories. So age alone doesn't prepare children to get the most out of books. Factors such as exposure to and experience with literature—factors that teachers can certainly influence—are equally important.

Social Perspective on Children's Literary Meaning Making

Social factors also affect children's literary meaning making, and this is particularly important to understand. The research that we discussed earlier in this chapter pointed to the potential richness of children's literary meaning making. However, we cannot simply assume that all children naturally respond in such rich and diverse ways. What happens in the classroom will likely have a significant impact on children's literary meaning making.

So what does research say about how educators can create classrooms that nurture children's thinking about literature? Just as teachers can't wait for children to become better readers or to master increasingly complex math concepts, they also shouldn't wait for children to think more deeply or critically about literature. Instead, teachers need to take the necessary steps to ensure that such growth occurs. Teachers who understand the social factors that influence children's thinking about literature are in the best position to nurture rich responses. In chapters 3, 4, and 5, we explore more fully how teachers can create classrooms that nurture children's literary meaning making.

Literature Discussion

Although the actual reading of a text is a solitary experience, "the literary transaction, the one-to-one conversation between author and the audience, is frequently surrounded by other voices" (Hepler and Hickman, 1982, 279). In the classroom, these other voices belong to the teacher and classmates. This is important because when readers come together to share their varied interpretations of a piece of literature, the "meaning potential of the text is expanded" (Peterson and Eeds, 1995, 21). Literature discussion is an especially powerful instructional vehicle for fostering children's literary thinking, and chapter 4 examines literature discussion at length, with particular emphasis on how teachers can ensure that their students have the opportunity to share their insights into literature.

Evolution of Response

Children's responses to stories can evolve over time, becoming deeper and more insightful. Reading stories repeatedly to children seems to be an effective vehicle for fostering such growth. Janet Hickman identified repeated readings of stories as one of the classroom factors that encourage rich responses. A number of investigators have looked specifically at what happens when children hear stories repeatedly.

Lesley Morrow (1988) compared the responses of young children who heard stories read repeatedly with those of other children who listened to different stories read only one time. The children who heard repeated readings of a story made more comments than did those who listened to different books, and they also shared a wider variety of responses and more complex interpretive responses. Amy McClure (1985) investigated responses to poetry in a combined fifth- and sixth-grade classroom. The teacher in this classroom frequently reread the same poems, and these rereadings enabled her students to move beyond hearing the words of the poem to reflecting more deeply on meaning.

Cultural Perspective on Reader Response

We are all cultural beings who belong to particular ethnic, class, and gender groups and, as members of these groups, share values, attitudes, assumptions, and knowledge with other group members. Patricia Enciso (1994) has observed that our cultural understandings are "everywhere and always a part of how we interpret the world and our place in it" (532). So, of course, cultural understandings shape readers' transactions with texts, either supporting or constraining them. For example, one teacher's initial response to Sherley Anne Williams's *Working Cotton* (1992) reflected her cultural perspective. In this book, Williams documents a day in the life of an African American child working in the cotton fields alongside her family, who are migrant workers. Upon first reading this Caldecott honor book, the teacher observed how impressed she was by the beauty of the illustrations and the straightforward manner in which the story is narrated; nonetheless, she put the book aside, finding this story about a child working in the fields from sunup to sundown too painful to share with children. Her first response was constrained by her own cultural experiences. Only later when she realized that *Working Cotton* is a book with which migrant students might connect did it come down off her shelf. Others whose background knowledge sensitizes their viewing of the illustrations even more deeply find the artwork almost too beautiful—that the images don't convey strongly enough the hardships endured by those who labor in the fields picking cotton.

We are increasingly aware of the likely impact of culture on children's responses to literature. For example, we know that middle-grade readers respond more positively and fully to literature that reflects their own cultural experiences (Brooks, 2006; Hicks, 2004; Sims, 1983). Elizabeth Smith (1995) found that fifth-grade African American students in her class who were reluctant readers avidly sought out books about African Americans and responded to these books differently than they did to other books. Carmen Martínez-Roldán and Julia López-Robertson (2000) found that bilingual first-grade students reached new understandings of text, self, and others when they saw their lives and language reflected in picture books.

Such research underscores the importance of bringing into the classroom literature that authentically represents students' cultures; moreover, books that authentically represent the cultures of others also have a place in classrooms. Rudine Sims Bishop (1990) has written about literature serving as "mirrors," "windows," and "sliding glass doors." When readers see reflections of their world in a book, the book serves as a mirror, and readers more readily connect to books that function as mirrors. Books serve as windows when children see people and places that may be different from their own world, and these books may become sliding glass doors when readers "walk through [them] in imagination to become part of whatever world has been created or re-created by the author" (Sims Bishop, 1990, x). Finding the right books that serve these different functions for your students may require an investment of time and energy, but the effort is worth making.

Carmen Martinez-Roldán (2003) investigated children's literary meaning making in a bilingual second-grade classroom and found that opportunities to share personal stories in literature circles were especially important, enabling children to draw on their "funds of knowledge" (or cultural experiences and knowledge) in responding to literature. In addition, coming together to talk about literature allows people with different perspectives to exchange ideas and step into the shoes of others. For example, Christina DeNicolo and Maria Franquiz (2006) found that when children in a bilingual fourth-grade classroom met in literature circles, they considered multiple perspectives and thought critically about issues of racism revealed through multicultural children's literature. In effect, participants in literature discussion can share cultural insights that will make the literary experience a richer one for everyone.

What Does the Expert Say?
Diversity in Children's Literature

Kwame Alexander
Author and winner of the Newbery Award for *The Crossover*

I believe that diversity is more than lip service. If teachers and librarians are interested in helping their students imagine a better world, then the books on the shelves need to reflect that kind of world. And we're not talking about going through a catalog and saying, "Oh, there's a black face on *that* cover"; you know, "There's a kid of color on *this* cover." My child is eight years old, and when her librarian recommends a book, I need her to recommend a book far beyond the surface. It needs to be more than symbolic; it needs to be substantive. We live in a diverse world, so the books need to reflect that.

If you want a kid to engage with a form of literature, then they need to see *you* engage with it. They have to see you excited about reading a poem by Naomi Shihab Nye. They need to see you engage with reading *Brown Girl Dreaming*. They need to see you excited about reading a Jason Reynolds novel. They do what we do and that's been one of the exciting things around *The Crossover*. A big part of its success had to do with librarians reading the book and then putting the book in kids' hands and saying, "You gotta read this," and they were reading it with the kids. They were getting excited; they were sort of bonding. They were having that "Sunday dinner" familial type of connection that we have as families.

We used to have dinner at my grandmother's house—it was about the food but it was also about the conversation and discussion and what it means to be a community. So you have these teachers around the country who were creating these communities in their classrooms, with kids in general and with boys in particular who weren't necessarily reading, [and] they were all reading this story that on the surface was about basketball but was really about family and friendship and love and all the things that I posit that kids—boys—really do care about, but we just haven't learned how to connect them and reach them. We've gotta read the literature, we've got to read all kinds of literature.

So people are reading the books, they're recommending them, and they're having family conversations. What if those conversations continually focus on what you said, that "it's for all of us, that which is the familiar, that which is the common interest." Is that enough?

(continues)

What Does the Expert Say? (cont.)

That's a good question. I think it's enough for the kids. It may not be enough for us, but the kids are often a lot more culturally, racially evolved than we are. As adults we've got our baggage and our perceptions and our misconceptions, and we want to bring that to the table and unfortunately sometimes that sort of taints, it sort of confuses, and kids are a lot more evolved than we are. A teacher asked me, "What color are the boys in your novel *The Crossover*," and I asked, "Why does it matter?" She said, "My sixth graders are going to want to know," and I said, "No, they're not. They're not going to ask." She said, "No, they're going to want to know." I said, "If they ask you what color they are, let me know." And she said, "You were right." Ultimately what we realize is that regardless of whether you are black or white, you laugh, you breathe, you dance, you smile, you cry, you feel, you think—you do those things and if we are in the business of trying to deny the humanity of all children, if we are trying to make this kid other and this kid the default, then that's problematic, and I think segregating the literature is not a good thing. Obviously there is value in books that are mirrors. I grew up reading *Stevie* and *Uptown* by John Steptoe. I grew up reading *And the Sun God Said: That's Hip*. In order to form your identity, in order to know who you are, you need to read books that reflect the culture and community that you come from. You also have a responsibility, if you are interested in becoming more human, to read books that are windows. To read books that are doors allow you to see another part of you. We are all connected, and if we can understand how other people move through the world, we become more empathetic, more connected, more human.

I'm not saying they don't need to know about the race. I'm saying it's a matter of fact. As adults we want to say, "he's a black writer" or "that's a white writer"; "oh this is an Asian writer." I'm saying that it is a matter of fact that I'm a black man and that's it. Let's not let that mean something other than I'm black. We try to make it mean more than it needs to mean. It is because of the construct of race. It's about how we view race in America. Race means we are separate. I posit that—and this may sound really cliché—but I posit that kids already understand that we are all one human race. It sounds kind of corny, I know. But if we are ever going to get to a point where we actually believe that, we have to start trying to convince ourselves to think that way, even if we may not believe it yet. Because eventually our hearts will catch up to us and our hearts will realize that. So it's not that the kids don't need to know. They know. It doesn't matter inasmuch as it is a matter of fact. It matters when we begin to label and separate and segregate based on that fact.

Kwame Alexander

Reaching *All* Students

Children respond most deeply to literature that offers them the opportunity to draw on their funds of knowledge (i.e., to connect with personal experiences). To ensure that this can happen, teachers must carefully select books for read-alouds that reflect their students' experiences. If you work with young Mexican American children, a book such as Yuyi Morales's *Niño Wrestles the World* might be such a book. *Niño Wrestles the World* features a young boy pretending to be a *luchador* (or a world-champion wrestling competitor) who confronts fearful competitors including Cabeza Olmeca (Olmec head) and La Momia (The Mummy) of Guanajuato. The secret to selecting appropriate books for your classroom is getting to know your students and the cultures from which they come.

Technology Tip

Though not all children have the opportunity to meet the creators of books face-to-face, the Internet provides access to many authors and illustrators of children's books. For example, visit TeachingBooks.net (www.teachingbooks.net) and listen to the author interview with Francisco Jimenez, who talks about the importance of readers seeing their own worlds reflected in books.

Although cultural differences often have a positive effect when students are encouraged to help their classmates interpret a book by sharing their related cultural experiences, it is also important to be aware that children's conversations about a book are sometimes constrained by their cultural perspectives (Dressel, 2005). Teachers should try to anticipate cultural roadblocks that may arise and put a damper on literature discussion, so that they can attempt to help students maneuver around those roadblocks. Constructivist theory maintains that an individual's interpretation of an event, influenced as it is by his or her unique culture-based experience, is the event. In light of this theory, it is important for teachers to encourage students to come together in literature study as diverse members of society and to consider actively the issues and experiences found in literature. The very act of considering literature will reveal how differently students think about things and will provide opportunities for understanding others' points of view.

Like students, teachers also bring cultural perspectives to texts. These perspectives can have an effect on the kinds of literature a teacher selects. More important, the way the teacher responds to and perceives the literature influences how she or he guides the literature discussion. Teachers need to monitor their own culturally based responses to texts to ensure that they do not constrain students' responses. Ladson-Billings (2003) found that even teachers who were being inclusive of multicultural literature through class readings were not always aware that the kinds of questions they asked their students to consider avoided issues of race relations, focusing instead on literary ideas more holistically. Yet critical race theory incites the need for recognizing power relations among races, and teachers who are effective in scaffolding literary discussion in line with such thinking can offer inclusive and even corrective impressions of culture (Yokota, 2013/2014).

Textual Perspective on Children's Literary Meaning Making

Reading is often described as a reader/text transaction in which the reader brings to bear on the text his or her experience, knowledge, beliefs, and feelings. Knowledge about how texts "work" is one type of knowledge that readers bring to the transaction, and textual theorists place special emphasis on it. The more experience readers (or listeners) have had with literature, the greater their store of knowledge about how literature works. This store may include knowledge of genre conventions, literary elements, literary language, and visual elements and design—the kind of information that we explore in chapter 2.

There is evidence that children respond differently to different genres of literature (Elster and Hanauer, 2002; Shine and Roser, 1999). Even very young children who have been read to have begun to build a store of literary knowledge, as evidenced by their use of "once upon a time" to begin their own stories or by the concern they express when a wolf enters the scene as they are listening to a story—they know full well that this stock character is not to be trusted. You can sometimes even anticipate how textual knowledge is likely to influence children's transactions with particular books. Children's delight in Jon Scieszka's *The Stinky Cheese Man and Other Fairly Stupid Tales* can be understood (at least in part) in light of a textual perspective on literary meaning making. Scieszka's wonderfully mixed-up fantasy violates every imaginable book convention. The book begins with text, which is then followed by the title page. Readers are invited to put their own name into the dedication (which happens to be written upside down). The table of contents is shown falling onto the characters in "Chicken Licken." One of the characters (the Little Red Hen) insists on narrating her story at the most inopportune times. Children love this story—if they have acquired an understanding of how stories work.

There are a number of ways in which teachers can help students build a rich foundation of textual knowledge. Immersion appears to be an important means of building this type of knowledge. In discussing how children acquire genre knowledge, Lucy Calkins (1994) argues that such knowledge is acquired when children inhabit a given literary genre. Immersion is especially powerful when accompanied by opportunities to reflect on a targeted textual feature (e.g., how authors develop character, how illustrators use color in developing a story). Instruction can also help students acquire insights into how texts work, especially when that instruction moves beyond the surface identification of text features. For example, in the following exchange, Ms. Gomez guided the second and third graders in her class to analyze the setting in a variety of familiar texts in order to better understand how this literary element functions in the fantasy genre.

> *Ms. Gomez:* Today we're going to talk about setting in relation to fantasy. Who can tell me what the setting is? We've talked about that in our class before and we've looked at it in other stories.
>
> *Greg:* Usually it's a place.
>
> *Ms. Gomez:* A place. And so, can we add anything else to that?
>
> *Mary:* It's where the book takes place. Like in *The Lion, the Witch, and the Wardrobe,* it takes place in Narnia. But like in the beginning, it's [*another student says "Earth"*] yeah, Earth.

Ms. Gomez: Okay, so *The Lion, the Witch, and the Wardrobe* might be one of those special cases where there's two settings. Do you remember *Thunder Cake*? When we read Patricia Polacco's *Thunder Cake*? Do you remember what the setting was in this story? Where did most of this story take place? I'll give you a few little reminders with some of the illustrations.

Terry: Just at the babushka's farm.

Ms. Gomez: Yes, the babushka's farm. So, this story took place at the farm. One place, one time, it all happened in one day. What about this story that you read last week [*holding up a copy of* Zathura]? What do you think about the setting in *Zathura*?

Sarah: In the beginning, it's like on the ground, on Earth. And then in the middle it turns and they go into space.

Ms. Gomez: Do you know, what Sarah just said makes me think about what Mary was saying with *The Lion, the Witch, and the Wardrobe*.

Guided discussions of this type in which children are invited to share their discoveries about particular features of books are likely to help young readers build a solid foundation of textual knowledge. In chapters 4 and 5, we explore strategies that teachers can use to help children acquire understandings about how texts work.

Try This
Inviting Children to Explore Color Shifts in Picture Books

Because illustrations and words work together to tell stories in picture books, it is important for children to attend closely to illustrations. Color is a particularly potent tool that illustrators use to develop stories, and illustrators sometimes use shifts in color to reveal character emotion. To help children explore how shifts in color can help them better understand the characters they meet in picture books, read aloud books such as *When Sophie Gets Angry—Really Really Angry . . .*, *A Ball for Daisy*, *Click Clack Moo*, and *Llama Llama Red Pajama*. Invite the children to talk about the color shifts they see in the books and what those shifts tell them about the characters.

In this chapter, we put forth goals—challenging goals—for reading in the twenty-first century. Research on children's literary meaning making suggests that these goals can be realized when teachers create classroom contexts that both motivate and challenge children. To do this, teachers must have a deep understanding of how literary texts work, how to create motivating classroom contexts, and how to organize and guide children's experiences with literary texts. These are the topics that we explore in subsequent chapters.

▪ RECOMMENDED BOOKS FOR YOUNG READERS

Aronson, Marc, and Marina Budhos. *Sugar Changed the World: A Story of Magic, Spice, Slavery, Freedom, and Science.* New York: Clarion, 2010. A historical exploration of how sugar and the sugar trade has impacted the world. Ages ten and older.

When Sophie Gets Angry—
Really, Really Angry . . . by Molly Bang.
Scholastic Inc./Blue Sky Press.
Reproduced by Permission.

Bang, M. *When Sophie Gets Angry—Really Really Angry . . .* New York: Blue Sky Press/Scholastic, 1999. Sophie becomes furious when her sister grabs her toy, but a walk in nature gives Sophie the opportunity to get her emotions under control. Picture book. Ages five through eight.

Becker, Aaron. *Journey.* Somerville, MA: Candlewick Press, 2013. In this wordless book, a bored child draws her way into a fantastic world where she is immersed in adventure and danger. Picture book. Ages six through ten.

Browne, Anthony. *Voices in the Park.* London: DK Children, 2001. The story of a visit to the park is told from four different perspectives. Picture book. Ages 6 and older.

Cohn, Diana. *Si, Si, Puede!/Yes, We Can! Janitor Strike in L.A.* Illustrated by Francisco Delgado. El Paso, TX: Cinco Puntos, 2005. In this fictional story set against the backdrop of the 2000 Los Angeles janitors' strike, Carlos rallies his classmates to show their support by joining the strikers. Picture book. Ages seven through eleven

Creech, Sharon. *Chasing Redbird.* New York: Joanna Cotler/HarperCollins, 1997. A young girl is determined to prove herself by clearing the long-lost trail that she discovers. Ages ten through twelve.

Cronin, Doreen. *Click, Clack, Moo: Cows That Type.* Illustrated by Betsy Lewin. New York: Simon & Schuster Books for Young Readers, 2000. When Farmer Brown refuses to bow to the demands of his cows, the animals decide to take action. Picture book. Ages six through nine.

Curtis, Christopher Paul. *The Watsons Go to Birmingham—1963.* New York: Delacorte, 1995. An African American family from Detroit visits in Birmingham in 1963, the summer of the fateful church bombing that set the civil rights movement into high gear. Ages ten through twelve.

Cushman, Karen. *The Midwife's Apprentice.* New York: Clarion, 1995. A homeless waif in medieval England is given the opportunity to become a midwife's apprentice. Ages ten through twelve.

Dewdney, Anna. *Llama Llama Red Pajama.* New York: Viking, 2005. When left alone in the dark, baby llama becomes increasingly afraid. Picture book. Ages five through seven.

DiCamillo, Kate. *Flora and Ulysses: The Illuminated Adventures.* Somerville, MA: Candlewick Press, 2013. Flora sets out to save the life of Ulysses, a squirrel with superhero powers, while simultaneously dealing with her relationship with her divorced parents. Ages nine through eleven.

Ellis, Deborah. *My Name Is Parvana.* Toronto: Groundwood Books, 2012. In this sequel to *Breadwinner,* Parvana remembers the past four years of her life after being reunited with her mother and sisters in war-torn Afghanistan. Ages ten through twelve.

Fleming, Candace. *The Lincolns: A Scrapbook Look at Abraham and Mary.* New York: Schwartz and Wade/Random House, 2008. Using a scrapbook format, Fleming explores the lives of Abraham and Mary and the complex intertwining of their lives. Ages ten through twelve.

———. *Oh, No!* Illustrated by Eric Rohmann. New York: Schwartz and Wade/Random House, 2012. Stalked by a tiger, a series of jungle animals fall into a deep, deep hole. Picture book. Ages five through eight.

Giff, Patricia Reilly. *Pictures of Hollis Woods.* New York: Random House, 2002. Hollis Woods longs to belong to a family, but every foster family seems to view her as a "mountain of trouble." Ages ten through twelve.

Hall, Bruce E. *Henry and the Kite Dragon.* Illustrated by William Low. New York: Philomel, 2004. When the Italian kids begin to destroy the beautiful kites made by Grandfather Chin, Henry Chu is ready to confront his nemeses. But when Henry and his pals talk to the Italian kids, they discover that compromise offers a solution to the problem. Picture book. Ages six through ten.

Johnson, Jen Cullerton. *Seeds of Change.* Illustrated by Sonia Lynn Sadler. New York: Lee & Low, 2010. A biography of the Kenyan environmentalist, Wangari. Picture book. Ages five through ten.

Lai, Thanhhà. *Listen, Slowly.* New York: Harper, 2015. Mai wants to spend her summer at home in Southern California—not in Vietnam, where she is expected to help her grandmother discover what happened to her husband during the Vietnam War. Ages ten through twelve.

Lewis, C. S. *The Lion, the Witch, and the Wardrobe.* New York: Macmillan, 1950. Four children enter a magical realm where they are caught up in a struggle between the forces of good and evil. Ages nine through twelve.

Morales, Yuyi. *Niño Wrestles the World.* New York: Roaring Brook Press, 2013. A young luchador (wrestler) confronts fearsome competitors including Cabeza Olmeca (Olmec head) and La Momia (The Mummy) of Guanajuato. Picture book. Ages five through eight.

Patron, Susan. *The Higher Power of Lucky.* New York: Simon & Schuster/Richard Jackson, 2006. Fearing that her guardian will abandon her, Lucky goes in search of a "higher power" in hopes of finding security and family stability. Ages ten through twelve.

Polacco, Patricia. *Thunder Cake.* New York: Philomel, 1993. A grandmother helps her granddaughter overcome her fear of thunder. Picture book. Ages five through nine.

Potter, Beatrix. *The Tale of Peter Rabbit.* London: Frederick Warne, 1902. Retrieved from www.gutenberg.org/ebooks/14838. When he disobeys his mother and visits Farmer McGregor's garden, a naughty rabbit finds himself in great danger. Picture book. Ages five through nine.

Raschka, C. *A Ball for Daisy.* New York: Random House, 2011. Daisy the dog becomes desolate when her favorite ball is destroyed. Picture book. Ages five through seven.

Recorvits, Helen. *My Name Is Yoon.* Illustrated by Gabi Swiatkowska. New York: Farrar, Straus, Giroux, 2003. Yoon is bewildered by her new life in America, and most bewildering of all is her father's expectation that she will write her name in English rather than Korean. Picture book. Ages six through ten.

Ryan, Pam Muñoz. *Echo.* New York: Scholastic, 2015. Deep in a forbidden forest, a young boy encounters three sisters imprisoned by a witch's curse. He promises to carry their spirits from the forest via a harmonica that in turn becomes the thread connecting the stories of three young people living in particularly dark eras of history—the rise of Nazi Germany, the Great Depression, and World War II. Ages eleven and twelve.

Sachar, Louis. *Holes.* New York: Farrar, 1998. When Stanley Yelnats is sent to a juvenile detention center for a crime he didn't commit, he is sure it is just another instance of the family curse, but his stay at Camp Green Lake presents him with the opportunity to finally break that curse. Ages ten and older.

Schlitz, Laura Amy. *Splendors and Glooms.* Somerville, MA: Candlewick Press, 2012. In Victorian London, the lives of two orphaned puppeteers, their evil master, and a powerful witch consumed by greed and regret become intertwined with the life of Clara, the child of a wealthy family.

Scieszka, Jon. *The Stinky Cheese Man and Other Fairly Stupid Tales.* Illustrated by Lane Smith. New York: Viking, 1992. A clever format is used in presenting humorous spin-offs of familiar European folktales and fairy tales. Picture book. Ages six and older.

Selznick, Brian. *The Marvels.* New York: Scholastic, 2015. Told through a creative blend of words and illustrations, Selznick's book is about a boy seeking family and about the creation of story.

Sendak, Maurice. *Where the Wild Things Are.* New York: Harper & Row, 1963. When he is punished and sent to bed without supper, Max sails off to an imaginary world where he is the king of the Wild Things. Picture book. Ages five through eight.

Skármata, Antonio. *The Composition.* Illustrated by Alfonso Ruano. Toronto: Groundwood, 1998. Living in harsh dictatorship, Pedro is faced with a dilemma when a soldier comes to school offering a possible reward to children who write truthfully about what their parents do in the evenings. Picture book. Ages eight through twelve.

Stead, Rebecca. *When You Reach Me.* New York: Wendy Lamb Books/Random House, 2009. Miranda's life in New York City takes a mysterious turn when she receives a series of notes from someone who appears to be from the future. Ages ten through twelve.

Timberlake, Amy. *One Came Home.* New York: Alfred A. Knopf/Random House Children's Books, 2013. Unconvinced that her sister is dead, Georgie sets out to solve the mystery of her sister's disappearance. Ages ten through twelve.

Tonatiuh, Duncan. *Separate Is Never Equal: Sylvia Mendez and Her Family's Fight for Desegregation.* New York, Abrams Books, 2014. This is the story of the Mendez family's fight to desegregate California schools, paving the way for the *Brown vs. Board of Education* ruling seven years later. Picture book. Ages eight through twelve.

Van Allsburg, Chris. *Zathura.* Boston: Houghton Mifflin, 2002. A game board becomes a portal to an outer space adventure. Picture book. Ages five through nine.

Vanderpool, Clare. *Moon over Manifest.* New York: Delacorte, 2010. Only as she gradually learns of events from 1917 to 1918 does Abilene come to understand why her father has sent her to live in the town of his youth while he travels the country seeking work during the Great Depression. Ages ten through twelve.

Wiles, Deborah. *Love, Ruby Lavender.* New York: Harcourt, 2001. When her beloved grandmother decides to spend the summer in Hawaii, Ruby Lavender is sure that she will be unable to cope with the obstacles she faces in her small Mississippi town. Ages nine through twelve.

———. *Revolution.* New York: Scholastic Press, 2014. Amid her personal struggle to come to terms with being part of a blended family, twelve-year-old Sunny is caught up in the tumultuous events of Freedom Summer in her hometown of Greenwood, Mississippi. Ages ten through twelve.

Williams, Sherley Anne. *Working Cotton.* Illustrated by Carole Byard. San Diego: Harcourt, 1992. A young girl describes a day spent in the fields with her migrant worker family. Picture book. Ages five through eight.

Woodson, Jacqueline. *Brown Girl Dreaming.* New York: Nancy Paulsen Books/Penguin, 2014. In her memoir, Woodson recounts her experiences growing up in both South Carolina and Brooklyn, New York, during the 1960s and 1970s. Ages eleven and twelve.

■ REFERENCES

Applebee, Arthur. *The Child's Concept of Story*. Chicago: University of Chicago Press, 1978.

Beach, Richard. *A Teacher's Introduction to Reader-response Theories*. Urbana, IL: National Council of Teachers of English, 1993.

Bloem, Patricia L., and Anthony L. Manna. "A Chorus of Questions: Readers Respond to Patricia Polacco." *The Reading Teacher* 52 (1999): 802–8.

Brooks, Wanda. "Reading Representations of Themselves: Urban Youth Use Culture and African American Textual Features to Develop Literary Understandings." *Reading Research Quarterly* 41 (2006): 372–92.

Cairney, Trevor H. "Fostering and Building Students' Intertextual Histories." *Language Arts* 69 (1992): 502–7.

Calkins, Lucy. *The Art of Teaching Writing*. Portsmouth, NH: Heinemann, 1994.

Cochran-Smith, Marilyn. *The Making of a Reader*. Westport, CT: Ablex, 1984.

Colman, Penny. "A New Way to Look at Literature: A Visual Model for Analyzing Fiction and Nonfiction." *Language Arts* 84 (2007): 257–68.

DeNicolo, Christina P., and Maria E. Franquiz. "'Do I Have to Say It?' Critical Encounters with Multicultural Children's Literature." *Language Arts* 84 (2006): 157–70.

Dressel, Janice H. "Personal Response and Social Responsibility: Responses of Middle School Students to Multicultural Literature." *The Reading Teacher* 58 (2005): 750–64.

Duke, Nell K. "3.6 Minutes Per Day: The Scarcity of Informational Texts in First Grade." *Reading Research Quarterly* 35 (2000): 202–24.

Elster, Charles A., and David I. Hanauer. "Voicing Texts, Voices around Texts: Reading Poems in Elementary School Classrooms." *Research in the Teaching of English* 37 (2002): 89–134.

Emery, Donna W. "Helping Readers Comprehend Stories from the Characters' Perspectives." *The Reading Teacher* 49 (1996): 534–41.

Enciso, Patricia E. "Cultural Identity and Response to Literature: Running Lessons from *Maniac Magee*." *Language Arts* 71 (1994): 524–33.

Galda, Lee. "Assuming the Spectator Stance: An Examination of the Responses of Three Young Readers." *Research in the Teaching of English* 16 (1982): 1–20.

Galda, Lee, and Lauren Aimonette Liang (2003). "Literature As Experience or Looking for Facts: Stance in the Classroom." *Reading Research Quarterly* 38 (2003): 268–75.

Hancock, Marjorie R. "Exploring the Meaning-making Process through the Content of Literature Response Journals: A Case Study Investigation." *Research in the Teaching of English* 27 (1993): 335–68.

Heller, Mary F. "Telling Stories and Talking Facts: First Graders' Engagements in a Nonfiction Book Club." *The Reading Teacher* 60 (2006): 358–69.

Hepler, Susan, and Janet Hickman. "'The Book Was Okay. I Love You'—Social Aspects of Response to Literature." *Theory into Practice* 21 (1982): 278–83.

Hickman, Janet. "A New Perspective on Response to Literature: Research in an Elementary School Setting." *Research in the Teaching of English* 15 (1981): 343–54.

Hicks, Deborah. "Back to Oz? Rethinking the Literary in a Critical Study of Reading." *Research in the Teaching of English* 39 (2004): 63–84.

Iser, Wolfgang. *The Act of Reading: A Theory of Aesthetic Response*. Baltimore: John Hopkins University Press, 1978.

Ladson-Billings, G. J. "Still Playing in the Dark: Whiteness in the Literary Imagination of Children's and Young Adult Literature." Paper presented at the 93rd annual National Council of Teachers of English Convention, Detroit, MI, November 2003.

Langer, Judith. *Envisioning Literature: Literary Understanding and Literature Instruction.* New York: Teachers College Press, 2010.

Lehr, Susan. "The Child's Developing Sense of Theme As a Response to Literature." *Reading Research Quarterly* 23 (1988): 337–57.

Lukens, Rebecca. J., Jacqueline E. Smith, and Cynthia M. Coffel. *A Critical Handbook of Children's Literature.* 9th ed. New York: Pearson, 2012.

Lysaker, Judith T. "Young Children's Readings of Wordless Picture Books: What's 'Self' Got to Do with It?" *Journal of Early Childhood Literacy* 6 (2006): 33–55.

Martínez-Roldán, Carmen. "Building Worlds and Identities: A Case Study of the Role of Narratives in Bilingual Literature Discussion." *Research in the Teaching of English* 37 (2003): 494–526.

Martínez-Roldán, Carmen M., and Julia López-Robertson. "Initiating Literature Circles in a First-grade Bilingual Classroom." *The Reading Teacher* 53 (2000): 270–81.

McClure, Amy A. "Children's Responses to Poetry in a Supportive Context." PhD diss., Ohio State University, 1985.

McGinley, William, and George Kamberelis. "*Maniac Magee* and *Ragtime Tumpie*: Children Negotiating Self and World through Reading and Writing." *Research in the Teaching of English* 30 (1996): 75–113.

McGuire, Caroline, Monica Belfatti, and Maria Ghiso. "'It Doesn't Say How?' Third Graders' Collaborative Sense-making from Postmodern Picturebooks." In *Postmodern Picturebooks: Play, Parody, and Self-referentiality*, ed. Lawrence Sipe and Sylvia Pantaleo, 193–206. New York: Routledge, 2008.

Morrow, Lesley M. "Young Children's Responses to One-to-One Story Readings in School Settings." *Reading Research Quarterly* 23 (1988): 89–107.

National Governors Association Center for Best Practices and Council of Chief State Officers. *Common Core State Standards for English Language Arts and Literacy in History/Social Studies, Science, and Technical Subjects.* Washington, DC: National Governors Association Center for Best Practices and Council of Chief State Officers, 2010.

Nikolajeva, Maria. *The Rhetoric of Character in Children's Literature.* Lanham: Scarecrow Press, 2002.

Oyler, Celia, and Anne Barry. "Intertextual Connections in Read-alouds of Information Books." *Language Arts* 73 (1996): 324–29.

Paley, Vivian. *Wally's Stories: Conversations in the Kindergarten.* Cambridge, MA: Harvard University Press, 1981.

Pantaleo, Sylvia. "Exploring the Artwork in Picturebooks with Middle Years Students." *Journal of Children's Literature* 1 (2014): 15–26.

———. *Exploring Student Response to Contemporary Picturebooks.* Toronto: University of Toronto Press, 2008.

Peterson, Ralph, and Maryann E., eds. "More Compelling Questions in Reading Education." *Reading Today* (June/July 1995): 21.

Rosenblatt, Louise M. *Literature As Exploration.* 4th ed. New York: Modern Language Association, 1938.

———. *The Reader, the Text, the Poem: The Transactional Theory of the Literary Work.* Carbondale: Southern Illinois University Press, 1978.

Shine, Stephanie, and Nancy Roser. "The Role of Genre in Preschoolers' Response to Picture Books." *Research in the Teaching of English* 34 (1999): 197–254.

Short, Kathy G. "Intertextuality: Searching for Patterns That Connect." In *Literacy Research, Theory, and Practice: Views from Many Perspectives: Forty-first Yearbook of the National Reading Conference*, ed. Charles K. Kinzer and Donald J. Leu, 187–97. Oak Creek, WI: National Reading Conference, 1992.

Sims, Rudine. "Strong Black Girls: A Ten-year-old Responds to Fiction about Afro-Americans." *Journal of Research and Development in Education* 16 (1983): 21–28.

Sims Bishop, Rudine. "Mirrors, Windows, and Sliding Glass Doors." *Perspectives: Choosing and Using Books for the Classroom* 6 (1990): ix–xi.

Sipe, Lawrence R. "Individual Literary Response Styles of First and Second Graders." In *Forty-seventh Yearbook of the National Reading Conference*, ed. Timothy Shanahan and Flora V. Rodriguez-Brown, 76–89. Oak Creek, WI: National Reading Conference, 1998.

———. *Storytime: Young Children's Literary Understanding in the Classroom*. New York: Teachers College Press, 2008.

Smith, Elizabeth B. "Anchored in Our Literature: Students Responding to African American Literature." *Language Arts* 72 (1995): 571–74.

Smith, Scott. *Teach a Donkey to Fish*. Illustrated by Andrea Smith. Mustang, OK: Tate Publishing, 2009.

Tower, Cathy. "'It's a Snake, You Guys!' The Power of Text Characteristics on Children's Responses to Information Books." *Research in the Teaching of English* 37 (2002): 55–88.

Wollman-Bonilla, Julie, and Barbara Werchadlo. "Literature Response Journals in a First-grade Classroom." *Language Arts* 72 (1995): 562–70.

Yokota, J. Realism in Picture Books for Children: Images of Our Diverse World." *Filoteknos* 4 (2013/2014): 64–72.

▪ RESOURCES

Dooley, Caitlin M., Miriam Martinez, and Nancy L. Roser. "Young Children's Literary Meaning Making: A Decade of Research 2000–2010." In *Handbook of Early Childhood Literacy*, ed. Joanne Larson and Jackie Marsh, 222–34. New York: Sage, 2012.

Lehr, Susan. *The Child's Developing Sense of Theme: Responses to Literature*. New York: Teachers College Press, 1990.

Martinez, Miriam, and Nancy Roser. "Children's Responses to Literature." In *Handbook of Research on Teaching the English Language Arts*, ed. James Flood, Diane Lapp, Jim R. Squire, and Julie M. Jensen, 799–813. New York: Erlbaum, 2002.

Pantaleo, Sylvia. *Exploring Student Response to Contemporary Picturebooks*. Toronto: University of Toronto Press, 2008.

Rosenblatt, Louise M. "The Literary Transaction: Evocation and Response." In *Journeying: Children Responding to Literature*, ed. Kathleen E. Holland, Rachael A. Hungerford, and Shirley B. Ernst, 6–23. Portsmouth, NH: Heinemann, 1993.

Roser, Nancy, and Miriam Martinez. *Book Talk and Beyond: Children and Teachers Respond to Literature*. Newark, DE: International Reading Association, 1995.

Roser, Nancy L., Miriam Martinez, and Karen Wood. "Recent Research on Students' Response to Literature." In *The Handbook of Research on Teaching the English Language Arts*, ed. Diane Lapp and Doug Fisher, 264–77. New York: Routledge, 2010.

Sipe, Lawrence R. "The Construction of Literary Understanding by First and Second Graders in Oral Responses to Picture Storybook Readalouds." *Reading Research Quarterly* 35 (2000a): 252–75.

———. "'Those Two Gingerbread Boys Could Be Brothers': How Children Use Intertextual Connections during Storybook Readalouds." *Children's Literature in Education* 31 (2000b): 73–90.

Temple, Charles, Miriam Martinez, and Junko Yokota. *Children's Books in Children's Hands: An Introduction to Their Literature*. 5th ed. New York: Pearson, 2015.

▪ WANT TO KNOW MORE?

1. Langer (2010) says readers assume different stances (or different relationships to a text) as they read. Review the discussion on pages 6–10 of the five stances Langer describes: being out and stepping in, being in and moving through, being in and stepping out, and stepping out and objectifying the experience. Then select a book to read—perhaps Rebecca Stead's *When You Reach Me*—and keep a journal in which you record your responses to the book. After reading the book, go back and identify the different stances you assumed as you responded to the book. Did you have any difficulty stepping into the book? In what ways were you "in and moving through"? Were you able to personally associate with a character? Did you find yourself mesmerized by the language of the text? When were you aware of "stepping out" (assuming you did)? Did you feel compelled to consider the world in which you live, any social issues, or a human condition? As you stepped out, did you recognize the literary devices used by the author? We want our students to be able to read for the sheer joy of it, but as they become aware of their stances, they marvel at the layers of meaning that reading can bring to their lives.

2. Discuss a piece of multicultural literature such as Jacqueline Woodson's *Brown Girl Dreaming* with a group of peers from different cultural backgrounds. How, if at all, do different cultural perspectives come into play in the discussion? What other perspectives were you aware of? Did you respond primarily from a cultural perspective? Were there elements in the story with which you made a personal connection? Perhaps the story stirred a social reaction in you, or it may have reminded you of another book you have read, thus eliciting an intertextual response. Take note of the various lenses through which you and your peers respond.

3. Picture book illustrators often include important clues about their stories before the first page of text. These clues may be found in any number of places—the cover, the endpapers, the frontispiece (the illustrated page before the title page), the dedication/copyright page, the half title page, or the title page. Carefully examine a book such as Candace Fleming's *Oh, No!* or Aaron Becker's *Journey* to see what important story clues the illustrator shares with readers prior to the first page of text. Are there clues to character? Story problem? Setting? Genre? Consider how these clues can help young readers "step into the story world."

CHAPTER 2

How Literature Works

"That was a good service, Shady."
"It was," he agreed, but didn't say more.
"Seems like everyone in this town's got a story to tell."
Shady nodded. "I believe you're right about that. The Lord himself knew the power
of a good story. How it can reach out and wrap around a person like a warm blanket."

—from *Moon over Manifest* by Claire Vanderpool (2010, 248)

Good stories *are* powerful, but if teachers are going to maximize the power of stories in classrooms, we believe it is important that they have an understanding of how stories—and other genres of literature—work. When teachers have a deep understanding of the inner workings of literature, they are better able to guide children's transactions with literature. For example, the teacher who understands the importance of setting in science fiction is likely to invite children to think about ways in which the futuristic world of a science fiction story is different than our own world (and perhaps the ways in which it is similar, as well). Or the teacher who realizes that illustrators sometimes plant important story clues in picture books on the endpapers (those pages that one encounters when first opening a picture book) is likely to encourage her students to look closely at this part of the book as a story is introduced.

Teachers need textual knowledge for a second reason, as well—so that they can help *students* learn about how texts work. The need to understand how texts work is reflected in today's educational standards. For example, to help students learn to read deeply and recognize craft and structure—two of the goals we discussed in chapter 1—we must help them acquire their own textual knowlexdge. When children have an understanding of how texts work, that understanding impacts their transactions with literature in positive ways (and it also helps them become more proficient writers). Though immersion in books is one way of helping students deepen these understandings (Meek, 1987), teachers also have an important role to play in helping them acquire textual knowledge. This means that teachers must have rich textual knowledge to share with students (Eeds and Peterson, 1991).

In this chapter we look at the three major genres of literature—fiction, nonfiction, and poetry—and the subcategories and formats of these genres. In addition, we consider how each genre works and the tools used by writers of each genre.

▪ FICTION

The writers of fiction weave webs—story webs—that pull readers in, and literary elements are the tools that writers use in crafting their webs. In this section we discuss the literary elements of setting, plot, character, theme, and style.

How Fiction Works: Literary Elements

In this section we focus on how literary elements work.

Setting

The setting of a story includes the time and place in which the story takes place. At the very least, an author (and illustrator) must make the setting believable, but in some stories, setting becomes central to the story's development. Such is the case in the picture book *Hey, Al!* (Yorinks, 1989). In this book, the janitor Al and his dog Eddie live in a drab, cramped apartment in the city. So the two gladly accept an invitation from a giant bird that ferries them to what at first appears to be a paradise island in the sky. *Hey, Al!* is a picture book, so important setting details are found in the illustrations. However, in longer works of fiction, setting is established by the author's inclusion of rich details. In Gary Blackwood's *The Shakespeare Stealer*, readers are introduced to London in the 1500s through the eyes of the main character, Widge, as he arrives in the great city, the first he has ever visited:

> Here there were no gold-plated buildings or great cathedrals, only shabby rows of houses, cheek by jowl. With no space to spread sidewise, they had arched over the street, like the trees on that desolate stretch of road where we had met the outlaws, nearly meeting above our heads, shutting out the sun.
>
> There were no street vendors here, nor prosperous merchants, only sullen wives emptying their slop jars into the street, sometimes missing the scrawny, shoeless children playing there, sometimes not. (1998, 42)

The setting details that Blackwood includes in this story about a boy who becomes an apprentice in the Globe Theater help the reader envision how dramatically different the London of Shakespeare's day was from cities of today. Particularly important to the story's development, Widge's attention to his new surroundings helps the reader see just how inexperienced with city ways the young apprentice is.

Technology Tip

ReadWriteThink (www.readwritethink.org) is a useful Web site sponsored by the International Reading Association and the National Council of Teachers of English. It offers a host of lesson plans for different grade levels, including ones designed to explore literary elements and literary genres with students.

Plot

Plot refers to the ordering of events in a story. The plot of most stories unfolds as a character is drawn toward a goal but encounters some kind of conflict. There are different kinds of conflict—conflict between characters, conflict within a character, conflict between a character and nature, or conflict between a character and society. Table 2.1 contains examples of stories with these different kinds of conflicts. In addition to being built around conflict, plots contain some near-universal features—introduction or exposition, complication, rising action, climax, falling action, and denouement. Definitions of each feature are offered in Table 2.2. Each of these elements is evident in Gianna Marino's picture book, *Too Tall Houses* (2012). In the beginning of this story, the reader is introduced to Rabbit and Owl, who live side by side in houses on top of a hill. The two friends have different interests; Rabbit is a gardener, whereas Owl's favorite pastime is watching the forest from the top of his house. The story's complication occurs when Owl complains that he cannot see the forest because the plants in Rabbit's garden are too high. Soon the action begins to rise: when owl builds his home higher and higher, Rabbit claims the sun can no longer reach his garden. So Rabbit makes his house higher and plants vegetables on the roof. Soon Rabbit and Owl are living in "the two tallest houses in the world." The story reaches its climax when fierce, high altitude winds batter the houses, which are then reduced to rubble. Rabbit and Owl seemingly have nothing left at all—until they realize that some of their building materials have survived—enough to build one small house. The story's denouement is revealed in the final illustration that shows the two friends sitting side by side on the roof of their new shared home.

Character

Many works of fiction are memorable because of their characters. Richly developed characters are ones that we feel we know well—we understand the type of person they are (e.g., shy, curious, clever), what motivates them, and how they feel. Such characters may also *grow* as a result of their experiences. Author Kate DiCamillo created such

Table 2.1 Stories with Different Kinds of Conflict

Conflict between Characters	Conflict within a Character	Conflict between a Character and Nature	Conflict between a Character and Society
Book: *Doctor De Soto* A mouse dentist agrees to accept as a patient a fox suffering from a toothache. Soon, though, the dentist discovers that the fox plans to eat him.	Book: *Because of Winn Dixie* Opal Buloni is lonely. Her mother left the family when Opal was three years old. Opal and her preacher father are new in town, and her father is completely wrapped up in his work.	Book: *Hatchet* A boy survives a plane crash, only to find himself stranded in the Canadian wilderness where he encounters one challenge after another armed only with a hatchet and his determination to survive.	Book: *Return to Sender* In this story told from two perspectives, Tyler worries that the Mexican laborers his dad has hired are undocumented. Mari and her family live in constant fear that the authorities will discover them and send them back to Mexico.

Table 2.2   Features of Plots

Introduction (or Exposition)	Complication	Rising Action	Climax	Falling Action	Denouement
The *exposition* provides background information needed to understand the story.	The *complication* occurs when conflict is introduced in the story.	The *rising action* follows from the complication as characters work to resolve the problem(s) they face.	The *climax* is the turning point in the plot.	The *falling action* consists of the rapid series of events that follow the climax.	The *denouement* reveals the characters' state of affairs following the resolution of the conflict.

Try This
Exploring Plot Structure with Young Children

When exploring plot structure with young children, plot-related terms like exposition, complication, rising action, climax, falling action, and denouement are not appropriate. Instead, invite young children to identify the problem in a story, the way(s) the character attempts to solve the problem, and the outcome (or resolution) of the problem. Try out this simpler plot language by talking with children in kindergarten, first grade, or second grade about the plot of Aaron Reynolds's *Creepy Carrots* or Philip Stead's *A Sick Day for Amos McGee*.

a character in *Because of Winn Dixie* (2000): Opal's kind nature begins to emerge in the first chapter when she rescues a stray mongrel running amuck in the local grocery store. But Opal is also lonely: she is new in town, her preacher father is wrapped up in his work, and her mother left when Opal was only three. It is her sense of loneliness and isolation that motivates Opal to begin connecting (with the help of her dog, Winn Dixie) to other lonely souls in town.

Writers bring characters like Opal Buloni to life in a number of different ways: by their actions, by their sense of self, by their relationships with others, and by what the narrator shares about the character. In *Because of Winn Dixie*, author DiCamillo relies on the first three of these techniques to help readers get to know Opal. In the beginning of the book, we are immediately attuned to Opal's kind nature through her actions when she rescues the dog and convinces her father that they must give it a home. We gain insight into Opal's sense of self as she talks to her newly adopted dog, Winn Dixie, while giving him his first bath (and trying to brush his teeth):

> You don't have any family and neither do I. I've got the preacher, of course. But I don't have a mama. I mean I have one, but I don't know where she is. She left when I was three years old. I can't hardly remember her. And I bet you don't remember your mama much either. So we're almost like orphans. (21)

Opal's sense of loneliness is also evident in her relationships with others. Though Gloria Dump is called a "witch" by other children, she provides Opal with something she sorely needs: "And the whole time I was talking, Gloria Dump was listening. . . . I could feel her listening with all her heart, and it felt good" (68).

Theme

The theme of a story is the issue or message that readers take from a story. Even simple stories intended for young children can offer important messages. Themes are not explicitly stated in most stories. Instead, readers must infer them. So not surprisingly, different readers sometimes find different messages in the same story. *Bear Has a Story to Tell* (Stead, 2012) by Phillip Stead is a good example. In this simple story, Bear yearns to share a story before hibernating for the winter, but all his friends are too busy with their own winter preparations to listen. So in-

Bear Has a Story to Tell
(Roaring Brook Press/Macmillan)

stead of telling his story, Bear graciously helps each of his friends with their preparations. When Bear's friends gather after the long winter, Bear finally has a chance to share—but he has forgotten his story! Now it is time for Bear's friends to lend Bear a helping hand. Some readers take a message from Stead's story about the importance of storytelling, whereas others see the story being about friends helping one another.

Don't Miss . . .
Picture Books That Invite Thematic Inferences

Hello! Hello! by Matthew Cordell

More by I. C. Springman, illustrated by Brian Lies

Too Tall Houses by Gianna Marino

Blackout by John Rocco

A Sick Day for Amos McGee by Phillip Stead, illustrated by Erin Stead

Because Amelia Smiled by David Ezra Stein

In some stories, themes are represented or symbolized by an image in the story. One of the characters in *Because of Winn Dixie* gives Opal some Littmus lozenges, candy that is at once sweet and sour. The candy evokes both happy and sad memories for all who taste it, and it comes to symbolize the complexities of life with its joys and sorrows.

Style

The way a writer uses language is what we call style. It encompasses word choice, the use of metaphors and images, and the sounds of language. In *Oh, No!* (Fleming, 2012) Candace Fleming's rhythmic, repetitive language is filled with onomatopoeia that is the perfect accompaniment for a lively tale about a pack of jungle animals that tumble into a hole: "Frog fell into a deep, deep hole. Ribbit-oops! Ribbit-oops!"

Author Robert Burleigh uses a distinctly different style in *Flight* (1991), the story of Charles Lindbergh's solo flight across the Atlantic. The reader is introduced to

Lindbergh on the airfield before he begins his historic flight. Burleigh's use of short, staccato sentences and phrases conveys the tension and anxiety that must surely have marked the feelings of all those gathered to watch Lindbergh embark on what was to become a historic flight:

> And yet—he is about to attempt what no one has done before:
>> To fly—without a stop—from New York to Paris, France.
>> Over 3,600 miles away.
>> Across the Atlantic Ocean.
>> Alone. (n.p.)

Subgenres of Fiction

We began this section by noting that writers of fiction weave story webs. And just as there is a multitude of different kinds of spiders in the world, there is also a wide array of story types. Included in this array are well-researched stories set in the past, futuristic stories set on other planets, stories that reflect the world in which we live today, stories about wily animals seeking to outsmart others, and many other types of stories as well. We call these different types genres (or subgenres) of fiction.

There are many reasons to help children learn about different fictional genres. For example, in the previous chapter we talked about ways in which readers attempt to "step into" text worlds. One helpful way of doing this is by drawing on one's genre knowledge—just one of the reasons we need to help children acquire genre knowledge.

In the following section, we briefly introduce different subgenres of fiction. Each is distinct in terms of the ways in which the literary elements are crafted. Some of the distinctive features of setting, character, plot, and theme across the subgenres of fiction are summarized in Table 2.3.

Traditional Literature

Traditional literature encompasses old stories (often hundreds and hundreds of years old) that were initially told orally and passed down by word of mouth. Only in relatively recent years have some of these old stories been written down. Because traditional tales come to us from around the world, they can be important vehicles in schools for exploring different cultures. One of the particularly interesting things about traditional tales is the commonalities found in so many tales from different parts of the world. For example, there are many variants worldwide of the "Little Red Riding Hood" story. In each, a child (or children) is warned to beware of strangers. The stranger (often a wolf) tricks the child by pretending to be a beloved relative.

Don't Miss . . .
Little Red Riding Hood Variants

Lon Po Po: A Red Riding Hood Story from China by Ed Young

Little Red Riding Hood by Trina Schart Hyman

Pretty Salma: A Little Red Riding Hood Story from Africa by Niki Daly

Although there are fascinating commonalities in variants such as the "Little Red Riding Hood" story, equally intriguing are the distinctive features of stories from within particular cultures. For example, stories from Scandinavia are replete with trolls and hags, whereas many of the stories from Africa are animal tales of cleverness and wisdom. The distinctive nature of traditional literature from different cultures makes the genre valuable for inclusion in units of study exploring particular cultures.

Reaching *All* Students

Teachers must strive to ensure that all students are included in today's diverse classroom communities. Traditional literature can serve as one vehicle for bringing children from diverse cultural backgrounds into that community. Many children come from cultures in which the oral tradition flourishes, and those children feel like valued members of the community when stories from their cultures are shared. Children from Mexico are likely to know one of the many variants of "La Llorona," whereas children from western Africa (or the West Indies) are likely to be acquainted with tales about Anansi the trickster. The teacher can seek out these tales and bring them into the classroom, and students can also be invited to share tales from their home community.

There is a wide array of traditional tales, and some of the particularly popular types include animal tales, trickster tales, numbskull tales, tall tales, pourquoi tales, fairy tales, fables, myths, and ghost stories. Each of these subgenres has characteristics that set it apart from other types, and in chapter 5 we discuss ways of constructing units to guide children in exploring the subgenres of traditional literature. See Table 2.4 for definitions of each of these types of traditional literature.

Contemporary Realistic Fiction

Works of contemporary realistic fiction are set in our own world, and although the stories are made up, everything that happens in them is actually possible in the world as we know it. The characters in realistic fiction resemble real people, perhaps ones we might encounter in our everyday lives. They live in places that are real or certainly could be real. Also, the characters in contemporary realistic fiction deal with problems with which real people must contend, and they discover realistic solutions to their problems. It isn't surprising that many children find this subgenre of fiction particularly appealing. After all, children often see their world and themselves—their problems and dreams—in contemporary realistic fiction stories. But given the wide range of subject matter explored within the subgenre, many stories provide a window onto the broader world for children. Writers of contemporary realistic fiction explore a wide range of topics including families, self-discovery, growing up, schools, sports, and animals. Other authors address thought-provoking topics including emotional and physical challenges, moral challenges, social diversity, death, and other types of loss.

Historical Fiction

Historical fiction is set in the past. The setting may be the distant past, but stories set during more recent times—such as the civil rights era or the cold war of the latter

Table 2.3 Literary Elements and the Subgenres of Fiction

	Setting	Character	Plot	Theme
Traditional Literature	• limited setting information (e.g., "once upon time" or "in a land far away") • limited variety of settings (e.g., cottage, castle, forest)	• sparsely described characters • frequent contrasts between main characters (e.g., good vs. bad; rich vs. poor) • clearly identifiable roles (e.g., hero, rival, helper) • frequent inclusion of stock characters (e.g., princess, prince, trickster)	• prominent plots • characters encounter a problem, make various attempts to solve problem, and find a solution • common motifs across many folktales including actors (e.g., princess, wicked stepmother); objects (e.g., flying carpet, magical items); or actions (e.g., hero facing impossible tasks, three attempts to achieve goal)	• important themes that are often relevant to our lives today
Contemporary Realistic Fiction	• set in the present in the real world	• characters behave like real people • characters are typically developed in detail	• explores problems that could happen in the real world	• explores issues and ideas relevant to children's real experiences (e.g., friendship, independence)
Historical Fiction	• set in the past • settings typically described in detail to bring the time and place to life for the reader	• characters are most often ordinary people rather than figures of historical importance, but they *may* be swept up in great historical events of their times • characters must speak and behave in ways consistent with the time period in which the story is set	• conflict must grow out of the time and place in which the story is set • events must unfold plausibly and the conflict must be resolved in a manner consistent with the historical time period	• explores themes significant for the time period in which the story is set—and for the present (e.g., prejudice, need for freedom, moral responsibility)

(continues)

Table 2.3 Cont.

	Setting	Character	Plot	Theme
Fantasy	• story may be set in our own world or in a fantastic world (e.g., Neverland or Narnia) • when setting is the fantastic element, details about place must be so vivid that readers can see, hear, and feel the setting	• characters may be the fantastical element in the story (e.g., talking animals, creatures such as unicorns, dragons) • rich details make fantastic characters believable	• conflicts (particularly in high fantasy) often center around struggles between good and evil • plots of high fantasy may involve quests, tests of endurance, journeys to other lands • even though fantastic events may occur in the fantasy world (e.g., people who travel on the backs of dragons), these events must be governed by internal consistency and logic	• significant themes that matter to real people often emerge from fantasies, especially high fantasy (e.g., triumph of good over evil)
Science Fiction	• takes place in a futuristic world • setting is a critical element in which technology and scientific invention may play a pivotal role • story may be set in our own world or in some other world	• characters may be real people or an invented species (e.g., robots) • character behaviors must be plausible in light of the futuristic society in which they live	• conflicts emerge from the realm of possibility the author establishes for the futuristic society • events must unfold plausibly and the conflict must be resolved within the realm of possibility established by author	• significant themes relevant to our own lives are typically explored

Table 2.4 Categories of Traditional Literature

Type of Tale	Features	Example
Animal tale	Tales in which animals talk and have human characteristics	"The Little Red Hen" "The Three Little Pigs"
Trickster tale	Tales in which a character (usually an animal) uses its wits to outsmart another	"Anansi Goes Fishing" "Brer Rabbit and the Briar Patch"
Numbskull tale	Tales that feature characters who are none too bright but who nevertheless sometimes come out ahead	"The Three Sillies" "Juan Bobo"
Tall tale	Tales that feature the highly exaggerated exploits of larger-than-life heroes	"Paul Bunyan" "Pecos Bill"
Pourquoi tale	Tales that explain some natural phenomenon	"Why Mosquitoes Buzz in People's Ears" "How Chipmunk Got His Stripes"
Fairy tales	Tales of magic and wonder	"Cinderella" "Sleeping Beauty" "Snow White and the Seven Dwarfs"
Fables	Brief tales featuring animals with human characteristics that conclude with an explicitly stated moral	"The Tortoise and the Hare" "The Fox and the Grapes"
Myths	Stories that explain how the world came to be	"Prometheus" "Demeter and Persephone"
Ghost stories	Scary stories about the supernatural	"Tailypo" "The Teeny-Tiny Woman"

twentieth century—are also considered historical fiction. Authors in the United States who write historical fiction for children most often set their stories in the United States. This means that relatively little historical fiction set in other parts of the world is available in our country. Further, American writers tend to set their stories during only a few historical eras including the American Revolution, and the Civil War and periods during slavery, the westward movement, immigration, and World War II.

We believe that historical fiction is of value as a genre in and of itself. In addition, integrating the genre into the social studies curriculum can enrich the study of history in many ways. A well-researched work of historical fiction can potentially extend children's understanding of history. Perhaps even more important, the genre can help children develop "historical empathy" (Tomlinson, Tunnell, and Richgels, 1993, 54), which some educators believe is necessary to develop historical understanding. Historical empathy enables readers to "perceive past events and issues as they were experienced by the people at the time" (Tomlinson, Tunnell, and Richgels, 54).

Fantasy

Modern fantasy is literature that has unexplainable magic. In well-crafted works of fantasy, readers willingly suspend their disbelief and enter into the fantasy world created by the author. There are two major categories of fantasy. Low fantasy is set in the primary world (that is, the here and now) and contains fantastic elements such as personified animals or toys, outlandish characters, magical powers or objects, or supernatural elements. *The Tale of Peter Rabbit* (Potter, 1902), Beatrix Potter's classic tale

Try This
Exploring Trickster Tales with Children

Create a language chart to guide children's explorations of trickster tales. (See chapter 5 for more information about language charts.) This large matrix for the wall poses questions to guide children's explorations of a related set of books. As each book on the chart is read, the children can decide (after discussion) how to answer the questions posed on the chart. For trickster tales, a chart might look like this:

	Who is the trickster?	Who is tricked?	What is the trick?	What is the outcome?
Coyote: A Trickster Tale from the American Southwest by Gerald McDermott				
Monkey: A Trickster Tale from India by Gerald McDermott				
Borreguita and the Coyote by Verna Aardema				
Anansi Goes Fishing by Eric Kimmel				

featuring rabbits that talk and dress in human clothing, is an example of low fantasy. Another is Tomie dePaola's *Strega Nona* (dePaola, 1979), which features an out-of-control magic pasta pot that produces such an abundance of pasta that it threatens to swallow up an entire town.

In contrast to low fantasy that is set in our own world, authors of high fantasy often create secondary worlds. Some high fantasies are set exclusively in the secondary world, whereas in others, characters move between the primary and secondary worlds. Gary Schmidt's *What Came from the Stars* (2012) is set in a distant and unnamed world as well as in the contemporary world of Plymouth, Massachusetts. Works of high fantasy are also distinguished by conflicts between good and evil.

Don't Miss . . .
High Fantasy

The Conch Bearer by Chitra Banerjee Divakaruni

The Sea of Trolls by Nancy Farmer

The Lion, the Witch, and the Wardrobe by C. S. Lewis

The Lightning Thief by Rick Riordan

Harry Potter and the Sorcerer's Stone by J. K. Rowling

Science Fiction

Science fiction is a variety of fantasy. The worlds created by writers of science fiction are not possible, and yet because the writers draw on scientific concepts, the worlds they craft seem believable. According to Jean Greenlaw (1982), "fantasy never could be [whereas] science fiction has the possibility of being—maybe not in our time or on our planet, but the possibility of happening within some time and in some place" (64). An example of science fiction is M. T. Anderson's *Feed* (2002). Set in a society in which television and computers are connected directly into people's brains when they are babies, this futuristic society driven by blatant consumerism is chillingly believable.

■ FORMATS OF FICTION

Our discussion of fiction is not complete without focusing on the two formats in which stories for children are most commonly told: picture books and chapter books. In addition, we talk briefly about two formats that are becoming increasingly popular: graphic novels and digital books.

Picture Books

In picture books, stories are told through the interplay of pictures and words (unless of course the picture book is wordless, in which case the story is told entirely through pictures). The way in which pictures and text work together varies. Sometimes pictures and words function in a parallel fashion with illustrations showing what the words say. In other instances, illustrations extend the words of the author by including information not found in the text. In Peggy Rathman's *Officer Buckle and Gloria* (1995), Officer Buckle is accompanied on his school visits by a police dog named Gloria. As Officer Buckle gives his safety presentations to children, he is unaware that Gloria is behind him engaging in all sorts of antics, but the reader is in on the joke because the illustrations show each of Gloria's increasingly outrageous capers.

The relationships between pictures and text can actually become quite complex in picture books, with illustrations even contradicting what is found in the words. For example, in Mark Teague's *Dear Mrs. LaRue* (2003), Ike the dog is sent to obedience school. The letters Ike writes home bemoan his cruel treatment by school officials, and the story told through the accompanying black and white illustrations parallel Ike's letters. But colored illustrations placed next to the black and white ones tell a very different (and more believable) story—life in obedience school is pretty cushy for Ike.

Development of Literary Elements in Picture Books

Since stories in picture books are told through pictures and words, literary elements are developed through the interplay of these two systems. Pictures appear to be especially important in developing the setting, characters, and plot of many picture books (Martinez and Harmon, 2012).

When setting is important in a picture book (and it isn't always), readers are likely to get much (if not all) of the setting information through illustrations. John Rocco's *Blackout* (2011) is an example of a book in which setting does matter. The narrator tells the reader that the story takes places in the city, but it is through illustrations that we learn just what kind of city it is. In one scene, readers see big skyscrapers—and the Brooklyn Bridge. Amid the blackout, when the family goes to the rooftop of their apartment building, the illustrations reveal that they live in a *tall* building, one as high as a billboard. The street scenes—shown visually—reveal that the neighborhood is one in which people live in brownstones intermingled with shops. This is a *big* city.

Illustrations in picture books are also likely to offer critical information about characters. Pat Hutchins's classic story *Rosie's Walk* (1971) features a hen that takes a walk around the farmyard, all the time being followed by a fox that repeatedly tries to snatch her. The entire time the hen is totally unaware of what is happening. The book features only these two characters—the hen and the fox. However, the verbal text makes no mention of the fox. Not only do readers learn through the illustrations that the fox is one of the two characters in the story, but they also find clues *only in the illustrations* that reveal how crafty the fox is—and how clueless the hen is. Oftentimes illustrations in picture books offer the richest information about character traits, motivations, and emotions, as well as changes in character.

In picture books, key elements of plot may also emerge through illustrations. In Kelly Bingham's zany picture book, *Z Is for Moose* (2012), Moose can hardly wait for his turn to appear in Zebra's theatrical presentation of the alphabet. The illustrations reveal an eager Moose lifting the curtain and peering out at the audience prior to the performance. Once the show begins, readers discern through the illustrations that Moose is trying to upstage the other actors–Ice Cream Cone, Jar, Kangaroo. When it is finally time for "M" to appear onstage, Moose discovers that he has been replaced by Mouse. The pictures reveal Moose's outraged reactions to this turn of events as he rampages across the stage, stomping on Pie, knocking over Queen, and drawing antlers on Ring. This is visual storytelling at its best.

Peritext

A book's peritext includes everything in the book except for the text (and, in the case of picture books, the illustrations that accompany the text). So, included in the peritext are the front and back covers, the endpapers, the title page, the dedication and copyright pages, and sometimes a frontispiece (an illustration before the title page). Increasingly in picture books, these features are being used to contribute to story-telling in important ways; hence, readers should closely attend to these features. For example, the front cover of *Oh, No!* (Fleming, 2012) features a tiger gazing in a threat-ening manner at a loris that peers down at the tiger with big, round eyes. The back cover, which for this book continues the scene represented on the front cover, features a timid looking frog and mouse cowering as they stare at the tiger. The setting for the story—a jungle—is also represented on the cover of the book. There is a wealth of information on the cover of this book: readers learn where the story takes place; they are introduced to some of the book's characters; but most important, the cover (which also includes the book's title) points to the central problem of the story: the tiger is out to get the smaller animals! As the book is opened to the front endpapers (the first pages one sees when opening the book), the reader sees the crouching tiger staring intently at the frog. Then, on the next page (the title page), we see the tiger in action, chasing the frog that has leaped halfway off the page. The story has started before the reader has even reached the first page of text. And in the case of this particular book, the back endpapers present the concluding scene of the story as the reader witnesses the tiger trying to climb out of the deep hole into which *he* has now fallen.

Tools of the Illustrator

In addition to conveying story elements via the content of illustrations (i.e., what is depicted), illustrators also use visual elements to convey important information. These visual elements include line, color, shape, space, and texture. Table 2.5 includes infor-mation about some of the many ways in which illustrators manipulate these elements to convey meaning visually.

My Friend Rabbit
(Roaring Brook Press/Macmillan)

Bear Has a Story to Tell, a story about friends helping one another, is an example of a book in which the illustrator, Erin Stead, manipulates many of the visual elements in partic-ularly effective ways to enhance sto-rytelling. For example, shifts in color convey important information about the changing seasons, which are cen-tral to this story's development. As the story begins, it is autumn, and Bear is seeking an audience for the story he wants to tell. In the early pages of the book as Bear wanders through the woods, we see orange, red, and yellow leaves drifting gently to the ground. But winter is approaching, and Bear's friends are too busy preparing for the coming cold to stop and listen to a story. Soon, we see a marked shift in color as Bear looks up into a blue gray sky from which snow is falling. Winter has come and Bear must hibernate. The next shift in color occurs with the coming of spring: the page is filled with green grass, newly leafing trees, and a bright orange sun in the sky. It is a new season, and once again a time for storytelling.

Table 2.5 Visual Elements

Visual Element	(Some) Uses to Enhance Storytelling	Picture Books in Which Element Is Used Effectively
Line	• horizontal lines convey repose • vertical lines convey stability • diagonal lines convey movement • curving lines convey gentle, peaceful qualities • angular lines convey tension and excitement	*The Paperboy* by Dav Pilkey *Don't Let the Pigeon Drive the Bus* by Mo Willems *Red Knit Cap Girl* by Naoko Stoop *Boot & Shoe* by Marla Frazee *One Cool Friend* by Toni Buzzeo, illustrated by David Small
Color	• color can convey temperature (e.g., reds and yellows are associated with heat whereas greens and blues are associated with cool) • color can convey emotion (e.g., red is associated with anger) • color can convey personality traits (e.g., strong colors suggest lively personalities) • color can convey status (e.g., purple is associated with royalty)	*When Sophie Gets Angry—Really, Really Angry . . .* by Molly Bang *The Relatives Came* by Cynthia Rylant, illustrated by Stephen Gammell *No, David!* by David Shannon *Extra Yarn* by Mac Barnett, illustrated by Jon Klassen *Hello! Hello!* By Matthew Cordell *Voices in the Park* by Anthony Browne
Shape	• rounded shapes can convey tranquility and gentleness • angular or geometric shapes can convey action, tension, excitement	*Kitten's First Full Moon* by Kevin Henkes *Zomo the Rabbit* by Gerald McDermott *Sleep Like a Tiger* by Mary Logue, illustrated by Pamela Zagarenski
Space	• extensive space moves eye to the central image(s) in illustration • minimal space forces the eye to seek out details in the illustration	*Wilfrid Gordon McDonald Partridge* by Mem Fox, illustrated by Julie Vivas *Leonardo the Terrible Monster* by Mo Willems *My Friend Rabbit* by Eric Rohmann
Texture	• conveys the illusion of a tactile surface	*Top Cat* by Lois Ehlert *Where the Wild Things Are* by Maurice Sendak *Smoky Night* by Eve Bunting, illustrated by David Diaz

In *Bear Has a Story to Tell*, Stead also uses shape masterfully to signal the gentle nature of the animals in this story. Bear may be big, but he is a gentle giant, round and soft. In a similar fashion, rounded shapes define each of Bear's friends—mouse, frog, duck, and mole.

The visual element of space is also used to great effect in the story. After Bear's friends have flown south or settled into their hideaways for the winter, we see a double-page spread featuring the winter sky, empty except for a few snowflakes. In the lower left-hand corner of this double-page spread, a diminutive-looking Bear stands gazing up into the sky. The wide expanse of empty space that is the winter sky conveys Bear's loneliness.

Red Knit Cap Girl
(Little Brown)

Don't Miss . . .
Picture Books That Convey Important Character Information Visually

When Sophie Gets Angry—Really, Really Angry . . . by Molly Bang

One Cool Friend by Toni Buzzeo, illustrated by David Small

Olivia by Ian Falconer

I Want My Hat Back by Jon Klassen

Click, Clack, Moo: Cows That Type by Doreen Cronin, illustrated Betsy Lewin

A Ball for Daisy by Chris Raschka

Art and Max by David Wiesner

Too many people dismiss the picture book as a simple format, so we hope our discussion of picture books has revealed some of its complexities. However, before concluding the discussion, it is important to note that the picture book is a continuously evolving format, and nowhere is this more evident than in postmodern picture books. To explore the postmodern picture book in more depth, we invite you to read Sylvia Pantaleo's discussion of postmodern picture books below.

What Does the Expert Say?
What Are Postmodern Picture Books?

Dr. Sylvia Pantaleo
Professor, University of Victoria

In picture books, the artwork and the words work together in a synergistic relationship to convey meaning (except in wordless picture books). The intentional spelling of picture book as a compound word by many scholars reflects the ecological relationship between the visual and written modes in this format of literature (Lewis, 2001). Throughout its history, the ecology of the picture book has been both impacted by and reflective of social and cultural changes. Bader (1976) is commonly quoted for her description of a picture book as a "social, cultural, historical document" (1).

Most children and youth today live in a multimedia and multimodal world characterized by fragmentation, juxtaposition of differing forms, and an ever-increasing diversity of symbolic representations. With respect to children's literature, a growing array of print and electronic texts is available to readers. Numerous individuals have written about how the changes in contemporary children's and young adult literature reflect the broader historical, social, and cultural movement referred to as postmodernism. Although confusion, ambiguity, and divergence surround a precise definition of postmodernism, it is commonly accepted that the term describes the tendencies, changes, and/or developments that occurred in architecture, art, literature, philosophy, and music during the latter half of the twentieth century. Many scholars (e.g., Coles and Hall, 2001; Lewis, 2001; Pantaleo and Sipe, 2008) have identified particular characteristics or concepts that typify living in the postmodern world, and reflective of the character or inclination of postmodernism itself, many of these features are connected and synergistic in nature. Lewis (2001) notes that because illustrators and writers have been exposed to "the same postmodernizing influences as everyone else . . . it would be reasonable to suppose that such influences might find their way into books" (99). In the book edited by the late Larry Sipe and me, *Postmodern Picturebooks:*

(continues)

What Does the Expert Say? (cont.)

Play, Parody, and Self-referentiality (2008), international scholars representing various disciplines provide a critical examination and discussion of postmodern picture books and reflect upon their unique contributions to both the field of children's literature and to the development of new literacies for child, adolescent, and adult readers.

A review of the literature (Pantaleo and Sipe, 2008) reveals much overlap and commonality regarding the features associated with postmodern picture books. The following list of postmodern characteristics, which is neither definitive nor exhaustive, includes attributes that are both encompassing and specific in nature: intertextuality, parody, playfulness, pastiche, genre eclecticism, collapse of traditional narrative structures, narrative discontinuities and fragmentation, abandonment of linear chronology, polyphony, boundary crossing and breaking, excess, chaos and disorder, indeterminacy and a "pervasive use of metafiction" (Watson, 2004, 55). Indeed, metafiction is one of the most prominent features exhibited in postmodern literature (Pantaleo, 2008, 2014). According to Waugh (1984), metafiction is "fictional writing which self-consciously and systematically draws attention to its status as an artefact" (2). Metafictive texts explicitly direct readers' and/or viewers' attention to how they work and to how meaning is created through the use of a number of devices or techniques. In picture books, metafictive devices can be employed with both words and images. For example, the picture book *No Bears* (McKinlay and Rudge, 2012) features multiple metafictive devices that work together in a synergistic manner. Ella, the young narrator, directly addresses readers and proclaims that her book will feature "NO BEARS." Using a faux spiral-bound notebook, Ella creates her own book, in front of readers, about a monster intent on stealing a princess (who is Ella herself) (Pantaleo, 2014). However, a bear is indeed a character in the picture book! Furthermore, unbeknownst to Ella, the bear's actions, which are represented exclusively through the illustrations, are integral to her unfolding tale.

Are there compulsory characteristics required for a picture book to be classified as postmodern? Larry Sipe and I stated that the answer to this question is no. We believe that formulating criteria would create a binary—postmodern/not postmodern—and the latter is antithetical to the propensity of postmodernism itself. As discussed in our book (Pantaleo & Sipe, 2008), we believe a continuum of postmodernism that includes consideration of both the quantity and the specific nature of the postmodern characteristics exhibited within a particular picture book makes more sense.

We hope that our discussion of picture books points to the need for teachers to immerse themselves in the format to learn as much as possible about how pictures and texts work together in the telling of the stories so that they, in turn, can more skillfully guide their students' interactions with picture books.

Chapter Books

Around second and third grades, many students begin to transition into chapter books (Roser, Martinez, McDonnold, and Fuhrken, 2004). This does not mean that picture books should simply be left behind. In fact, there are many sophisticated picture books that are more appropriate for older readers. Nonetheless, it is important for learners to become proficient readers of chapter books. To successfully scaffold children in learning to read in this format, it is important to recognize that a chapter book is more than just a book with chapters.

Chapter books differ from picture books in a variety of ways. One difference is that chapter books offer minimal, if any, pictorial support. Another particularly obvious difference is length. Chapter books designated as "beginning chapter books" are relatively short. One analysis of beginning chapter books revealed a range between 29 and 133 pages (Roser, Martinez, McDonnold, and Fuhrken, 2004). However, length can be deceiving because short chapter books can be emotionally complex. Such a book is the Newbery-winning book *Sarah, Plain and Tall* (MacLachlan, 1985), which is only sixty-four pages in length. In this book Patricia MacLachlan tells the story of a nineteenth-century farmer in the Midwest who advertises for a wife and mother for his two children. In response to the ad, Sarah arrives from Maine. The children come to love her, but knowing how much Sarah misses her native state, the children fear that she will leave them.

The complexity of chapter books is also evident in terms of characterization. Chapter books typically have more characters and more complex characters than do picture books. Also, characters in a chapter book are more likely to grow and change in the course of the book. At the beginning of Kimberly Brubaker Bradley's *The War That Saved My Life* (2015), readers meet ten-year-old Ada, who has never left her London apartment because of her mother's embarrassment about Ada's twisted foot. Ada knows little to nothing of the world beyond her window. Then, World War II breaks out. Ada's brother is sent to live in a small town to escape the German blitz, and Ada manages to go with him. In her new home, the world opens up for Ada. She teaches herself to ride a horse, she learns to read, and she even begins to trust and love the woman who has taken Ada and her brother into her home.

Chapter books are also more structurally complex than picture books. There are two types of structures commonly associated with chapter books—episodic structures and epic structures. In a book with an episodic structure, chapters are connected by common characters, settings, or themes but not by a unifying story problem. Chapter books for younger readers often have episodic structures, and these books are frequently memorable due to characterization. Books in Beverly Cleary's Ramona series and Barbara Park's Junie B. Jones series have episodic plot structures. Because each chapter in a book with this structure can stand alone, the books "demand less on the part of the reader in terms of keeping plot points straight" (Cadden, 2011, 305). Books with episodic plot structures work particularly well as read-alouds for younger children.

Chapter books with epic or problem-centered plots tend to be more complex structurally and have multiple plot strands centering around different (but related) problems. For example, the Newbery honor book *Splendors and Glooms* (Schlitz, 2012) set in Victorian England has three major plot strands. The first focuses on Lizzie Rose and Parsefall, orphans who work as assistants to Grisini, the sinister puppeteer/magician. The second plot strand presents the story of Clara, a child from an aristocratic family who vanishes after Grisini and his assistants perform at her birthday party. The final strand centers on Cassandra, the witch—and rival to Grisini—who wears a powerful phoenix stone around her neck, a stone that threatens to destroy her. These intertwined story strands play out in unexpected and intriguing ways.

Given the potential complexity of chapter books, it is important for teachers to thoughtfully analyze the books they plan to use with students and develop ways of supporting students' reading of these books. In chapter 5 we offer a variety of instructional strategies that can be used with chapter books.

Graphic Novels

It is no exaggeration to say that graphic novels aimed at children and teen audiences have undergone a revolution in the past decade. Prior to that, such graphic materials were typically written for adult audiences or for a very specific audience of teen readers. Those aimed at children were largely comic books designed as humorous, short creations that were not viewed as having literary quality. Inspired by graphic novels like *Maus* (Spiegelman, 1997) and *Persepolis* (Satrapi, 2003) that were created for adults but increasingly read by teenagers and eventually incorporated into many high school English literature classrooms, authors and illustrators increasingly pushed the boundaries younger and younger. Currently, there are numerous graphic novels published specifically for elementary-aged readers. Many are part of a series—Babymouse, Lunch Lady, and Bone, for example—but others are individual titles—*Bake Sale* (Varon, 2011), *Artemis Fowl: The Graphic Novel* (Colfer, 2007), and award winners *To Dance: A Ballerina's Graphic Novel* (Siegel, 2006), *Little Mouse Gets Ready* (Smith, 2009), and *This One Summer* (Tamaki, 2014).

A graphic novel is neither solely graphic nor necessarily a novel. It is a book-length work of fiction or nonfiction told with images and verbal text using the conventions of a comic book. The process of reading a graphic novel is different from reading a chapter book or even a picture book, because it involves understanding how the panels work to create "sequential art" (Eisner, 1985). Also, although the illustrations in a graphic novel tell much of the story, one reads a graphic novel by continually going back and forth between text and picture; it is the interweaving of the two forms of input that typically reveals the whole story.

William Teale, Jung Kim, and William Boerman-Cornell (2008) discuss two especially important ways that graphic novels can profitably become part of the literacy and subject area curricula of elementary schools: as a source of independent reading that can support children's development of word recognition, fluency, and comprehension skills and also as content-area reading material for lessons in reading/language arts and social studies.

Digital Books

The rise of digital publishing has brought about a wide array of reading materials for children, ranging from scanned PDFs of books that originally appeared as print books to multimedia apps that barely resemble anything one might call a "book" in the traditional sense. Likewise, how those materials are read ranges from computer screens to tablet readers to smartphone screens to dedicated e-book readers. Libraries make digital books available through online checkout systems so borrowers don't even have to leave their own device screen to download them—they can simply go online, use their library cards, and temporarily download the digital book onto their own device wherever they are. Schools provide access through licensed agreements with publishers, and teachers may use a projection device to share them with the whole class. However, the home market largely drives digital material sales. This, therefore, creates a digital divide, because not all children have access to digital reading materials. Moreover, rather than children entering libraries or bookstores to select books for their own reading, parents are often the ones who download the books that they select for their children and pay for them through their app store accounts.

What are these digital materials, and how should parents, teachers, and librarians evaluate and select digital materials? The first iteration of digital materials for children was in the form of scanned PDF pages of physical books. Historically, some were turned into what was known as "living books," which included primitive animation, narration, and interactive mouse-click animation like birds flying and tweeting, bread popping out of toasters, or characters clumsily walking. In the early 2000s, the International Children's Digital Library made a worldwide effort to scan the world's children's books and to make them freely available through their web site. To date, it remains the only such internationally cooperative effort to scan books in their entirety and in their original languages. However, its collection development policy is based on donations of copyright and therefore varies enormously in quality and quantity across countries.

In time, subscription-based libraries were offered through public or school library accounts or privately through individual accounts. Such libraries tended to have relatively current books with audio narration and sound effects; some added follow-up games and quizzes. It was the arrival of touch-screen tablets that changed the digital world of reading materials for children the most with the onset of apps that were based on the interactivity of the readers. Increasingly gamelike, these features call for the reader to make decisions about their experience with the story. Most recently, the app world has been offering stories that were never in print originally; apps such as David Wiesner's *Spot* have been created specifically for the touch-screen format. The ways in which readers enter and move within such stories—and how the stories play out—are entirely dependent on reader decision making.

Junko Yokota and William Teale (2014) outline a set of guidelines for evaluating and selecting digital picture books for children:

- Is the story appropriately presented in digital format?
- Does the story take appropriate advantage of features the digital world allows, beyond what is possible in print?
- Do the interactive features maintain the integrity of the main story?
- Do supplementary features align with the story?
- Do the features make sense in terms of how children learn to read and learn in general?

All of these questions should be preceded by the expectation of a well-told story, skillfully crafted language, and artistically successful illustrations that illuminate, extend, and cocreate the story. In short, no compromises should be made for digital materials, and they should uphold all the literary and artistic standards of print. In addition, they should be evaluated for their multimedia elements.

What Do You Think?

The digital age impacts every facet of our lives, and this includes the world of children's literature. Today a wide array of e-books and book-related apps are available for use in the classroom. Many educators welcome this proliferation, noting the motivational potential of these formats for children of the twenty-first century. Others laud the capability of e-books to support readers, particularly those who struggle. For example, many e-books have speech capabilities so that stories can be read to a child or a child can receive help in identifying words. There is also a wide assortment of book-related apps available that can extend children's engagement with stories.

Yet educators have also expressed legitimate concerns about e-books and apps. They believe that reading e-books provides less personal experiences than reading print books. Further, e-books originally designed as print books often lose important features when cast in a digital format—features such as shape and size, which are important elements of book design. Also, in many instances the interactive features that accompany digital books are largely gamelike and often lead readers away from the story rather than into deeper engagement. Educators also express concern that the interactive features of e-books may impede the kinds of discussion about books that can enrich a child's reading experience.

What do you think? Given the potential value of digital books and apps as well as the potential problems associated with them, what steps might teachers take to ensure that they strike an appropriate balance between the use of print books and e-books?

▪ NONFICTION

By definition, nonfiction is "a genre created mainly to inform" (Mitchell, 2003, 326), but a definition does not provide the full picture. It is true that nonfiction informs, but nonfiction can do so much more. High quality nonfiction can satisfy readers' curiosity, extend their experiences, build knowledge about the wider world, provide opportunities to engage in critical literacy, and introduce children to text structures used by writers of nonfiction. Given the potential benefits of reading in the genre, there is little wonder that educators increasingly call for the wide reading of nonfiction. However, we need to add one more important reason for ensuring that nonfiction has an established place in our classroom: nonfiction can provide readers with satisfying reading experiences. Once begun, it is hard to put down a book like Deborah Hopkinson's *Titanic: Voices from the Disaster* (2012). Readers are bound to become engrossed in the stories of *Titanic* passengers like young Jack Thayer, who jumped into the icy waters of the Atlantic just before the great ship sank into the ocean—and survived! Equally intriguing is Caitlin O'Connell and Donna Jackson's investigation of the mysteries of elephant communication documented in *The Elephant Scientist* (2011). Nonfiction for young people offers a wealth of tantalizing information and ideas, but too often the genre is neglected in classrooms (Colman, 2007; Duke, 2000; Venezky, 2000). It is time for this to change.

How Nonfiction Works

In our discussion of nonfiction, we consider four facets: structure, style, organizational and support tools, and graphic and visual features.

Structure

In describing how fiction works, we focused on literary elements. However, writers of nonfiction organize their works differently. Some nonfiction writers utilize a narrative style, incorporating elements such as suspense and pacing, tools also utilized by writers of fiction. For example, in *Titanic: Voices from the Disaster*, the author shares the stories of different survivors, but no individual's story is told as a whole from beginning to end. Rather, the author shares each story piecemeal, and as the narration reveals the escalating danger on the doomed ship, readers are left wondering about the fate of the passengers whose stories they have been following.

Rather than utilizing a narrative style to inform, most writers of nonfiction rely on an expository style of writing to explain, inform, persuade, or describe. Expository writing uses various organizational patterns to present information; these patterns include description, sequence, comparison/contrast, problem/solution, and cause and effect. Table 2.6 includes definitions of each pattern as well as examples of books that are organized using these patterns. It is important that readers learn to recognize these different text patterns, because they reflect the line of thinking put forth by the writer of a book. A reader who is attuned to the way the writer has organized a book is in a far better position to comprehend the work.

Style

Writers of nonfiction use a variety of literary techniques to engage readers. They may approach their topic in an unusual way, craft an interesting title, or create an engaging introduction. Writers of nonfiction sometimes use humor or highly descriptive language and imagery to hook readers. Author Steve Sheinkin uses at least two of these tools in launching his 2013 Sibert award–winning book. The title is intriguing—*Bomb: The Race to Build—and Steal—the World's Most Dangerous Weapon* (2012)—and promises not just a historical analysis but something of a thriller as well. The hint of suspense suggested by the title is reinforced by the book's opening in which the reader meets Harry Gold as he rushes around his apartment, desperately attempting to hide evidence of his spying before opening the door to his accusers.

Table 2.6 Organizational Patterns Commonly Used in Informational Books

Organizational Pattern	Definition	Sample Books
Description	This pattern provides information about an object, event, or person, often qualifying the listing in terms of criteria such as size or importance.	¡Ole Flamenco! by George Ancona
Sequence	This pattern puts information such as events or steps into a sequence.	Island: A Story of the Galapagos by Jason Chin
Comparison/Contrast	This pattern reveals ways in which two or more things are alike and/or different.	Those Rebels, John & Tom by Barbara Kerley
Problem/Solution	This pattern identifies a problem and provides a possible solution or solutions.	Kakapo Rescue: Saving the World's Strangest Parrot by Sy Montgomery
Cause and Effect	This pattern shows how events, facts, or ideas happen because of other events, facts, or concepts.	Ocean Sunlight: How Tiny Plants Feed the Seas by Molly Bang and Penny Chisholm

Organizational and Support Tools

Writers of many works of nonfiction—particularly longer works—include different organizational and support tools such as a table of contents, index, glossary, timeline, and appendixes. These tools can help readers in many ways—if they learn how to use them. For example, a table of contents can provide a road map to a book's content, signal the structure of the book, and even serve to entice readers. A look at the table of contents of Stewart Ross's *Into the Unknown: How Great Explorers Found Their Way by Land, Sea, and Air* (2011) reveals that the first chapter is entitled "340 BC: Pytheas the Greek Sails to the Arctic Circle." How was such a feat possible in 340 BC? Readers will find answers to this and many other questions inside Ross's book. Table 2.7 lists organizational and support tools found in many nonfiction books and the ways in which each can facilitate reading.

Graphic and Visual Features

A wide variety of visuals can be found in nonfiction for children. These can include photographs, drawings, charts, diagrams, graphs, maps, and copies of documents. Visuals typically play a central role in nonfiction, particularly in nonfiction picture books, and they require the same meticulous research that is conducted for the text. The importance of visual elements in the Sibert honor book, *Electric Ben* (Byrd, 2012) by Robert Byrd, is signaled by the author/illustrator note found at the end of this biography about the remarkable Benjamin Franklin. In the note, Byrd discusses his research for the ink and watercolor paintings that fill the pages of the book.

Visuals serve a variety of functions in nonfiction. They can help to clarify abstract concepts, convey specific facts, or clarify specialized vocabulary. Visuals can provide background knowledge necessary for readers' understanding. In *Electric Ben*, visuals convey a wealth of information including details about daily life in Boston in the 1700s and the work of printers and firefighters. Visuals help readers better understand Franklin's remarkable scientific experiments, and a reproduction of a page from Franklin's *Poor Richard's Almanack* helps the reader to better appreciate Benjamin Franklin, the writer. Byrd also includes visual representations of major historical events including the Boston Tea Party and the Battle of Lexington.

Table 2.7 Organizational and Support Tools Often Found in Informational Books and Biographies

Organizational Tool	Purpose
Table of contents	• Provides a road map to the book's content • Signals structure of book • Serves to entice readers • Helps in locating information within book
Index	• Assists in locating information within book
Glossary	• Includes definitions of key vocabulary words
Timeline	• Gives an overview of the order of important events
Bibliography and source notes	• Provides information that readers can use to evaluate the thoroughness of author's research
Note about the author	• Provides information about the author's credentials

Subgenres of Nonfiction

We use the term "nonfiction" as an umbrella term, and under that umbrella we include biographies, autobiographies, memoirs, and informational books. Biographies are nonfiction books that inform about an individual's life, whereas autobiographies are books that individuals write to document their own lives. In a memoir, an author also shares events from his or her life. However, authors of memoirs typically focus on one particular event (or time period) in their life, reflecting on what was personally significant about it.

Snakes (Scholastic)

Informational books refer to books intended to inform about subjects, issues, or ideas. They largely present factual information about which there is general agreement. *Snakes* (Bishop, 2012) by Nic Bishop is such a book. The author presents information about the anatomy of snakes, their physical characteristics, their diet, and their defense mechanisms, as well as other topics. Other informational books move beyond the presentation of factual information to present researched information with interpretation. These are what author Marc Aronson (2012) described as books that "take you on a journey." *Titanic: Voices from the Disaster* by Deborah Hopkinson does just this. The author weaves together the voices of *Titanic* survivors to tell the gripping story of the maiden voyage and subsequent sinking of the great ocean liner. A final type of informational book is the nonfiction of inquiry or what Myra Zarnowski and Susan Turkel (2011) have described as the "literature of inquiry" (31). Like writers of interpretive informational books, writers of the nonfiction of inquiry also conduct in-depth research and then synthesize and interpret the findings. However, what sets the nonfiction of inquiry apart is that the author makes explicit the inquiry process engaged in by the researcher. That is, the reader gains insight into the investigative process. This type of nonfiction can be a valuable tool for content teachers who want their students to better understand what the inquiry process is all about. Marc Aronson's *If Stones Could Speak: Unlocking the Secrets of Stonehenge* (2010) is an example of such a work.

■ POETRY

Poetry is an almost indefinable genre. Poetry is often marked by its conciseness and insight, and yet a particular poem may be notable because it tells a humorous story. Poetry can be striking for its distinctive use of rhythm and rhyme, but, once again, many poems that touch us do not rhyme and have no distinctive rhythm. Poetry is indeed an elusive genre to define.

The importance of poetry is recognized in educational standards that call for the wide reading, interpretation, and analysis of poetry. Children as young as first grade are often expected to identify words and phrases in poems that suggest feelings or that appeal to the senses, whereas older students are expected to explore the structure of poems, among other things. Yet a word of warning is called for: we know that poetry in the form of Mother Goose rhymes is often children's first introduction to literature, and young children delight in listening to and joining in the narration of these engaging rhymes. But all too often, within a span of a few years, too many children insist that they do not like poetry. Part of the problem may be their limited exposure to poetry beyond Mother Goose rhymes; there is no excuse for this to happen given the wealth of poetry for children that can delight and engage. One way of finding appealing poetry for use in the classroom is by becoming familiar with the work of poets who have won the National Council of Teachers of English Award for Excellence in Poetry for Children.

How Poetry Works

Many of the poems we love are distinctive because of their sounds and images. Poets work with a variety of tools in crafting their work. These tools range from rhyme and rhythm to onomatopoeia and personification. In Table 2.8, we list some of these elements of poetry and present definitions and examples.

Categories of Poetry

A variety of subgenres of poetry are written for children ranging from Mother Goose rhymes that young children find so appealing to narrative poems that tell stories to free verse, which has no discernible form. In Table 2.9 we list and define a few of the many forms of poetry that are written for children. For a guide to still other poetic forms, you can turn to Paul Janeczko's *A Kick in the Head* (2009), a guide that children also find intriguing.

Table 2.8 Tools of the Poet

Tool	Definition	Example
Rhythm	Rhythm refers to the beat of a poem.	Humpty Dumpty sat on a wall.
Rhyme	Rhyme is created when words end in the same sound.	Humpty Dumpty sat on a *wall.* Humpty Dumpty had a great *fall.*
Alliteration	Alliteration is the repetition of the same sounds within a sentence or phrase.	Peter Piper picked a peck of pickled peppers.
Onomatopoeia	Onomatopoeia is the use of words in a poem that imitate the actual sounds of things.	Bam! Pow! Wham! Meow, moo, quack.
Sensory imagery	Sensory imagery is language that appeals to the senses—visual, auditory, etc.	The red and orange of autumn leaves burn bright. . . .
Simile	A simile is an explicit comparison that uses the word "like" or "as."	The moon is like a rocking chair.
Metaphors	A metaphor is a direct comparison in which one thing is described as if it was another.	All the world's a stage.
Personification	In personification, an inanimate object is given human characteristics.	Rain, rain, go to Spain, Never show your face again!

Technology Tip

The Internet offers many Web sites related to children's literature. For an extensive collection of nursery rhymes and intriguing information about their origins and history, visit www.rhymes .org.uk.

Table 2.9 Types of Poems

Type of Poem	*Definition*
Mother Goose rhymes	These traditional poems include rhymes such as "Jack and Jill" and "Hey Diddle Diddle," which are much loved by children. They are marked by the distinctive use of rhythm and rhyme.
Lyric or expressive poems	Poems in this category are works of emotion, observation, or insight. An example is Robert Louis Stevenson's poem entitled "Happy Thought": The world is so full of a number of things, I'm sure we should be as happy as kings.
Narrative poems	Narrative poems are those that tell stories and include familiar works such as "'Twas the Night before Christmas" or the popular baseball poem "Casey at the Bat."
Limericks	Limericks are form poems identifiable by their distinctive rhythm and rhyming pattern: AABBA An example of a limerick: There was an Old Man who said, "How Shall I flee from this horrible Cow? I will sit on this stile, And continue to smile, Which may soften the heart of that Cow."
Haiku	Haiku is another type of form poem. It consists of three lines with five syllables in line one, seven syllables in line two, and five syllables in line three. Traditional haikus make observations about nature.
Dialogue poems	Dialogue poems are poems for two voices to read aloud: Pussy cat, pussy cat, where have you been? I've been to London to look at the queen. Pussy, pussy cat, what did you there? I frightened a little mouse under her chair.
Free verse	Free verse is poetry with no discernible form and no rhyme or particular rhythm.

■ CONCLUSION

We have covered a great deal of ground in this chapter! We envision it as a foundational chapter to which you will return repeatedly as you read the remainder of this book. We hope that you will see this chapter as a repository of textual information to use as you select books for your classroom, as you guide students' experiences with literature, as you plan instructional activities for literature, and as you develop literary units and literature-based content units.

■ RECOMMENDED BOOKS

Picture Books

Aardema, Verna. *Borreguita and the Coyote.* Illustrated by Petra Mathers. New York: Knopf, 1991. In this Mexican folktale, the *borreguita* proves to be far more clever than the coyote that wants to eat her. Ages five through nine.

Bang, Molly. *When Sophie Gets Angry—Really, Really Angry. . . .* New York: Scholastic, 1999. We see the power of a young child's emotional outpouring when required to share a toy with her sister. Ages five through seven.

Barnett, Mac. *Extra Yarn.* Illustrated by Jon Klassen. New York: Balzer & Bray, 2012. When a little girl finds a magic yarn box, she transforms her drab and dull town by creating colorful clothing for everyone and everything. Ages five through eight.

Bingham, Kelly. *Z Is for Moose.* Illustrated by Paul Zelinsky. New York: Greenwillow, 2012. Moose can't wait for his turn to appear on stage in Zebra's alphabet play, but when the time finally arrives, Moose discovers that he has been replaced by Mouse. A monumental (and hilarious) tantrum follows! Ages six through nine.

Browne, Anthony. *Voices in the Park.* New York: Knopf, 1998. A visit to the park is told from four very different viewpoints. Ages eight and older.

Bunting, Eve. *Smoky Night.* Illustrated by David Diaz. Boston: Houghton Mifflin Harcourt, 1999. When Daniel's neighborhood is threatened by rioters, he and his mother connect with neighbors from different cultures for the first time. Ages eight and older.

Burleigh, Robert. *Flight.* Illustrated by Mike Wimmer. New York: Philomel, 1991. This book chronicles Charles Lindbergh's 1927 solo flight across the Atlantic from New York to Paris. Ages eight through twelve.

Buzzeo, Toni. *One Cool Friend.* Illustrated by David Small. New York: Dial, 2012. When a boy brings a penguin home from the aquarium, his dad appears to be oblivious to the antics of the boy and his new pet. The ending of this book holds a wonderful surprise for the reader. Ages six through ten.

Cordell, Matthew. *Hello! Hello!* New York: Hyperion, 2012. A little girl ventures alone into the natural world because her family is so engaged with their technologies that they have no time for her. Ages five through eight.

Cronin, Doreen. *Click Clack Moo: Cows That Type.* Illustrated by Betsy Lewin. New York: Simon and Schuster, 2000. When Farmer Brown's cows go on strike, they spell out their demands on a typewriter in the barn. Ages five through eight.

Daly, Niki. *Pretty Salma: A Little Red Riding Hood Story from Africa.* New York: Clarion, 2007. In this African version of "Little Red Riding Hood," a girl sent to market by her grandmother is tricked by Mr. Dog. Ages five through eight.

dePaola, Tomie. *Strega Nona.* New York: Simon & Schuster, 1979. Events get out of hand when Big Anthony makes the magic pasta pot cook. Ages five through eight.

Ehlert, Lois. *Top Cat.* Boston: Houghton Mifflin Harcourt, 2001. Top Cat has to mentor the new kitten in his home. Ages five through seven.

Falconer, Ian. *Olivia.* New York: Atheneum, 2000. Through text and illustration, readers meet Olivia, a little pig whose daily life is lived fully and expressively. Ages five through eight.

Fleming, Candace. *Oh, No!* Illustrated by Eric Rohmann. New York: Schwartz & Wade, 2012. Tiger is on the prowl, and one by one the jungle animals are trapped in a deep, deep hole. Who will come to their rescue? Ages five through eight.

Fox, Mem. *Wilfrid Gordon McDonald Partridge.* Illustrated by Julie Vivas. San Diego: Kane Miller, 1989. Determined to help Miss Nancy, who has lost her memory, Wilfrid sets out to learn what a memory is by talking to all the old folks in the retirement home. Ages five through eight.

Frazee, Marla. *Boot and Shoe.* New York: Beach Lane Books, 2012. When two devoted puppies are separated, a comic search (and touching loneliness) culminate in a joyful reunion. Ages five through eight.

Henkes, Kevin. *Kitten's First Full Moon.* New York: Greenwillow, 2004. Mistaking the moon for a bowl of milk, kitten sets out to capture the elusive treat. Ages five through seven.

Hutchins, Pat. *Rosie's Walk.* New York: Aladdin, 1971. The illustrations tell the *real* story of what happens when Rosie the hen goes for a walk around the barnyard. Ages five through eight.

Hyman, Trina Schart. *Little Red Riding Hood.* New York: Holiday House, 1987. This is a retelling of the Grimm version of "Little Red Riding Hood." Ages five through eight.

Kerley, Barbara. *Those Rebels, John & Tom.* Illustrated by Edwin Fotheringham. New York: Scholastic, 2012. John Adams and Thomas Jefferson had their differences, but these patriots set those differences aside to work for the good of the American colonies. Ages seven through ten.

Kimmel, Eric. *Anansi Goes Fishing.* Illustrated by Janet Stevens. New York: Holiday House, 1992. The tables are turned when Anansi tries to trick Turtle into getting him a fish for dinner. Ages five through eight.

Klassen, Jon. *I Want My Hat Back.* Somerville, MA: Candlewick Press, 2011. A bear goes searching for his lost hat in this humorous picture book told through the clever interplay of pictures and text. Ages five through eight.

Logue, Mary. *Sleep Like a Tiger.* Illustrated by Pamela Zagarenski. Boston: Houghton Mifflin Harcourt, 2012. In this bedtime story, a little girl avoids saying goodnight by repeatedly asking her parents about the sleeping habits of various animals. Ages five through eight.

Marino, Gianna. *Too Tall Houses.* New York: Viking, 2012. When two good friends begin to compete to see who can build the tallest house, they learn a valuable lesson about cooperation. Ages five through nine.

McDermott, Gerald. *Coyote: A Trickster Tale from the American Southwest.* Boston: Houghton Mifflin Harcourt, 1999. Coyote decides he wants to fly with the crows—without success, of course. Ages five through nine.

———. *Monkey: A Trickster Tale from India.* Boston: Houghton Mifflin Harcourt, 2014. To get the mangoes on the distant island, Monkey asks Crocodile to help him. Ages five through nine.

———. *Zomo the Rabbit: A Trickster Tale from Africa.* Boston: Houghton Mifflin Harcourt, 1996. Zomo the Rabbit sets out to trick other animals into doing his work, only to find the joke is on him. Ages five through nine.

McKinlay, Meg, and Leila Rudge. *No Bears.* Somerville, MA: Candlewick Press, 2012. Believing there are too many bears in books, a girl constructs her own book, but unbeknownst to her, a bear is integrally involved in the creation of her book. Ages five through nine.

Pilkey, Dav. *The Paperboy.* New York: Scholastic, 1999. On a cold winter morning, a boy and his dog awaken in the dark to deliver newspapers. Ages five through nine.

Potter, Beatrix. *The Tale of Peter Rabbit.* London: Frederick Warne, 1902. Retrieved from www.gutenberg.org/ebooks/14838. In this classic story, Peter, a naughty rabbit who disobeys his mother, ends up caught in Mr. McGregor's garden. Ages five through eight.

Raschka, Chris. *A Ball for Daisy.* New York: Schwartz & Wade, 2011. In this wordless book, Daisy the dog is heartbroken when her beloved ball is destroyed. Ages five through eight.

Rathman, Peggy. *Officer Buckle and Gloria*. New York: Putnam, 1995. As Officer Buckle makes school rounds, giving safety tips to children, it is actually his dog, Gloria, who keeps the children amused—all unbeknownst to Officer Buckle. Ages six through nine.

Reynolds, Aaron. *Creepy Carrots*. Illustrated by Peter Brown. New York: Simon & Schuster, 2012. Jasper the rabbit is convinced that the carrots in Crackenhopper Field are out to get him. Ages five through nine.

Rocco, John. *Blackout*. New York: Hyperion, 2011. A blackout in the big city brings a family and neighbors together for a memorable evening—without technology. Ages five through nine.

Rohmann, Eric. *My Friend Rabbit*. New York: Roaring Brook, 2002. When Mouse's new plane is caught in a tree, Rabbit finds a clever solution. Ages five through seven.

Rylant, Cynthia. *The Relatives Came*. Illustrated by Stephen Gammell. New York: Bradbury, 1985. When the relatives arrive after traveling through the Appalachian Mountains, a wonderful family reunion ensues. Ages five through eight.

Sendak, Maurice. *Where the Wild Things Are*. New York: Harper & Row, 1963. When Max is sent to bed without any supper, he sails off in a magic boat to become king of the Wild Things. Ages five through seven.

Shannon, David. *No, David!* New York: Blue Sky/Scholastic, 1998. David's antics repeatedly elicit "No, David"—until he receives a reassuring hug from his mother. Ages five through seven.

Springman, I. C. *More*. Illustrated by Brian Lies. Boston: Houghton Mifflin, 2012. Page by page, frame by frame, magpie gathers, gathers, and gathers—until the she is literally overwhelmed by all her acquisitions. With the help of animal friends, magpie makes an important life change. Ages five through eight.

Stead, Phillip. *Bear Has a Story to Tell*. Illustrated by Erin Stead. New York: Roaring Brook Press, 2012. Bear wants to share a story with his friends, but with the approaching winter, no one has time to listen. Ages five through eight.

———. *A Sick Day for Amos McGee*. Illustrated by Erin Stead. New York: Roaring Brook Press, 2010. When the zookeeper calls in sick, his animal friends leave the zoo and travel to his home to comfort their friend. Ages five through eight.

Steig, William. *Doctor De Soto*. New York: Farrar, 1982. Doctor De Soto, a mouse dentist, faces eminent danger when he agrees to treat a fox. Ages five through eight.

Stein, David Ezra. *Because Amelia Smiled*. Somerville, MA: Candlewick Press, 2012. As Amelia runs through the streets of New York City in the rain, she smiles, a smile that sets into motion a chain of events that extends across the world. Ages five through eight.

Stoop, Naoko. *Red Knit Cap Girl*. New York: Little Brown, 2012. More than anything Red Knit Cap Girl longs to talk to the moon. Ages five through seven.

Teague, Mark. *Dear Mrs. LaRue: Letters from Obedience School*. New York: Scholastic, 2003. When Ike the dog is sent to obedience school, he pens a series of letters home telling of his cruel mistreatment—but the illustrations tell another story. Ages six through ten.

Wiesner, David. *Art and Max*. New York: Clarion 2010. This is the story of two very different lizard artists—and also an exploration of the creative process. Ages seven through ten.

Willems, Mo. *Don't Let the Pigeon Drive the Bus*. New York: Hyperion, 2003. A persistent pigeon uses every ploy in the book to convince the reader to let him drive the bus. Ages five through eight.

———. *Leonardo the Terrible Monster*. New York: Hyperion, 2005. Leonardo is determined to find someone to "scare the tuna salad out of," but to his surprise, he discovers that being a friend is better than being a monster. Ages five through seven.

Yorinks, Arthur. *Hey, Al!* Illustrated by Richard Egielski. New York: Square Fish/Macmillan, 1989. When a giant bird ferries Al and his dog to a paradise island in the sky, they make some discoveries about what is really important in life. Ages five through nine.

Young, Ed. *Lon Po Po: A Red Riding Hood Story from China.* New York: Puffin, 1989. In this Chinese version of "Little Red Riding Hood," three girls left at home alone are approached by a menacing wolf. Ages seven through ten.

Chapter-length Fiction

Alvarez, Julia. *Return to Sender.* New York: Yearling, 2010. Tyler worries that the Mexican laborers his dad has hired are undocumented, while Mari and her family live in constant fear that the authorities will deport them to Mexico. Ages ten and older.

Anderson, M. T. *Feed.* Somerville, MA: Candlewick Press, 2002. In this futuristic world shaped by consumerism and corporate gain, individuals' minds are connected directly to a computer network through which they receive constant messages from advertisers. Ages eleven and older.

Blackwood, Gary. *The Shakespeare Stealer.* New York: Dutton, 1998. Ordered by a cruel master to steal the script of *Hamlet* from the Globe Theatre, Widge confronts a new world when he is taken in and befriended by the Globe company members. Ages ten and older.

Bradley, Kimberly Brubaker. *The War That Saved My Life.* New York: Dial, 2015. Ada has been confined to a London apartment her entire life because of her crooked foot. To escape the German blitz during World War II, she is evacuated to the countryside where a new life opens up for her. Ages ten and older.

Colfer, Eoin. *Artemis Fowl: The Graphic Novel.* Illustrated by Rigano Giovanni. New York: Disney-Hyperion, 2007. This is the graphic novel version of the adventure story of the twelve-year-old criminal mastermind Artemis Fowl. Ages ten and older.

DiCamillo, Kate. *Because of Winn Dixie.* Somerville, MA: Candlewick Press, 2000. Her newly adopted dog, Winn Dixie, becomes the means by which Opal connects to others in her small town and thereby comes to terms with her mother's leaving. Ages nine through twelve.

Divakaruni, Chitra Banerjee. *The Conch Bearer.* New York: Roaring Brook, 2003. Twelve-year-old Anan's quest begins in modern-day Calcutta and takes him on a dangerous journey through the Himalayas with his companion, Nisha, to return a magical conch to its rightful place. Ages ten and older.

Draper, Sharon. *Stella by Starlight.* New York: Atheneum, 2015. Growing up in the Depression-era South, Stella witnesses a meeting of the Ku Klux Klan that signals the troubles that will come to her African American community. Ages ten and older.

Farmer, Nancy. *The Sea of Trolls.* New York: Richard Jackson/Atheneum, 2004. Jack, a bard's apprentice, and his little sister are kidnapped by Viking "berserkers," and Jack is sent on a quest across the dangerous Sea of Trolls to try and reverse a spell gone awry. Author Nancy Farmer draws on Norse mythology in crafting this epic adventure. Ages eleven and older.

Lewis, C. S. *The Lion, the Witch and the Wardrobe.* Illustrated by Pauline Baynes. New York: Macmillan, 1950. Four children discover that they can go through the back of a wardrobe to enter the magical world of Narnia, where they meet the lion Aslan who is trying to free Narnia from the spell cast by the evil White Witch. First in a series. Ages nine through twelve.

MacLachlan, Patricia. *Sarah, Plain and Tall.* New York: Harper Collins, 1985. In this Newbery Award book, a brother and sister hope that Sarah will choose to stay on the prairie and become their mother. Ages nine through twelve. Sequels: *Skylark, Caleb's Story, More Perfect Than the Moon.*

Paulsen, Gary. *Hatchet.* New York: Viking, 1987. Brian survives a plane crash, only to find himself stranded in the Canadian wilderness where he encounters one challenge after another armed only with a hatchet and his determination to survive. Ages ten through twelve.

Riordan, Rick. *The Lightning Thief.* New York: Miramax, 2005. Young Percy Jackson, a demigod, finds his life entangled with mythological monsters and the warring gods of Mount Olympus. Ages nine through twelve.

Rowling, J. K. *Harry Potter and the Sorcerer's Stone.* New York: Scholastic, 1998. An orphaned boy begins his education at Hogwarts School of Witchcraft and Wizardry and discovers that he is the most famous wizard alive. First in the series. Ages nine and older.

Schlitz, Laura Amy. *Splendors and Glooms.* Somerville, MA: Candlewick Press, 2012. This complex story set in Victorian England has three major plot strands—the story of orphans who work as assistants to a sinister puppeteer, the story of an aristocratic child who vanishes, and the story of a witch who may be destroyed by the phoenix stone she wears around her neck. Ages eleven and older.

Schmidt, Gary. *What Came from the Stars.* New York: Clarion, 2012. As the Valorim is about to fall to an evil enemy, they send a chain containing the art of their civilization into the universe where it finds its way into the lunchbox of Tommy Pepper, a sixth grader in Plymouth, Massachusetts. Ages ten and older.

Siegel, Siena Cherson. *To Dance: A Ballerina's Graphic Novel.* Illustrated by Mark Siegel. New York: Atheneum, 2006. The author shares her early years of studying at the School of American Ballet. Ages eight through twelve.

Smith, Jeff. *Little Mouse Gets Ready.* New York: Toon Books, 2009. Little Mouse is faced with the challenge of getting dressed in this Geisel Honor book. Ages four through seven.

Tamaki, Jillian. *This One Summer.* Illustrated by Mariko Tamaki. New York: First Second, 2014. Told in graphic novel format, a young girl not yet ready to leave childhood is nonetheless surrounded by the world of adolescence one summer. Ages twelve and older.

Vanderpool, Claire. *Moon over Manifest.* New York: Delacorte, 2010. Only as she gradually learns of events from 1917 and 1918 does Abilene come to understand why her father has sent her to live in the town of his youth while he travels the country seeking work during the Great Depression. Ages ten and older.

Varon, Sara. *Bake Sale.* New York: First Second, 2011. In this graphic novel, Cupcake encounters problems in the kitchen and is not sure where to find answers to the problems. Ages six through nine.

Wiles, Deborah. *Each Little Bird That Sings.* Boston: Houghton Mifflin Harcourt, 2006. Ten-year-old Comfort thinks she knows all about death; after all, her family lives in the local funeral home. But the events Comfort must deal with one summer put her touch with loss and life in ways she never imagined. Ages nine through twelve.

Nonfiction

Ancona, George. *¡Ole Flamenco!* New York: Lee & Low, 2010. The author explores the history, traditions, and techniques of the flamenco. Picture book. Ages seven through ten.

Aronson, Marc. *If Stones Could Speak: Unlocking the Secrets of Stonehenge.* Washington, DC: National Geographic, 2010. A documentation of the investigative quest to determine why Stonehenge was created. Ages nine through twelve.

Bang, Molly, and Penny Chisholm. *Ocean Sunlight: How Tiny Plants Feed the Seas.* New York: Blue Sky Press/Scholastic, 2012. The authors explore the food chains and life cycles deep within the oceans. Picture book. Ages nine through twelve.

Bishop, Nic. *Snakes*. New York: Scholastic, 2012. Bishop's book contains a variety of information about snakes and includes remarkable photographs of the creatures. Ages six through ten.

Burleigh, Robert. *Flight*. New York: Puffin, 1997. This works captures the drama of Lindbergh's heroic solo flight across the Atlantic. Picture book. Ages seven through ten.

Byrd, Robert. *Electric Ben: The Amazing Life and Times of Benjamin Franklin*. New York: Dial, 2012. This wonderfully illustrated award-winning biography is filled with information about the adult life of the remarkable Benjamin Franklin. Ages eight through twelve.

Chin, Jason. *Island: A Story of the Galápagos*. New York: Roaring Brook Press, 2012. Chin explains the evolution of a fictional island in the Galápagos across six million years. Ages eight through twelve.

Hopkinson, Deborah. Titanic: *Voices from the Disaster*. New York: Scholastic, 2012. Through the voices of survivors, Hopkinson chronicles the events leading up to the *Titanic*'s collision with the iceberg and the dramatic hours following the disastrous accident. Ages ten and older.

Montgomery, Sy. *Kakapo Rescue: Saving the World's Strangest Parrot*. Photographs by Nic Bishop. Boston: Houghton Mifflin Harcourt, 2010. The author documents ten days of work by a scientific team attempting to save from extinction the kakapo, a flightless New Zealand parrot. Ages nine and up.

O'Connell, Caitlin, and Donna Jackson. *The Elephant Scientist*. Photographs by Timothy Rodwell. Boston: Houghton Mifflin, 2011. Part of the Scientists in the Field series, this book presents information about elephant communication and the ways in which scientists have uncovered the information. Ages eight through twelve.

Ross, Stewart. *Into the Unknown: How Great Explorers Found Their Way by Land, Sea, and Air*. Illustrated by Stephen Biesty. Somerville, MA: Candlewick Press, 2011. Ross relates the stories of fourteen brave explorers beginning with the explorations of a little-known Greek who set sail for the Arctic Circle in 340 BC and culminating with the story of astronauts Armstrong and Aldrin in 1969. Ages nine through twelve.

Sheinkin, Steve. *Bomb: The Race to Build—and Steal—the World's Most Dangerous Weapon*. New York: Flash Point/Roaring Brook Press, 2012. Sheinkin documents the intrigue associated with the race to develop the atomic bomb. Ages ten and older.

Poetry

Janeczko, Paul. *A Kick in the Head: An Everyday Guide to Poetic Forms*. Illustrated by Chris Raschka. Somerville, MA: Candlewick Press, 2009. This is a playful guide to a host of poetic forms. Ages eight and older.

■ REFERENCES

Aronson, Marc. "Mad Max: Digital Nonfiction in the Graveyard of Previous (Expensive) Tools." Presentation at the International Reading Association's 57th annual convention, Chicago, IL, April 29, 2012.

Bader, Barbara. *American Picturebooks from "Noah's Ark" to "The Beast Within."* New York: Macmillan, 1976.

Cadden, Mike. "Genre As Nexus: The Novel for Children and Young Adults." In *Handbook of Research on Children's and Young Adult Literature*, ed. Shelby A. Wolf, Karen Coats, Patricia Enciso, and Christine A. Jenkins, 302–12. New York: Routledge, 2011.

Coles, M., and C. Hall. "Breaking the Line: New Literacies, Postmodernism and the Teaching of Printed Texts." *Reading: Literacy and Language* 35 (2001): 111–14.

Colman, Penny. "A New Way to Look at Literature: A Visual Model for Analyzing Fiction and Nonfiction." *Language Arts* 84 (2007): 257–68.

Duke, Nell K. "3.6 Minutes Per Day: The Scarcity of Informational Texts in First Grade." *Reading Research Quarterly* 35 (2000): 202–24.

Eeds, Maryann, and Ralph Peterson. "Teacher As Curator: Learning to Talk about Literature." *The Reading Teacher* 45 (1991): 118–26.

Eisner, Will. *Comics and Sequential Art: Principles and Practices from the Legendary Storyteller.* New York: Norton, 1985.

Greenlaw, M. Jean. "Science Fiction: Images of the Future, Shadows of the Past." *Top of the News* 39 (1982): 64–71.

Lewis, David. *Reading Contemporary Picturebooks: Picturing Text.* New York: RoutledgeFalmer, 2001.

Martinez, Miriam, and Janis M. Harmon. "Picture/Text Relationships: An Investigation of Literary Elements in Picturebooks." *Literacy Research and Instruction* 51(2012): 323–43.

Meek, Margaret. *How Texts Teach What Readers Learn.* Somers, NY: Richard C. Owen Publishers, 1987.

Mitchell, Diana. *Children's Literature: An Invitation to the World.* Boston: Pearson, 2003.

Pantaleo, Sylvia. *Exploring Student Response to Contemporary Picturebooks.* Toronto: University of Toronto Press, 2008.

———. "The Metafictive Nature of Postmodern Picturebooks." *The Reading Teacher* 67 (2014): 324–32.

Pantaleo, Sylvia, and Lawrence Sipe. "Postmodernism and Picturebooks." In *Postmodern Picturebooks: Play, Parody, and Self-referentiality*, ed. Lawrence Sipe and Sylvia Pantaleo, 1–8. New York: Routledge, 2008.

Roser, Nancy L., Miriam Martinez, Kathleen McDonnold, and Charles Fuhrken. "Beginning Chapter Books: Their Features and Their Support of Children's Reading." In *Fifty-third Yearbook of the National Reading Conference*, ed. Colleen M. Fairbanks, Jo Worthy, Beth Malock, James V. Hoffman, and Diane L. Schallert, 308–20. Oak Creek, WI: National Reading Conference, 2004.

Satrapi, Marjane. *Persepolis: The Story of a Childhood.* New York: Pantheon, 2003.

Sipe, Lawrence, and Sylvia Pantaleo. *Postmodern Picturebooks: Play, Parody, and Self-Referentiality.* New York: Routledge, 2008.

Spiegelman, Art. *Maus.* New York: Pantheon, 1997.

Teale, William H., Jung Kim, and William Boerman-Cornell. "It's Elementary–Graphic Novels for the K–6 Classroom." *Book Links* 17, no. 5 (2008): 6–13.

Tomlinson, Carl M., Michael O. Tunnell, and Donald J. Richgels. "The Content and Writing of History in Textbooks and Trade Books." In *The Story of Ourselves: Teaching History through Children's Literature*, 51–62, ed. Michael O. Tunnell and Richard Ammon. Portsmouth, NH: Heinemann, 1993.

Venezky, Richard L. "The Origins of the Present-day Chasm between Adult Literacy Needs and School Literacy Instruction." *Scientific Studies of Reading* 4 (2000): 19–39.

Watson, K. "The Postmodern Picture Book in the Secondary Classroom." *English in Australia* 140 (2004): 55–57.

Waugh, Patricia. *Metafiction: The Theory and Practice of Self-conscious Fiction.* New York: Methuen, 1984.

Yokota, Junko. "The Past, Present and Future of Digital Picturebooks for Children." In *Digital Literature for Children: Texts, Readers, and Educational Practices*, ed. M. Manresa Potrony and N. Real Mercada, 73–86. Brussels: Peter Lang, 2015.

Yokota, Junko, and William Teale. "Picture Books and the Digital World: Educators Making Informed Choices." *The Reading Teacher* 67 (2014): 577–85.

Zarnowsky, Myra, and Susan Turkel. "Nonfiction Literature That Highlights Inquiry: How Real People Solve Real Problems." *Journal of Children's Literature* 37 (2011): 30–37.

■ RESOURCES

Bang, Molly. *Picture This: How Pictures Work.* New York: Chronicle Books, 2000.

Gill, Sharon Ruth. "What Teachers Need to Know about the 'New' Nonfiction." *The Reading Teacher* 63 (2010): 260–67.

Gonyea, Mark. *A Book about Design: Complicated Doesn't Make It Good.* New York: Henry Holt, 2005.

Horning. Kathleen T. *From Cover to Cover.* New York: HarperCollins, 2010.

Lukens, Rebecca J., and Ruth K. Cline. *A Critical Handbook of Literature for Young Adults.* Boston: Addison-Wesley, 1995.

Matulka, Denise I. *A Picture Book Primer: Understanding and Using Picture Books.* Westport, CT: Libraries Unlimited, 2008.

Nodelman, Perry. *Words about Pictures: The Narrative Art of Children's Picture Books.* Athens: University of Georgia Press, 1988.

Sipe, Lawrence R. "How Picture Books Work: A Semiotically Framed Theory of Text-picture Relationships." *Children Literature in Education* 29 (1998): 97–108.

Sipe, Lawrence R., and Caroline E. McGuire. "Picturebook Endpapers: Resources for Literary and Aesthetic Interpretation." *Children's Literature in Education* 37 (2006): 291–304.

Temple, Charles, Miriam Martinez, and Junko Yokota. *Children's Books in Children's Hands.* 5th ed. Boston: Pearson, 2015.

Wolfenbarger, Carol, and Lawrence R. Sipe. "A Unique Visual and Literary Art Form: Recent Research on Picturebooks." *Language Arts* 84 (2007): 272–80.

Zarnowski, Myra, and Susan Turkel. "Nonfiction Literature That Highlights Inquiry: How Real People Solve Real Problems." *Journal of Children's Literature* 37 (2011): 30–37.

■ WANT TO KNOW MORE?

1. Literary elements in picture books are developed through the interplay of pictures and words. With a partner, select a picture book to analyze this interplay. *Art and Max* by David Wiesner would be a good choice for this activity. One partner should read only the words of the story. The second person "reads" only the illustrations. After completing the reading, each partner writes a summary of the story to share with the partner. Then discuss the critical information about literary elements that each person included in the retelling. How do the pictures and words seem to work together in the story?

2. Reading deeply is an important goal of twenty-first century reading, and this means—in part—exploring themes of books. To support students in making inferences about theme, a teacher needs to be prepared to guide students in identifying textual information that may point to particular thematic understandings.

Examine a book such as *Stella by Starlight* by Sharon Draper or *Each Little Bird That Sings* by Deborah Wiles and identify one of the themes that you believe emerge from the book. What textual information can you draw on to support this theme? Invite a classmate to read the same book and think about theme. Then share your thinking with one another.

Looking Closely at a Picture Book:
Freedom in Congo Square

By Carole Boston Weatherford
Illustrated by R. Gregory Christie

reedom in Congo Square brings powerful storytelling, combining text and illustration into a comprehensive experience that begins with the front cover and lingers in the mind and heart long after closing the back cover. Set in the days of slavery, the story describes slaves looking forward to Sundays, their one day with a bit of freedom, when they met other black people, both free and enslaved, in Congo Square.

Research: Congo Square is a historic place designated as an open area for meeting ever since the city of New Orleans was established in 1718. The book's front matter and end matter give some background information, and more can be learned by reading various documents readily available in print and online. Of course, it is important to consider what it might have meant to have a half a day once a week to gather freely when enduring being enslaved the rest of their week. Children may better understand the book by being introduced to the historic setting, seeing images of musical instruments common then, and discussing the activities of Congo Square. When children gain background knowledge prior to reading the book, they will be more likely to be able to read the book more closely and enhance their understanding. Although teacher/librarian research prior to the first reading is encouraged to enhance the introduction of the book, perhaps it is best to wait until after the first reading to engage children in research so they have the book's context on which to base their research.

Reading the text: The poetic text of Carole Boston Weatherford offers readers a soulful peek into the lives of enslaved African Americans in New Orleans. Alluding to harsh realities explicitly yet in terms child readers can readily understand, Weatherford uses the power of language to convey emotions. Without the weight of wordiness, the use of economy in expression is entirely effective.

Reading the illustrations: R. Gregory Christie used acrylic wash and collage to create artwork that reflects the earthy colors of the landscape, along with colors that inspire dreams. His choice of silhouetted faces and exaggerated body language communicates effectively.

Reading the book as a whole: After introducing the book with salient background information to set the stage for the reading, we suggest that that the entire book be read aloud without much more than a few "think-alouds" by the teacher that scaffold ways in which children might respond to the story as a whole.

The book cover: Serving as an "advertisement" to entice readers to select the book, this introduction adds text that informs us of the title, author, and illustrator. Reading the title offers an opportunity to briefly introduce the concept of Congo Square, as well as that of "freedom" during the days of slavery. Depending on what the children may already know, teachers can adjust the amount of background knowledge on slavery that the children may need to have introduced prior to the reading of the book. Naming the author and illustrator is important, but a richer introduction about who they are and their accomplishments (e.g., Coretta Scott King honorees) may come after the first reading. The visual introduction of the cover includes an enslaved protagonist, but shown here depicting the "freedom" felt in Congo Square, with its characteristic circular patterned cobblestones.

Each of the double-spreads begins with a day of the week. With a repeated reading of the book, it may be interesting to read all seven pages by lines: first read all the double lines about the days of the week and the work to be done, then only the third lines of each page, and finally all the last lines of each page. The couplets that begin with the name of the day serve as a brief list of the major work being done. The third line of each page drives a description of the hardships. Reading them together punctuates the difficulty of life, line after line. Finally, reading all the last lines consecutively offers a rhythmic countdown, demonstrating that the slaves looked forward to Congo Square every single day.

Little Bee Books. Reprinted with permission of Carole Boston Weatherford and R. Gregory Christie, copyright 2016.

Tuesdays, there were cows to feed,
fields to plow, and rows to seed.

The illustrations depict the lives of the slaves by using repeated angular shapes showing extremely bent backs, for example. Yet the silhouetted faces look toward the right, toward the page-turns that come next in anticipation of the

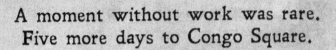

A moment without work was rare.
Five more days to Congo Square.

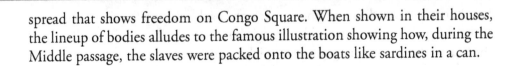

spread that shows freedom on Congo Square. When shown in their houses, the lineup of bodies alludes to the famous illustration showing how, during the Middle passage, the slaves were packed onto the boats like sardines in a can.

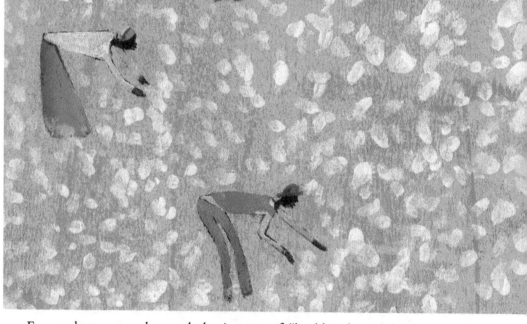

Week in, week out, from sun to sun, with always more chores to be done.

For students to understand the impact of "backbreaking labor," have them make the pose and keep it awhile, imagining being in that position all day, in the heat of the orange and golden sky, picking cotton that tears at their hands all the while. The extreme angularity of the bodies emphasizes the unnaturalness

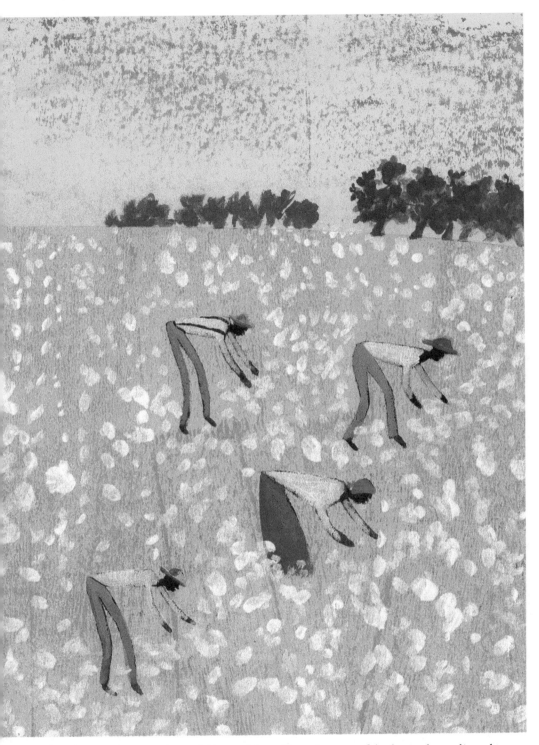

of enduring this position while working. Emotions are felt through reading the slaves' body language rather than the emotions on their faces. The regularity of the rows of cotton emphasizes the seemingly endlessness of the task.

It was a market and a gathering ground
where African music could resound.

This page marks an opportunity to understand that Congo Square was for more than dancing: it was a gathering place to share a musical heritage, to inspire new musical growth, a place to be together with others who endured enslavement. Upon repeated reading, pausing on this page to consider what such

Beneath the sun in the open air,
the crowd abuzz with news to share.

a gathering place might have meant could lead to discussions about Congo Square's continued importance during the decades before, during, and after slavery. What influences of today have roots in Congo Square?

Women in gauze, silk, and percale,

men in fringe and furry tails

Music played a major role in Congo Square. Sharing music through instruments, song, and dance was central to the time slaves spent together. In particular, long African drums were prominent. The illustrations depict both people

shook tambourines and shouted chants

as rhythms fueled a spirited dance.

and text swinging across the page, body poses rounded and joyful, brushstrokes in rhythmic motion.

Reference Material in the Book

The foreword, written by Freddi Williams Evans, researcher and author of a reference book about Congo Square, introduces and sets the stage for the reader. Back matter includes a glossary and author's note. These materials firmly ground the reality on which this book is based.

A compilation of resources about the book:
www.teachingbooks.net/tb.cgi?tid=48149&a=1

Illustrator Gregory Christie blogs about his thoughts in creating the art:
https://forum.teachingbooks.net/2016/02/guest-blogger-r-gregory-christie

Author Carole Boston Weatherford describes her thoughts about writing the text in an audio interview and recording of her reading:
www.teachingbooks.net/book_reading.cgi?id=12101&a=1

The Web site BrassyBrown.com includes a contemporary recording of drumming in Congo Square:
www.brassybrown.com/2015/12/interview-with

and an audio interview with the author:
https://soundcloud.com/brassybrown

An interview with Carole Boston Weatherford in "School Library Journal":
www.slj.com/2016/02/interviews/freedom-in-congo-square-an-interview-with-carole-boston-weatherford/#_

A lengthy interview with Gregory Christie prior to publication of *"Freedom in Congo Square"*:
http://blaine.org/sevenimpossiblethings/?p=1553

CHAPTER 3

Inviting Children into Literature

Classroom Libraries, Read-alouds, and Storytelling

Brother Hugo . . . knew that once a bear has a taste of letters, his love of books grows much the more.
          —from *Brother Hugo and the Bear* by Katy Beebe (2014, np)

Teachers work hard. They work hard to teach children *how* to read, but that is not enough. It is equally important that children *choose* to read, and if that is to happen, teachers must also nurture their students' love of books so that—like the bear in *Brother Hugo and the Bear*—their love grows "much the more."

Too many children do not choose to read. In fact, one study found that 50 percent of fifth graders read voluntarily for four minutes a day or less, 30 percent read for two minutes a day or less, and almost 10 percent reported never reading any books during their leisure time (Fielding, Wilson, and Anderson, 1986). It's little wonder that less than half of adult Americans don't read books either (National Endowment for the Arts, 2004).

The challenge for teachers is finding ways to help children discover the joys of reading. In this chapter we explore this issue.

THE LITERATURE-RICH CLASSROOM

Many years ago Janet Hickman (1981) conducted pioneering work in classrooms on children's spontaneous responses to literature. She noticed the ways in which classroom contexts shaped the children's responses, and she carefully described those classroom contexts. Hickman found that the teachers in her study invited responses to literature through the physical context they created, the way they used time, and the methods they used to encourage response. Some of the recommendations that Hickman offered based on her research included the following:

- Build extensive book collections and fill the classroom with attractive displays of high-quality books.

- Set aside ample time for all children to interact with books daily.
- Share literature with children daily by reading aloud and by introducing new books before putting them on display in the classroom.
- Provide children with opportunities to revisit some books repeatedly.

Those recommendations are as relevant today as they were thirty-five years ago, and in the following sections we explore these recommendations in greater depth.

The Classroom Library

When children walk into your classroom, it should be evident at a glance that it is a place where books matter! One feature that can send this signal is a good classroom library. Good classroom libraries are *not* bookshelves tucked away in the corner of the room. Rather, good classroom libraries are *focal areas* within classrooms. They are places where children can go to find and read high-quality children's literature. Is it really necessary to have a library center in the classroom, especially if your school has a well-stocked central library? We think it is essential. Estimates are that children in classrooms containing literature collections read 50 percent more than children in classrooms where literature is not available. What a difference!

Designing the Classroom Library Center

Not all library centers are equally appealing. Children beg to visit some centers, while others stand almost unused. Research by Lesley Morrow (1982) has shown that there are a number of design features you can implement to create classroom libraries that children find appealing and choose to use. These features are summarized in Table 3.1.

Often, when you step into a classroom, your eye is drawn to one area of the room; that eye-catching part is known as the focal area. The focal area isn't always the library center, but we think it should be. It isn't easy to define what makes a library center a focal area; in fact, it may be all the design features taken together that create such a space. Whatever the explanation, it is important to establish an eye-catching center that announces to students: "Literature matters in this classroom." In one school, teachers created centers built around themes. One teacher built an apple tree, using chicken wire covered with paper for the trunk and paper chains for the limbs. Across

Table 3.1 Characteristics of an Appealing Library Center

- The library center is a focal area of the classroom.
- The library center is partitioned off from the rest of the room.
- The library center is large enough to seat five or six children comfortably.
- The library center has two types of bookshelves: some that display the spines of books and others that display the covers of books.
- The library center offers comfortable seating.
- The library center offers a variety of other materials—literature-related displays, stuffed animals, and the like.
- The library center has an organizational system.
- The library center has books, books, and more books!
- The library center may include books borrowed from the school and public library.

the tree hung a banner that read "Don't Sit under the Apple Tree without a Good Book to Read." The apple motif was reflected throughout the center; for example, red beanbag chairs looked just like big apples. Another teacher used a sidewalk café theme and called her center "Café Escape." It was a perfect invitation to escape into a good book. To build ownership of the library center, some teachers invite their students to help them come up with the theme and a name for the library center.

You may also want to partition your library center off from the rest of the classroom. Like adults, children prefer to read in areas that are away from lots of hustle and bustle. So it makes sense to use something—for example, bookshelves or old sofas—to create a partition. One teacher turned her library center into the "O.K. Corral," using mesquite posts to build a fence around it. The possibilities are limited only by your imagination.

It is also important to create a library center that is large enough for at least some of your students to sit and read books. This means you will have to devote a chunk of floor space to the center. Why not just store the books in a bookcase instead and let students read at their desks? Many children prefer to lounge around in a library center. Besides, there are many times when reading becomes a social activity. Children may choose to read with a buddy or to share something they're reading. Imagine reading a riddle book without trying to stump someone! And the questions threaded through-out Steve Jenkins and Robin Page's *What Do You Do with a Tail Like This?* (Jenkins and Page, 2003) simply must be posed to a friend.

Of course, when the entire class is reading (and there should be times *every day* when this happens), the library center will not be able to accommodate everyone. During these times the center will function primarily as the place that students go to find books, and they will then need to spread out all over the classroom to read. Some may curl up under their desks; others may choose to stretch out on the floor, whereas still others may sit together at tables.

You will likely need to have some traditional bookshelves in your classroom; these are bookshelves that display only the spines of books. After all, this type of shelving is practical; it can hold a lot of books. But the spines of books don't make for interesting viewing. You will want to display the covers of at least some of the books in the class-room collection. Book covers are carefully designed to entice children into choosing them. (This is why most booksellers try to display as many book covers as possible).

Bookshelves that are designed to display the covers of books are expensive, and many schools can't stretch their budgets to buy them. So you will need to use some in-genuity to ensure that students see the covers of books. Slightly open books can stand alone on standard shelves or along a window ledge. Chalkboard trays can function as bookracks. To display paperback picture books, visit a home supply center and buy a plastic chain to which clothespins are attached. Hang the chain in an accessible spot, and use the clothespins to attach paperbacks to the chain.

Comfortable seating is important in a library center. After all, where do you choose to read for pleasure? Sofas and upholstered chairs are far more appealing than straight-back chairs. Carpeting, beanbag chairs, pillows, and cushions are also com-fortable and make the library center a cozy place for reading. And if you can find an old-fashioned bathtub and fill it with pillows, you will find that children clamor for turns to read in the tub.

Materials that highlight literature are also assets in the library center. Posters showing the covers of featured books can be obtained from publishers. Displays of book jackets also catch students' attention. Student-created artistic responses to literature may be an even better choice of material for decorating the library center, because they function as kid-to-kid book recommendations. Older students can contribute to a book recommendation log in the center where they rate books they read and perhaps write brief comments about them. For young children, a container of stuffed animals can be useful, because many enjoy cuddling up with a favorite creature when they read. Some teachers include flannel boards or puppets in the center, which young children can use to act out stories.

Children also like organizational systems in their libraries for the same reason adults do: organizational systems help them find books, and when children can readily find books, they spend more time actually reading.

No one particular system is best for organizing books. In fact, some teachers nurture ownership of the classroom library by inviting students to create their own system. Classifying books on the basis of difficulty level can be a good approach, especially for beginning readers and for students who may struggle with reading. We once had the opportunity to spend a semester observing children in three second-grade classrooms as they read books they selected from their classroom library centers (Martinez, Roser, Strecker, and Gough, 1997). Each of the three classrooms had a large, well-stocked classroom library, but the centers were organized quite differently. One teacher arranged her books by theme and author/illustrator, and the categories she created were clearly marked. The second teacher organized her books by difficulty level and, like the first teacher, used clearly marked categories. The third teacher had no organizational system. Rather, her books were all mixed together in a large bookcase. We documented the amount of time that the children in each classroom spent reading. Not surprisingly, the children in the first two classrooms (in which the books were clearly organized) spent far more time reading than the children in the third classroom. In this latter classroom, we witnessed children making repeated trips to the library center as they attempted to find books they wanted to read. This was time that should have been spent reading. We suspect an organizational system would have eliminated the problem we observed.

Some teachers set up organizational systems to reinforce the literary language they want students to acquire, grouping the books by genre. In determining the best system for your classroom, consider the interests and abilities of your students. Organizing by topics—such as sports, animals, and music—can help children find books of interest. Whatever system you use, be sure that your students understand how the books are organized.

Finally, the library center must have books, books, and more books! Unless the center is well stocked with a rich variety of quality books, children are not likely to use it. The more books you have, the richer the literature context you create in your classroom, so you will want to have *at least* four to eight books per child (Fractor, Woodruff, Martinez, and Teale, 1993). Unfortunately, school budgets rarely stretch far enough to allow teachers to buy books for classroom libraries. However, some teachers persuade their administrators to let them order children's literature instead of reading workbooks or other materials. Even if your school provides monetary assistance for

Try This
Stocking the Classroom Library

Although you will probably want a set of core books to remain in your library center all year, you should rotate additional books through regularly (probably every month or so). When you rotate new books into the library center, don't just place them there without fanfare. Introduce the books one by one, helping students to make connections between the new books and ones they already know: "We've been reading and writing a lot of trickster tales, so I've brought in *Tops and Bottoms* by Janet Stevens. I think you'll like the way you read this book from top to bottom—just as the title says." These brief introductions by the teacher build enthusiasm for the new selections, piquing student interest to eagerly delve into the books.

purchasing books, you'll probably still need to find creative ways of supplementing the collection. If your students have the financial means to order books from book clubs, the class can earn bonus points that can be redeemed for books. Secondhand bookstores and yard sales can also be good sources of inexpensive but worthwhile books. Many public libraries allow teachers to check out large numbers of books for extended periods of time.

Stocking the Classroom Library

The most important reason for having a classroom library—though not the only one—is to promote wide reading. Teacher Donalyn Miller writes about creating a "book frenzy" (2009, 22) in her classroom in which teacher and students are immersed in finding, reading, and sharing good books. A well-stocked classroom library can feed this type of book frenzy, especially when stocked with books that appeal to children. Although we offer guidelines for selecting books for the library center in this section, the lists of recommended books found at the end of each chapter of this book also serve as good resources for identifying worthwhile books.

Our first recommendation for stocking the library center is to include a variety of books. We suspect that too often teachers may tend to favor their own reading preferences when selecting books for the classroom library. Yet given the range of reading interests in any classroom, it makes sense to include all genres of literature in the center: fantasy, traditional literature, contemporary realistic fiction, historical fiction, nonfiction, and poetry. Also, you will want to find room for "odds and ends" for which there is no clear genre niche: predictable books, lift-the-flap and pop-up books, and joke and riddle books. Students will spend countless hours reading joke books, especially if they have the opportunity to share jokes—perhaps in a five-minute "joke spot" at the end of the school day. You will also want to include—across most grade levels—both chapter books and the increasingly popular graphic novel format. The more choices you provide for students, the more they'll read.

Although it is important to feature a variety of genres in your classroom library, we want to emphasize the inclusion of nonfiction. Penny Colman (2007) argues that classroom libraries are overwhelmingly stocked with fiction—at the expense of nonfiction. Many students particularly enjoy this genre (and reading nonfiction is also critical because it builds students' world knowledge and extends experience). There is an increasingly exciting array of nonfiction available for young readers. To find high-quality nonfiction for the classroom library, take a look at the books that have won the Sibert Informational Book Award (sponsored by the American Library Association) or the Orbis Pictus Award for Outstanding Nonfiction for Children (sponsored by the National Council of Teachers of English). The latter award not only identifies a winner and honor books each year, but also offers a list of recommended nonfiction books.

Don't Miss . . .
Chapter Books with Strong Story Lines

Dory Fantasmagory by Abby Hanlon

Three Times Lucky by Sheila Turnage

When You Reach Me Rebecca Stead

Splendors and Glooms by Laura Amy Schiltz

Dragon Rider by Cornelia Funke

Flora and Ulysses by Kate DeCamillo

Unusual Chickens for the Exceptional Poultry Farmer by Kelly Jones

When selecting fiction for the center, pay special attention to the story line. A strong story line sells itself: well-paced, action-oriented stories are a must when promoting independent reading. One such book for younger children is *One Cool Friend* (Buzzeo, 2012) by Toni Buzzeo in which a boy brings a penguin home from the aquarium, unbeknownst to his father who, throughout the story, is oblivious to the antics of the boy and his new pet. The ending of the book features an unexpected (and engaging) twist. Older children will be captivated by books such as Cornelia Funke's *Inkheart* (2003), in which young Meggie's father brings the malevolent characters of a book to life with his magical read-aloud skills. Soon, Meggie and her father are swept up in danger and intrigue as they are pursued and captured by the evil henchmen who have stepped out of the book and into the real world. Many fantasies and mysteries tend to have strong story lines and a lot of "kid appeal."

Dear Mrs. LaRue: Letters from Obedience School (Scholastic)

Children also love books with humorous and unusual story lines. Kate DiCamillo's *Flora and Ulysses* (2013) offers both humor and moments of poignancy. It is the story of a squirrel, the victim of an accident that has given him super strength and the ability to write poetry, and the girl determined to save him. Stories with unusual formats and distinctive illustrations also make good additions to the library center. One such book is Mark Teague's *Dear Mrs. LaRue: Letters from Obedience School* (2002), which is written as a series

Don't Miss . . .
Humorous Picture Books

Oh, No! by Candace Fleming, illustrated by Eric Rohmann

One Cool Friend by Toni Buzzeo, illustrated by David Small

Z Is for Moose by Paul O. Zelinsky

Creepy Carrots! by Aaron Reynolds, illustrated by Peter Brown

That Is Not a Good Idea! by Mo Willems

Boot & Shoe by Marla Frazee

The Wolf's Chicken Stew by Keiko Kasza

I Yam a Donkey! by Cece Bell

Don't Let the Pigeon Drive the Bus by Mo Willems

of letters composed by a disgruntled dog that has been sent away to obedience school. The illustrations in which the letters of complaint are embedded tell a far different tale than do the actual letters written by the dog!

Stocking the classroom library with books containing humor and strong story lines may be especially important for motivating the reluctant reader. You may also want to include relatively easy-to-read chapter books to help reluctant readers progress into longer works. Series books can also serve as a bridge for moving children into chapter books. Books in a series share the same setting, characters, and story arc, and familiarity with these elements serves as scaffold for reluctant readers as they pick up new titles in the series. Mystery series such as Nancy Drew and the Hardy Boys have been read for generations, and updated versions of books in these series remain popular with many children. Jon Scieszka's Time Warp Trio, Mary Pope Osborne's Magic Treehouse, and Rick Riordan's Percy Jackson and the Olympians books are newer popular fantasy series. Realistic series like the Diary of a Wimpy Kid, Junie B. Jones, and the Cam Jansen mysteries are also in demand by children.

The Children's Choice list is a useful resource for identifying books with "kid appeal." This list appears annually in the October issue of *The Reading Teacher*, a journal published by the International Reading Association.

Don't Miss . . .
Action Heroes in Picture Books

Traction Man Is Here! by Mini Grey

Robot Zot by Jon Scieszka, illustrated by David Shannon

Niño Wrestles the World by Yuyi Morales

Boy and Bot by Ame Dyckman, illustrated by Dan Yaccarino

Where the Wild Things Are by Maurice Sendak

It is also important to include books for a variety of reading levels in your classroom library. If a child believes that a book will be too challenging to read, in all

Niño Wrestles the World
(Macmillan)

likelihood, she or he won't give it a try. To motivate children to do lots of reading, it's necessary to provide books with which they feel comfortable. Anticipate a wide range of reading levels in your classroom. A typical second-grade classroom may have some students who are beginning readers and others who are reading at a sixth-grade level. The mythical classroom of "grade-level readers" is just that—a myth—and it is also important not to rely primarily on individual students' reading levels when helping students find books to read (Pierce, 1999). Reading level information provides only an estimated level and does not take into account a student's motivation to read a particular book. Perhaps the most valuable way of getting information about whether your students are comfortable with the books in your classroom library is simply by watching them.

Reaching *All* Students

As described in this chapter, predictable books are ones with repetitive structures or repetitive language. For example, Bill Martin Jr.'s *Brown Bear, Brown Bear* includes the following phrases repeatedly:

> Brown Bear, Brown Bear, what do you see?
> I see a _____ looking at me.

Books with this type of repetition can provide support for young children acquiring English as a second language, particularly when the picture book offers strong visual support (Linse, 2007). Teachers can read predictable books aloud repeatedly and then make them available in the classroom library for children to read themselves. To provide additional support for independent reading by English-language learners, the teacher can record predictable books on AudioBoom (see the Technology Tip on page 93) and make the recordings available for children to listen to while reading the books.

Kindergartners who have not yet learned to read conventionally also need books with which they can feel comfortable. Kindergartners are far more likely to engage in emergent reading (or "pretend reading") if predictable books are available. Predictable books contain repetitive structures or repetitive language, books such as Bill Martin Jr.'s *Brown Bear, Brown Bear, What Do You See?* (1967) or Mo Willems's *Let's Say Hi to Friends Who Fly!* (2010). In an observational study of kindergartners visiting their classroom library, we found that the mean number of times each non-predictable book in the library was selected by the children was 5.5 compared to 11.1 times for each predictable book. Further, when the kindergartners selected predictable books, they were far more likely to engage in emergent readings of the books than when they selected non-predictable books (Martinez and Teale, 1988).

Beginning readers—whether in first grade or higher grades—also respond well to predictable books. They also need limited text and lots of illustration cues. Jon Klassen's *I Want My Hat Back* (2011) fits this bill, as do Mo Willems' Elephant and Piggie books. If you teach beginning readers, you should become familiar with books that have won the Geisel Award, an annual award given by the American Library Association for the most distinguished book for beginning readers.

As young readers become more proficient, they will enjoy books with longer and somewhat more demanding vocabulary, such as Keiko Kasza's *The Wolf's Chicken Stew* (1987) and Mary Ann Hoberman's *You Read to Me, I'll Read to You* (2004). Beginning readers soon graduate to beginning chapter books, which are typically somewhat longer than picture books but contain minimal text per page and offer extensive illustration support (Roser, Martinez, McDonnold, and Fuhrken, 2004). Examples of beginning chapter books include Cynthia Rylant's Henry and Mudge series, James Marshall's comical series about Fox, and Kate DiCamillo's Bink and Gollie books.

More challenging picture books for developing readers also have a place in the classroom library, books like *The Great Fuzz Frenzy* (Stevens and Crummel, 2005), in which a great, fuzzy, round thing lands in the middle of a prairie dog town. Children who are reading these more demanding books with fluency should also be invited to read what have been called "transitional chapter books." These chapter books, which range from approximately sixty to one hundred pages, have a significant number of words per page, offer minimal illustration support, and generally contain a main plot line as well as secondary plot lines (Graves and Liang, 2004; Roser, Martinez, McDonnold, and Fuhrken, 2004). Examples of books that fit this description include those in Lois Lowry's Gooney Bird series and Paula Danzinger's Amber Brown series.

The library center can also be a tool to support and extend children's learning in content areas as well as reading. For example, if you are doing a unit on the civil rights movement, stock the library with books such as Kathleen Krull's *Harvesting Hope: The Story of Cesar Chavez* (2003) and Doreen Rappaport's *Martin's Big Words: The Life of Dr. Martin Luther King, Jr.* (2001). Such special collections within the library center can support students' learning in the content areas. Simultaneously students' content studies can support their voluntary reading by building background and interest. (See chapter 5 for a detailed discussion of literature-based content units.)

Including culturally relevant literature in the library is important for all children, but especially for those from diverse backgrounds who need to see themselves in the books they read. A Latino child once said to one of us, "They don't have people like us in books." Fortunately, today there is more culturally relevant literature available— though not as much as we need. Rudine Sims Bishop (1990) reminds us of the importance of ensuring that students have ample opportunities to read books that serve as mirrors so that they can see their worlds reflected in authentic ways in literature.

Sometimes teachers assume that it is not necessary to bring multicultural literature into their classrooms because their class is not ethnically diverse. Nothing could

What Does the Expert Say?

Moises Hernandez, teacher

Children live in a digital world, and many of today's youth are particularly passionate about video games. I recently had the opportunity to work in a summer tutoring program with a diverse  group of four boys who struggled with reading and were generally disaffected with literacy experiences in school. The boys were at different grade levels—first, second, fourth, and fifth—and struggled with diverse aspects of literacy ranging from decoding to fluency to comprehension. Despite the differences, the boys had one thing in common: they loved playing video games! I suspected this was one way I could engage all of them in literacy. So I took a deep breath and stepped into a world that was relatively unknown to me, all in the hope of helping the boys become stronger, more motivated readers.

Moises Hernandez

The boys had wide-ranging expertise in the video game world. Their expertise included experience with Minecraft, Five Nights at Freddy's, Halo, and Modern Warfare. We launched our inquiry project by generating a list of questions the boys had about video games: Where do video game designers get their ideas? What types of characters make great video games? How are games designed? Online resources (and teacher adaptations of online resources) provided much of the information the boys needed to answer their questions. However, I initially struggled with ways of incorporating children's literature into the inquiry project. The answer came when the boys decided on their culminating project for the summer tutoring program. They wanted to create a video game prototype to share with other students and parents at the end-of-semester celebration.

Online reading had provided the boys with a wealth of information for their prototype design, but they still had to determine who the hero of the game would be. This was the opening for bringing children's literature into the project. Characters from an array of genres offered opportunities to think about heroes (and heroines). What does it mean to be heroic? What traits define heroes? What challenges do heroes face? How do they rise to their challenges? Traditional literature offered heroes like Hercules, Paul Bunyan, and King Arthur. Fantasy offered still other possible heroes, such as the young girl in *Oh No! Not Again! (Or How I Built a Time Machine to Save History) (Or at Least My History Grade)* (Barnett, 2012). The quirky main character of *Westlandia* (Fleischman, 1999) offered the opportunity to consider whether creativity and leadership abilities might be characteristics of a hero. And, of course, biographies offered the opportunity to learn about real-life heroes and heroines such as Harriet Tubman in *Moses: When Harriet Tubman Led Her People to Freedom* (Weatherford, 2006) and Mexican American activist Cesar Chavez in *Harvesting Hope: The Story of Cesar Chavez* (Krull, 2003). Ultimately, the boys did not choose to "borrow" a hero from children's literature for their prototype. Nonetheless, children's literature had provided rich opportunities for reading and thinking more deeply about what it means to be a hero.

Moises, what do you do these days professionally, and why do you choose to do that?

Currently, I am the middle school language arts/instructional coach for Harlandale Independent School District in San Antonio, Texas. I took this position in order to facilitate the instructional goals of my English language arts teachers and build a strong collaboration amongst our school campuses.

Would you name one children's book you hope everybody reads, and why you think they should?

I hope young children read *Nico y los Lobos Feroces* by Valerie Gorbachev, because if they are scared of the dark and their imagination creates eerie thoughts of monsters and ghosts, then they share the same feelings as Nico, who screams for help in the middle of the night. In the end, the story is one that will bring comfort to children.

be further from the truth. It is important for children of mainstream cultures to see children from diverse backgrounds involved in situations both similar to and different from their own. Schools are preparing children to live in a diverse society, and it is important for them to understand this society.

If you have tablets available for use in your classroom library, you can extend your book collection with e-books. You can likely check out e-books for free from your local library. Most libraries use a service called Overdrive for checking out e-books, and you can access the service by downloading the Overdrive app on the tablets.

Audiobooks can also be included in the classroom library. By listening to audiobooks, beginning readers can gain access to books that are more complex than ones they might read on their own. Audiobooks can be a wonderful means of making multicultural literature accessible to children from other cultures. (Audiobooks and a CD player with headphones can even be part of the library center.) When multicultural literature is set in a different place, features dialects, or includes characters whose lives are very unfamiliar to children, then children may avoid these selections—unless they are mediated by an adult. In effect, a well-narrated audiobook helps to mediate the story for listeners when the narrator selects appropriate tones, brings character voices to life, and makes dialects accessible. Fortunately, there are numerous quality multicultural audiobooks on the market today that offer authentic listening experiences to children.

Assessing Individual Student Interests

Table 3.2 suggests some typical interests of students in different grades. However, just as you have particular reading preferences and reading interests, so will your students. To ensure that all your students find books they will love in your classroom library, you need to know as much as possible about your own students' reading preferences and reading interests. Take the time to discover those interests. To identify students who may be reluctant readers, you can begin the year by administering a reading attitude inventory such as the one created by Michael McKenna and Dennis Kear (1990). This can be administered in conjunction with a reading interest inventory to learn more about topics and types of books a student may be interested in. These are beginning steps. The most important way to get to know your students' interests is by talking to them about the things they enjoy doing and the books they are reading. These should be ongoing conversations. You can also have them keep logs of their independent reading in which they record the author and title of each book they read and rate the book using a four-star scale. By monitoring their reading logs, you will

Table 3.2 Children's Interests at Different Grade Levels

Grades	Interests
Grades 1–2	Animals, nature, fantasy, child characters, general and science informational materials, history
Grades 3–4	Nature, animals, adventure, familiar experiences
Grades 5–6	History, science, mystery, adventure, travel, animal stories, fairy tales
Grades 7–8	Science fiction, mystery, adventure, biography, history, animals, sports, romance, religion, career stories, comedy

have information you can use as you seek books to include in the classroom library. Also, as we discussed in chapter 1, it is worth remembering that many readers respond especially positively to literature that reflects their own cultural experiences.

Creating a Classroom Context That Promotes Reading

We have talked at length about creating and stocking the classroom library, but simply having a classroom library does not guarantee its use. To make that happen, the teacher must work from the first day of school to build a *classroom literacy community* —a community in which books are valued and shared. From the first day of school, students must know that their teacher is an enthusiastic book advocate. This means the teacher sets aside time for reading every day, helps students learn strategies for selecting books, models reading, and enthusiastically shares and recommends books.

Try This
Setting up a Book Recommendation Venue

Students are happy to share their opinions about the books they read. You can invite their input on what some teachers refer to as a "graffiti wall." Legitimize that desire to leave one's mark that seems to be as old as cave drawings. Simply tear off a long section of bulletin board paper and invite students to write the title of the book they wish to recommend directly on the paper. They should include their comments about the book and sign the response. The routine activity of lining up can become a learning experience when the "wall" is displayed in the hallway. Students will linger over their peers' latest reads.

Students need to know that reading is a central activity in their literacy community. The best way to do this is by establishing a reading workshop—a daily time for everyone to read—beginning on the first day of the school year.

Sometimes teachers tell students they can read "once their work is done." Perhaps that works for strong students who consistently finish their work early, but many students never finish early. To ensure that all students get to read every day, teachers must build in a block of time when everyone in the classroom stops what they are doing and chooses a book, magazine, or newspaper to read. These blocks of reading time are known by various terms such as DEAR (drop everything and read) or SSR (sustained silent reading). We prefer the name "reading workshop."

At the beginning of the school year, students sometimes struggle to settle into reading for a sustained period of time, particularly those for whom reading workshop is a new experience. To launch a reading workshop in your classroom, begin by establishing expectations for students. Together talk about what should happen during this block of time and what students' responsibilities are. Students need to know that during the workshop *everyone* reads. It is also important to recognize that readers often want to share with someone what they have read; so readers can agree to wait until the end of the workshop to share their books with others.

In launching reading workshop, students might need to read for shorter blocks of time at the beginning of the year (ten to fifteen minutes) and then work up to longer stretches (thirty to forty-five minutes). And reading workshop time is for *all* students. Even those not yet reading conventionally can engage in emergent reading, and there is no reason why beginning readers, for whom silent reading may not be appropriate, can't read their books out loud.

Initially, some students may avoid settling in to read. They may spend as much time visiting the library center to get new books as they spend actually reading. To alleviate this problem, students can each have a browsing box that they fill with a number of books from the classroom or school library. If during reading workshop one book doesn't hold their interest, they can move on to another book in their box.

Students may also benefit from mini-lessons focused on how to select books. Some teachers introduce the "five finger rule" for the purpose of helping students decide if they have selected books written at an appropriate level of difficulty. The process works like this: Students read any page from their chosen book and put up one finger for each unknown word encountered. If at the end of the page no fingers are up, then the book might be too easy. (However, there are times when we all want to read an easy book, and that is fine.) If one or two fingers are up, then the book is likely a good fit. If they encountered three or four unknown words, then the book is probably one worth trying, whereas if there are five or more unknown words, then there is a good chance the book is too difficult. Of course, there is more to consider in selecting books than level of difficulty. Mini-lessons can also be used to introduce students to new types of books that might be of interest, such as postmodern or wordless books.

Finally, if a true reading community is going to be established in the classroom, the teacher must also become part of the community, reading during the workshop and sharing with others at the end of workshop. It cannot be a time for the teacher to grade papers or finalize lesson plans. Table 3.3 contains a list of suggestions for making readers workshop successful.

Most readers are members of communities (typically informal ones) that enthusiastically share with others what they are reading. In the classroom, the teacher must model this kind of reading behavior. One way of doing this is by talking with your students about the children's books you are reading and by recommending books to children based on their interests. Just as important (maybe more so), the teacher must build in time for children to make book recommendations to others based on what they are reading.

In the literature-rich classrooms in which she observed, Janet Hickman (1981) found that teachers regularly added books to their classroom libraries, but they did not

Table 3.3 How to Make Reading Workshop a Success

- Make reading workshop a part of students' daily routine.
- Let students choose their own reading materials.
- Ensure that everyone, including the teacher, reads during reading workshop.
- For students who have a difficult time reading for long stretches, begin with a few minutes of reading time (perhaps ten minutes) and build to longer blocks of time (thirty to forty-five minutes).
- For younger readers, don't require that the reading time be silent; beginning readers frequently need to hear themselves read aloud.
- Let kindergartners participate in reading workshop by engaging in emergent reading of stories.

What Do You Think?
Does Transmedia Storytelling Have a Place in the Literacy Program?

In our digital world, the line between printed texts and digital texts is becoming increasingly blurred. Nowhere is this more evident than in the world of transmedia storytelling. Annette Lamb (2011) explains transmedia storytelling this way:

> Transmedia storytelling involves a multimodal, multimedia story with nonlinear, participatory elements. Resources connected to the story might include print materials; documents; maps; web-based clues; mobile apps; cell phone calls; social media connections; activities and games; and media such as audio, video, or animation. (15)

The Infinity Ring series is an example of this genre. In this adventure series, characters travel through time to fix "breaks" in history. Because the books are linked to a dedicated Web site (www.infinityring.com), readers can join characters online to participate in their own adventure.

Advocates of transmedia storytelling argue that the format has the potential to engage children who embrace the gaming world while resisting the world of print books. They believe that the brisk action typifying books in transmedia series appeals to reluctant readers, and the links to the digital world help to ensure that readers stay engaged in the print world. Lamb contends that multiplatform experiences provide opportunities for readers "to seek out content, explore information in different contexts, evaluate ideas across formats, and interact with other readers" (2011, 16).

Not all educators welcome transmedia storytelling into the classroom. Students already spend what some consider to be excessive amounts of time engaged in gaming. A national survey of young people funded by the National Institute on Media and the Family (2001) found that 92 percent of children and adolescents between the ages of two and seventeen play video games, and many children spend a considerable amount of time doing so. For example, between the ages of eight and thirteen, boys spend an average of forty-seven minutes a day involved in gaming. This is considerably more time than is spent reading. Many educators fear that the introduction of transmedia storytelling into the classroom will pull children even further away from print reading. What do you think?

simply place new books in the library. Rather, they talked with the children about the new additions: "Last week we finished reading aloud *The Tale of Despereaux* (DiCamillo, 2003) by Kate DiCamillo, so I brought in two new books by DiCamillo for the library." Or, "Halloween is almost here, so I thought you might enjoy reading *Creepy Carrots!* (Reynolds, 2012) by Aaron Reynolds. If you read it, I hope you tell me what you think about it." Books that teachers introduce are especially likely to be selected from the library for independent reading.

When choosing books for independent reading, children are most likely to select books that have been introduced or read to them. Beginning readers are especially likely to feel more confident picking up a book they have heard read aloud. So be

Technology Tip

AudioBoom (http://audioboom.com) is a free online recording service that teachers and other readers can use to share recorded read-alouds of books that are available in the classroom library. Recording segments are ten minutes in length.

sure to include these books in the classroom library. Later in this chapter we focus on read-alouds—an activity that may do more than any other to promote children's independent reading (as well as their literacy and literary learning).

Author Visits

Teachers who foster a love of literature devote ample time to reading, listening, and responding to literature. But there is probably no better way to bring to life both literature and the process of creating literature than through a visit by a recognized children's author (or illustrator). A good way of arranging for an author visit is by looking at the author's Web site, where you will likely find directions for making arrangements for a visit.

A visit by an author should be viewed as an opportunity to celebrate literature and literacy. Some schools do this by hosting a young authors' conference in conjunction with the author's visit. Presentations by the visiting author typically get top billing at the conference. Ideally, the author will be able to present to small groups of students. Visiting authors often have wonderful stories to share with students about the inspiration for their work as well as their writing process, and illustrators frequently offer fascinating demonstrations of their work. If time permits, it is ideal to organize more informal sessions in which small groups of students can talk to the visitor. Some authors will even work with small groups of students on their writing.

The author or illustrator is the celebrity of the young authors' conference, but this doesn't mean that other important things aren't happening. Students who attend the conference should be authors or illustrators themselves and should come to the conference prepared to join peer groups in which they share stories and illustrations they have created. A third type of event can center on children's literature selections. Students can attend sessions offered by teachers or members of the community where they participate in a story read aloud and a response activity based on the story.

Teachers need to prepare students for an upcoming author visit. First, they must ensure that the students know the featured author's work. In the weeks preceding the visit, the teacher should read the visiting author's stories aloud, and children should have the opportunity to respond to the author's work through discussion, writing, and artwork. Their responses can be displayed throughout the classroom or school. If students will have the opportunity to interview the visiting author, the teacher needs to help them generate questions about some of the author's stories as well as questions that will yield insights into how writers (or illustrators) go about their work: where they get ideas, how they budget their time to ensure that their work gets finished, the special techniques they use, and advice they might offer young writers (or artists).

Not every school has the resources to bring an author to campus for a visit. Yet in our digital age, there are other options. With the availability of technologies such as Skype and Zoom, more and more authors are doing virtual classroom visits (Springen, 2012). Some authors even do these visits at no cost. Online author and illustrator visits may not be effective with younger children who have a more limited attention span, but they can be engaging for older ones.

▪ READING ALOUD TO CHILDREN

In its report *Becoming a Nation of Readers*, the Commission on Reading declared, "There is no substitute for a teacher who reads children good stories" (Anderson, Hiebert, Scott, and Wilkinson, 1985). That is our sentiment exactly! Research indicates that reading to children has many positive outcomes (Teale, 2003). First, it whets their appetite for reading. Young children who are read to discover the rewards of reading and are motivated to learn to read. Second, literature nurtures children's language development and comprehension abilities (Sipe, 2008; Teale, 2003). Through read-alouds, children become acquainted with the cadences of written language and discover how print functions, especially if the adult reader draws attention to print conventions. Finally, through read-alouds, children acquire the real-world knowledge that is critical for success in school.

Read-alouds also support children's literary development (Sipe, 2008): children are introduced to conventional story openers ("Once upon a time"); they discover literary devices such as the transformation motif; and they meet stock characters like the sly fox and the tricky coyote. Read-alouds are the ideal vehicle for encouraging children to think in response to literature, and when discussion is a part of the read-aloud experience, children learn how to participate in literary conversations.

Like the Commission on Reading, we believe that read-alouds are an essential instructional activity for children of *all* ages. Although older children may have acquired a basic understanding of how print functions and how stories are structured, their language, reading, and literary development must continue. Also, there are many books that developing readers do not have the skill to read on their own but will delight in if the books are read aloud to them. In fact, by the time most children are able to read books such as A. A. Milne's *Winnie-the-Pooh* (1924) and Philip Pullman's *The Scarecrow and His Servant* (2004) on their own, the books are no longer age appropriate.

Research on Read-aloud Programs

James Hoffman, Nancy Roser, and Jennifer Battle (1993) conducted a comprehensive study on read-aloud programs in the United States. The results were disappointing. Reports from 537 classrooms revealed that 74 percent of teachers read to their students on a given day. However, there was a steady decline in the percentage of teachers reading aloud at each successive grade level. In kindergarten, 84 percent of the teachers read to their students, but in fifth grade, only 64 percent did so. No comprehensive studies have been conducted since Hoffman and his colleagues did this work, but with the growing emphasis on testing in recent years, we have little reason to believe that the situation has improved. If anything, we fear that teachers may be reading aloud even less today.

Teachers at every grade level should read aloud *at least* once a day. All too often teachers at upper grade levels believe that their students should be reading books on their own—which is true, of course. However, it is not an either/or situation. We hope teachers will recognize the special value of read-alouds. Another argument made by some intermediate-level teachers is that they have too much content to cover to devote time to reading aloud to students. One way of dealing with this time restriction is by "double dipping"—that is, using read-alouds to achieve both literary and curricular goals. If the class is studying the Civil War, then read aloud Patricia Polacco's *Pink and Say* (1994) and Barbara Kerley's *Walt Whitman: Words for America* (2004). Deborah Ellis's *A Company of Fools* (2002) or Avi's *Crispin* (2002) would make excellent read-alouds for a unit on medieval times.

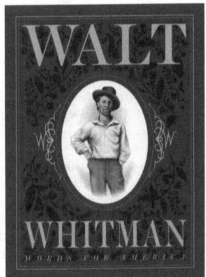

Walt Whitman: Words for America
(Scholastic)

Hoffman and his colleagues also found that the nature of the typical read-aloud session was not what it should be. The teachers who responded to their survey reported read-alouds lasting only ten to twenty minutes, with minimal discussion following. In addition, the literature selections were typically unrelated to a unit of study, and generally no response activity followed the read-aloud. The researchers cautioned that this "typical" read-aloud was *not* a model, arguing that a daily read-aloud of at least twenty minutes should be scheduled in a specific time slot. Instead of selecting unrelated literature, these educators called for organizing read-aloud programs around units. After all, mature readers often read books that are related in some way, and literature units encourage students to develop this habit. The investigators also questioned the adequacy of five minutes of literature discussion. The kind of sustained conversation that can enrich the understanding of all participants does not occur in five minutes.

When to Read Aloud

The read-aloud experience is one of the highlights of the school day for children who have the opportunity to participate in them. This is especially true when the teacher carefully selects each book and spends time preparing to read it aloud.

Read-alouds shouldn't be used merely to fill time between activities. By scheduling a read-aloud each day, you communicate to students that this is a valued activity. Besides, there is the all-too-real danger that on many days there won't be any extra time between activities.

At lower grade levels, teachers should read aloud several times a day, especially if their students have had only limited experiences with stories before entering school. Some children enter school having listened to thousands of storybook readings; others have not been read to at all. The latter children especially deserve a rich read-aloud program.

Selecting Books for Read-alouds

In selecting books for read-alouds, look for high-quality books with strong plots and interesting crafting. We especially encourage you to choose books that deal with significant themes, for these books have the potential to evoke insightful discussions. A picture book such as Matt de la Peña's *Last Stop on Market Street* (2015) is such a book. This book, about a little boy and his nana who volunteer at the local soup kitchen, is the kind of book that offers rich fodder for conversation focused on issues of social justice.

It is important to read books from a variety of genres, including poetry and nonfiction. Remember, your preferences might not be the same as those of your students. We know a first-grade teacher who decided to let her students select the daily read-aloud books. The girls selected the same kinds of books the teacher had been selecting—picture storybooks—but much to her surprise, the boys overwhelmingly favored nonfiction, a genre from which she had never read aloud.

Select age-appropriate books. There are no firm and fast guidelines about books that are most appropriate for particular grade levels. In fact, many books appeal to students across grade levels. Nonetheless, as a general rule, simpler, shorter books are more appropriate for both younger children and those with limited literature experience. However, this does not mean that picture books are for younger children and chapter books are for older ones. Many picture books, such as Chris Van Allsburg's *The Widow's Broom* (1992) or Anthony Browne's *Voices in the Park* (1998), are wonderful for older children. Conversely, many younger children enjoy listening to chapter books such as Grace Lin's *The Year of the Dog* (Lin, 2005).

Preparing to Read Aloud

To make read-alouds a success, remember one cardinal rule: never read aloud a book that you have not previously read. In fact, you really should read a book out loud to yourself or to someone else before reading it to children, because sometimes a book you loved when you read it silently just doesn't flow when it is read aloud. If you plan to read a book with unfamiliar words or words from a language in which you are not fluent, it is especially important to practice pronunciations prior to reading aloud.

In preparing for a read-aloud, thoughtfully read the book you select (see Table 3.4). Consider the focus that will shape your read-aloud. For example, if character is particularly important in the story, consider the clues that reveal character and how you might invite children to attend to those clues. Or if the book's peritext contains important story information, be prepared to remind the children to look closely at these features at the beginning of the book. Also, look for difficulties the book presents that might interfere with comprehension. Be alert to stopping points where you might invite predictions or discussion. Also, be sure to monitor your own responses to the story. The things you notice or wonder about are worth remembering because these spontaneous responses can become conversation starters after the reading.

The Year of the Dog
(Little Brown)

If you have never read the story aloud before, it makes sense to practice pacing and expression before reading it to an audience. What feelings and moods can you convey with your voice? Is a character surprised? Does a character become angry? Is a character especially wise, silly, or confused? Get to know the characters so that you can bring them to life. Don't be shy. Try out different voices and even facial expressions or gestures. And if you are reading a picture book, don't forget to practice holding the book so that the children can see the illustrations as you read. The result of all this preparation is likely to be an engaging read-aloud experience for your students.

Introducing the Story

Before introducing the story, gather the students together for the read-aloud. If there is room, let the students sit on the floor around you. If a picture book is to be read aloud, make sure everyone can see the illustrations. Keep your book introduction in

Table 3.4   How to Prepare for a Read-aloud

- Anticipate difficulties the story may present to students, and prepare to help them through those difficulties.
- Watch for interesting places to stop reading and invite children's predictions or discussion.
- Heed your own responses to the story for after-reading discussion.
- Practice varying your reading pace to highlight particular portions of the story.
- Become acquainted with the characters and changing moods of the story so that you can read with appropriate expression.
- Try out different voices for different characters.

proper perspective: time and attention should be devoted primarily to the read-aloud and to subsequent discussion. Nonetheless, an introduction offers you an opportunity to help children expand their store of literary understandings and allows you to "prime" them for the book.

In addition to introducing the story (or poem) by title, remember to mention the name of the author (and the illustrator if a different person). This is an excellent way of helping students begin to develop a sense of what authors and illustrators do. Also, mention other books written by the same author, especially those with which the children are likely to be familiar. Mentioning the book's genre is a way of gently introducing children to some of the language of literature.

Before starting to read, you might also need to build background. This may be especially important for nonfiction. If some concepts necessary for understanding the book are not adequately explained within the book, pay attention to these concepts in your introduction. If reading a story, you might want to invite children to make predictions about what the story will be about. A book's peritext (which include the cover, endpapers, and title page) will often offer clues that children can use to make predictions. For example, the cover of Candace Fleming's *Oh, No!* (2012) shows a tiger slyly peering up at a loris high in a tree. The initial endpapers show the same tiger, this time with a furtive eye on a frog. Then, as the page is turned, the title page reveals the tiger chasing the fleeing frog. These clues will give young children lots to draw on in making predictions about the upcoming story.

Reading the Story

When you begin to read the story, use everything you tried out in preparing for the read-aloud. Vary your reading pace to reflect changes in mood and emotion, read expressively, and use different voices when appropriate.

Some teachers believe that stories should be read straight through without any interruptions so as not to distract from the story line. However, we encourage you to feel free to interrupt the reading of a story to talk with your students. There may be times when you need to guide students through a tricky part of the story or to briefly fill in information that is important in understanding the story. Also, be open to children sharing their own responses to stories, especially younger ones. Older children may be able to hold their responses until the read-aloud is complete, but younger children often forget their observations if required to wait until the read-aloud is finished to talk. So if a child interrupts to make a prediction, ask a question, or share a response, honor that interruption. Finally, when you read predictable books, young children enjoy joining in on repeated phrases.

After Reading

The read-aloud experience should not be over as soon as you've read the final page of the story. The literary transaction will continue after the reading if you provide ample opportunity for children to discuss the story. Chapter 4 focuses on literary discussion as well as other modes of response.

▪ STORIES AND STORYTELLING

Storytelling is yet another way of engaging children in story worlds. Children's literature starts with the telling of stories. For thousands of years before the first story was written down, humans told stories and recited poems. The thousands of years of human experience with stories (compared to a little over a century of mass literacy) surely adapted the human mind to storytelling in a special way and nourished an art of storytelling that still moves listeners deeply. Further, many students in today's classroom—especially those from culturally and linguistically diverse backgrounds—come from cultures in which the storytelling is a living tradition (Parsons, 2016). This is why teachers must make storytelling a regular feature in the classroom.

Storytelling: The Tenacious Art

Many cultures have specific storytelling styles and rituals. In Jamaica today, a storyteller still begins a session by asking "Cric?" This means, "Do you want a story?" If the people want one, they answer "Cric," and the storyteller begins. But if they say "Crac," the storyteller looks for others willing to hear the tale. Japanese storytellers use *kamishibai*, a large set of pictures with text on the back; these pictures are presented in a box that looks like a traditional theater. Whatever the style, storytelling has never passed out of vogue, even with the proliferation of books. In fact, some children's books celebrate the power of storytelling, including Allen Say's *Kamishibai Man* (2005) and Jane Kurtz's *The Storyteller's Beads* (Kurtz, 1998).

Because storytelling is so active—from the point of view of both tellers and listeners—it is an especially appropriate activity to do with younger children. Storytelling is also a useful tool to use with reluctant readers because it offers a bridge to literature. A wise teacher advocated telling stories to students. "Most children," said Edmund Henderson, "will come running when you read a story. But if one does not, tell the story instead. The told story is the older form. Hence it will have more appeal." Telling a story allows you to look your students in the eye and invite them to help you bring the story to life.

Storytelling (like reading aloud) should exercise the often-neglected art of using the voice. The teller must provide the excitement, drama, and cadences that pull listeners in and play their emotions like a violin. To tell a story well, the storyteller must decide how the characters sound, where the suspenseful parts are, and what parts should be slow or fast, loud or soft.

Children enjoy telling stories, too, and there are many good reasons why they should. In this section, we present ways to choose, practice, and tell stories, and most of our advice applies to both the adult and the child storyteller.

Common Story Types: Personal Tales to Tall Tales

Stories differ in the amount of effort they require to learn or improvise. They also differ in the kind of attention they require of listeners and the sorts of participation they invite. These points will be made clear as we talk about different types of stories. Story types vary from personal tales, which usually evoke more inventiveness from the teller but offer less form for guidance, to already-heard stories, which offer more form but pose a challenge because they must be learned—they cannot be improvised.

Personal Stories

Personal stories are anecdotes from your own experience—about a camping trip, about being lost, about raising a pet. They can be rambling, especially if you haven't honed them down through practice. That's okay, especially when you're giving an example for children to copy when they do the telling. You can work with personal stories over time to give them more shape.

Family Stories

Family stories are true (well, maybe slightly embellished) stories about someone in your family. Because these stories may have been passed along through several generations, they are usually better formed than personal stories. Family stories often portray what people think is funny about themselves and their relatives. They can be a lot like stories that are written down; the Ramona Quimby stories come to mind, as do many of Patricia Polacco's stories. After all, writers come from families.

Friend-of-a-Friend Stories

Friend-of-a-friend stories, or "urban legends," are accounts of bizarre events in a community told by people who believe that they might have happened. When you try to check them out, though, it always turns out that they happened to someone the teller almost knows—"a friend of a friend."

Friend-of-a-friend stories are close to the folktale tradition. In his fascinating collections, the folklorist Jan de Brunvard compiled urban legends from newspapers, radio, and personal accounts of hundreds of people. Although the tales are generally recounted breathlessly, as if they just happened last week, de Brunvard (1981) has found variations that are hundreds of years old. For example, the story of the vanishing hitchhiker, set in contemporary Georgia, has a song version, "The Phantom 409." Some years ago in West Africa, children's author Frances Temple heard a version of the story from a nervous nun who claimed to have been in the Jeep when the hitchhiker disappeared.

Scary Stories

Scary stories usually lie somewhere in between friend-of-a-friend stories and folktales. Alvin Schwartz's popular collection *Scary Stories to Tell in the Dark* (1986) was collected from folktale sources. Xavier Garza has collected stories from the Southwest in two collections, *Creepy Creatures and Other Cucuys* (2004) and *The Donkey Lady Fights La Llorona and Other Stories* (2015). Some teachers find ghost stories good fare to tell to middle-grade children or for them to learn and tell. If the children are to do the telling, prepare to screen their choices.

Jokes and Riddles

Jokes and riddles aren't stories exactly, but they are so engaging that telling them in front of a group is good practice for children. Also, they are short enough that many children can participate in a single storytelling session.

Folktales

Folktales, the traditional stories we discussed in chapter 2, provide excellent fare for storytelling. Because they were passed down orally, folktales have been pared down to their essentials that make them well formed and memorable, but this also leaves room for embellishments by the storyteller. Fables, those brief instructive tales that end with a moral, can also be fun to tell, especially when you stop and ask students to guess the moral.

Myths

Myths range from serious creation stories, such as the Iroquois tale of Da-Ga-Na-We-Da, to the lighter pourquoi tales that explain various natural phenomena, such as the African tale *Why Mosquitoes Buzz in People's Ears* (Aardema, 1975) retold by Verna Aardema. Teachers should have no trouble finding collections from many cultures that offer abundant fare suitable for storytelling.

Legends

Legends are stories about famous cultural heroes that usually have a core of truth to them. The characters may be real; for example, George Washington is the subject of a number of legends, as is the Mexican revolutionary figure Pancho Villa. Legends make good choices for oral telling, especially in conjunction with social studies units.

Tall Tales

One or two (or maybe three) steps removed from legends are tall tales, which tell of exaggerated fictitious characters. These characters usually have qualities that real people like to claim for themselves. For example, Paul Bunyan didn't exist, but lumberjacks like to be thought of as tough.

Learning Stories to Tell

As Margaret Read MacDonald (1993) reminds us, it is easiest to learn a story from another teller. A story well told is so much more than the words; it's the voices of the characters, the pauses and dramatic flourishes, the joy and sorrow and excitement and dread, all communicated by the storyteller. If you have a chance to listen to a storyteller who can show you all those things, you're way ahead. If you can't find a live storyteller, you can watch videotapes of live performances.

Learning the story is the first task of the storyteller. Most storytellers agree that the way to prepare a story is not to memorize it. Memorizing makes a story sound flat or sets the teller up for a mental block during the telling. Besides, the beauty of a told story is that it is forever invented.

But a story is not random either. A well-told story is crisp, with the beginning, ending, and repeated parts told just so. How does a storyteller achieve this crispness without memorizing the story? Here's one way.

Get some index cards, and read through the story four times, each time with a different purpose:

1. On the first pass, read for the sense of the whole tale.
2. Next time, pay close attention to the different events in the story. Jot down each event in a few words on a separate card.
3. On the third read-through, pay close attention to the characters. On a separate card, name each character and make notes about the way she or he should sound and move. Note any gestures that you want to associate with each character.
4. Read through the story again and jot down the beginning and ending, as well as any repeated phrases. This is important. If you know exactly how a story begins, you can launch into it confidently. If you know exactly how the story ends, you can wrap it up crisply. So memorize both. In between, pay attention to repeated phrases (such as "Little pig, little pig, let me come in. Not by the hair on my chinny-chin-chin") or repeated patterns of actions.

Practicing the Story

Once you have the cards prepared and arranged in the order you find most useful, tell the story repeatedly (to yourself, to a friend, to your dog) until you can tell it confidently without looking at the cards. Later, when you tell the story, keep the cards unobtrusively in your lap—but have them handy in case you begin to forget.

If children are learning stories, have them pair up and tell their stories to each other. Also have them tell the story at home a certain number of times as they learn it (e.g., three times a day).

Once you have the gist of the story down, the fun part begins. This is when you refine the characterization, gestures, pauses, and other dynamics of narration.

Determine the sorts of word choices appropriate to the story you're telling. A story in a traditional setting requires the teller to say "a certain boy" or "There was an old woman who" instead of "this guy" or "this old lady." If your story is an Old English folktale, perhaps you want to sound modest and precise. If it's a Western tale from Texas, your language should be relaxed, expansive, and given to exaggeration.

You don't need to describe the characters fully to the audience, but you should have a clear idea of what they are like so that your voice and gestures will convey this information. You should decide the following for each main character in your story:

- How short or tall is she or he? How heavy? How does the character's size make her or him move?
- Is this character dignified? Sly? Lazy? Vain? How do these traits affect the way he or she talks?
- What is the character's usual mood?

If you're helping children learn storytelling, ask these questions and follow up with activities that will give the children practice in developing their characters. Have each child "get into" one of his or her characters as they all parade around the room. Call on several characters to introduce themselves in their own voices and say what's on their minds.

It also helps to visualize the setting. When Jack steps out onto the clouds at the top of the beanstalk, how is his footing? How does he step? When he gets to the giant's castle, how big is the door? How does Jack knock on it? Having thought through such details enables you to use voices and gestures that will help the audience to visualize—and believe—the setting.

You will also want to practice gestures. As a storyteller says the wolf's lines in "The Three Little Pigs," she or he will probably make a fist and pound on an imaginary door. When the storyteller says a pig's lines, she or he may pull at imaginary chin whiskers. A few gestures like these help the story, but too many will distract. Use only gestures that will give a hint of the setting, provide the signature of a character, or display a strong emotion.

It is also important to practice facial expressions. Boston storyteller Jay O'Callahan says that storytelling is the theater of the face. Gestures are important, but facial expressions and voices convey most of the story's meaning. Storytellers must learn to make facial expressions that project the way their characters feel: innocent, cunning, frightened, and so on.

If you're working with children, have them stand in a circle. One student decides on a facial expression and, without identifying the expression, "passes" it on to the next, who duplicates it and passes it on in turn. This continues until the expression has gone completely around the room. Take time to debrief: did the students understand the expression correctly? Then another student "passes" a different expression.

The storyteller's voice must be both loud enough to carry to the back of the audience and expressive enough to portray the characters in the tale. For practice, say the line "Twinkle, twinkle, little star" in the voice of each of these characters:

- a pitiful child with a big problem who wants to make an important wish
- a mean giant who is demanding that the star twinkle
- a crafty wizard who is making a magic charm

Many stories are told in the dialect of a region or of an ethnic group, and, after watching storytellers on television, you might believe that using dialect is an important part of the storyteller's art. As a general rule, though, if a dialect is not yours, don't use it. It is very easy to insult other people if you appear to make fun of their speech.

Once children have learned stories, they should tell them before audiences that have not heard them practice, such as children in other classes or parents on parents night. They will make many friends and bring good cheer if they perform their stories at a head start center or a senior citizens' activity center. You might even arrange a story swap: senior citizens can tell stories of their own in exchange for the children's stories.

■ CONCLUSION

Teachers are responsible for many facets of literacy instruction, but in attending to those different facets, it is important not to forget the "big picture"—creating a classroom context that motivates students to want to be readers. In this chapter, we examined critical features of that context including the classroom library, the read-aloud program, and storytelling. When your students have opportunities to listen to and read wonderful literature each day, the likelihood that they become lifetime readers is greatly enhanced.

▪ RECOMMENDED BOOKS

Avi. *Crispin: The Cross of Lead.* New York: Hyperion, 2002. Accused of a crime he did not commit and having lost his mother—his only living relative—Crispin flees his village and is swept up in the political intrigues of medieval England. Ages ten and older.

Barnett, Mac. *Oh No! Not Again! (Or How I Built a Time Machine to Save History) (Or at Least My History Grade).* Illustrated by Dan Santat. New York: Hyperion, 2012. A young girl travels back in time to save history—or, perhaps, just to save her own history grade. Picture book. Ages seven through ten.

Beebe, Katy. *Brother Hugo and the Bear.* Illustrated by S. D. Schindler. Grand Rapids, MI: Eerdmans Books for Young Readers, 2014. When a bear devours his borrowed illuminated manuscript, Brother Hugo must make a replacement and get it back to the monastery before the bear eats this one as well. Picture book. Ages six through ten.

Bell, Cece. *I Yam a Donkey!* New York: Clarion, 2015. A yam finds an unexpected outcome when trying to teach a donkey proper grammar. Picture book. Ages eight through twelve.

Browne, Anthony. *Voices in the Park.* New York: Knopf, 1998. A trip to the park is told and illustrated from four different perspectives. Picture book. Ages nine and older.

Buzzeo, Toni. *One Cool Friend.* Illustrated by David Small. New York: Dial, 2012. When Elliot brings home a penguin from a visit to the aquarium, his father appears oblivious to the antics of Elliot and his new pet. Picture book. Ages seven through ten.

DiCamillo, Kate. *Flora and Ulysses: The Illuminated Adventures.* Somerville, MA: Candlewick, 2013. When Ulysses the squirrel gains super strength and the ability to write poetry due to an unfortunate accident, Flora steps up to save the remarkable animal and learns more about herself in the process. Ages six through ten.

———. *The Tale of Despereaux: Being the Story of a Mouse, a Princess, Some Soup, and a Spool of Thread.* Somerville, MA: Candlewick, 2003. A mouse named Despereaux falls in love with the human Princess Pea and is banished to the dungeon for his unmouselike behavior. Good overcomes evil, while hope and forgiveness persevere in this story. Ages nine through twelve.

de la Peña, Matt. *Last Stop on Market Street.* Illustrated by Christian Robinson. New York: G. P. Putnam, 2015. After church each Sunday, a little boy and his nana take the bus to the local soup kitchen where they work as volunteers. Picture book. Ages six through nine.

Dyckman, Ame. *Boy and Bot.* Illustrated by Dan Yaccarino. New York: Knopf, 2012. A boy and his robot share wonderful adventures until the robot is accidentally switched off. The tables are turned when the boy is put to bed. Picture book. Ages five through seven.

Ellis, Deborah. *A Company of Fools.* New York: Fitzhenry and Whiteside, 2002. When the plague sweeps through Paris in the year 1348, the world of the choir boys at St. Luc's is forever transformed. Ages nine through thirteen.

Fleischman, Paul. *Weslandia.* Illustrated by Kevin Hawkes. Somerville, MA: Candlewick, 1999. A boy's ingenious creations transform his backyard into a remarkable space that draws in all the neighborhood kids, even those who once bullied the boy. Picture book. Ages seven through ten.

Fleming, Candace. *Oh, No!* Illustrated by Eric Rohmann. New York: Schwartz and Wade, 2012. As he flees from Tiger, Frog falls into a deep, deep hole and is soon followed by animal after animal as they try to come to his rescue. Picture book. Ages five through eight.

Frazee, Marla. *Boot and Shoe.* New York: Beach Lane, 2012. One little dog spends his days on the front porch while the other spends his time on the back porch—until a mischievous squirrel upsets their routines. Picture book. Ages five through eight.

Funke, Cornelia. *Dragon Rider.* Translated by Anthea Bell. New York: Chicken House/Scholastic, 2004. Set in a world of dragons, brownies, and other fantastic creatures, a boy becomes the Dragon Rider of a silver dragon who derives energy from moonlight. Ages eight through twelve.

———. *Inkheart.* New York: Chicken House/Scholastic, 2003. Through a magical read-aloud, Meggie's father has brought the evil characters of a book to life, and Meggie and her family find themselves caught up in a real-world adventure centering around these book characters. Ages ten and older.

Gorbachev, Valerie. *Nico y los Lobos Feroces.* New York: North South, 2000. Thanks to Mother Rabbit's clever plan, Nico conquers his fear of the wolves that bring him nightmares. Ages five through eight.

Grey, Mini. *Traction Man Is Here!* New York: Dragonfly, 2012. A boy and his superhero doll find adventure all over the house as they search for the Lost Wreck of the Sieve, confront dangers in the bathtub, and become engaged in a host of other adventures. Picture book. Ages five through eight.

Hanlon, Abby. *Dory Fantasmagory.* New York: Dial, 2014. Dory's older siblings may think she is a baby, but her other (fantastic) friends think otherwise. Ages five through eight.

Hoberman, Mary Ann. *You Read to Me, I'll Read to You.* Illustrated by Michael Emberley. New York: Little, Brown, 2004. This collection features very short fairy tales with a twist that are organized for two readers to read together. Picture book. Ages six through nine.

Jenkins, Steve. *Actual Size.* Boston: Houghton Mifflin, 2004. Animals and their body parts are illustrated in their actual sizes. Picture book. Ages five through eight.

Jenkins, Steve, and Robin Page. *What Do You Do with a Tail Like This?* Boston: Houghton Mifflin, 2003. In this interactive picture book, readers discover some of the wonderful things animals can do. Picture book. Ages five through nine.

Jones, Kelly. *Unusual Chickens for the Exceptional Poultry Farmer.* New York: Knopf, 2015. When her family moves to Great-uncle Jim's farm, Sophie is not prepared for the chickens who keep returning to their home. Ages eight through twelve.

Kasza, Keiko. *The Wolf's Chicken Stew.* New York: Putnam, 1987. A chicken outsmarts the wolf who wants her for his dinner. Picture book. Ages five through eight.

Kerley, Barbara. *Walt Whitman: Words for America.* Illustrated by Brian Selznick. New York: Scholastic, 2004. This biography of Walt Whitman focuses primarily on his role in the American Civil War. Picture book. Ages ten and older.

Klassen, Jon. *I Want My Hat Back.* Somerville, MA: Candlewick, 2011. Bear asks animal after animal if they have seen his hat—only to realize that he knows just where it is. Picture book. Ages five through eight.

Krull, Kathleen. *Harvesting Hope: The Story of Cesar Chavez.* Illustrated by Yuyi Morales. New York: Harcourt, 2003. This biography traces Chavez's life from his boyhood to his achievements as leader of the Mexican American farmworkers. Picture book. Ages eight and older.

Kurtz, Jane. *The Storyteller's Beads.* Illustrated by Michael Bryant. New York: Harcourt, 1998. Fleeing their drought- and violence-stricken land, two young Ethiopian strangers overcome their prejudices and find solace in the old stories passed down by one of their grandmothers. Ages nine through twelve.

Lin, Grace. *The Year of the Dog.* New York: Little Brown, 2005. Grace is an American girl of Taiwanese heritage, and throughout the "year of the dog" in the Chinese calendar, she navigates the differences of her two cultures. Sequel: *The Year of the Rat* (2008). Ages eight through ten.

Martin, Bill, Jr. *Brown Bear, Brown Bear, What Do You See?* Illustrated by Eric Carle. New York: Holt, 1967. Patterned, repetitive language is used to introduce colors and animal names. See also *Polar Bear, Polar Bear, What Do You Hear?* (1991) and *Panda Bear, Panda Bear, What Do You See?* (2003). Picture book. Ages five through seven.

Milne, A. A. *Winnie-the-Pooh.* Illustrated by Ernest H. Shepard. New York: Dutton, 1924. Winnie-the-Pooh has marvelous adventures in the Hundred Acre Wood with his host of friends—all stuffed animals like him. Ages five through eight.

Morales, Yuyi. *Niño Wrestles the World.* New York: Roaring Brook, 2013. Niño bravely faces his enemies: he conquers the Guanajuato mummy with his daring tickles and uses doll decoys to stun La Llorana. He is the ultimate hero—until his little sisters wake up from their nap! Picture book. Ages five through seven.

Polacco, Patricia. *Pink and Say.* New York: Philomel, 1994. During the Civil War, an African American Union soldier befriends a white Union soldier. Picture book. Ages eight through young adult.

Pullman, Philip. *The Scarecrow and His Servant.* New York: Knopf, 2004. Accompanied by an orphaned boy, Scarecrow sets out in a world filled with danger to seek adventure and the place where he belongs. Ages six through ten.

Rappaport, Doreen. *Martin's Big Words: The Life of Dr. Martin Luther King, Jr.* New York: Hyperion, 2001. Dr. King's own words are integrated throughout this biography of the great civil rights leader. Picture book. Ages eight and older.

Reynolds, Aaron. *Creepy Carrots!* Illustrated by Peter Brown. New York: Simon and Schuster, 2012. Jasper Rabbit loves carrots and can never pass by Crackenhopper Field without stopping to eat, but then the carrots begin to follow Jasper. Picture book. Ages five through eight.

Say, Allen. *Kamishibai Man.* Boston: Houghton Mifflin, 2005. Missing the old days when he told stories on the streets of Japan, the kamishibai man finds a receptive audience when he decides to revive the old tradition. Picture book. Ages eight through twelve.

Schiltz, Laura Amy. *Splendors and Glooms.* Somerville, MA: Candlewick, 2012. In this story set in Victorian England, two young orphans flee their cruel master, the great puppeteer Grisini, and set out to solve a mysterious kidnapping. Ages ten and older.

Scieszka, Jon. *Robot Zot.* Illustrated by David Shannon. New York: Simon and Schuster, 2009. A determined robot lands on earth—in the middle of a kitchen—where he confronts blenders and toasters and other daunting dangers of the kitchen. Picture book. Ages five through eight.

Sendak, Maurice. *Where the Wild Things Are.* New York: Harper and Row, 1963. When he is punished and sent to bed without supper, Max sails off to a land where he is the king of the Wild Things. Picture book. Ages five through eight.

Stead, Rebecca. *When You Reach Me.* New York: Wendy Lamb Books, 2009. Miranda's orderly world turns upside down when her best friend refuses to even speak to her and she begins to receive mysterious notes that appear to predict the future. Ages ten and older.

Stevens, Janet. *Tops and Bottoms.* San Diego, CA: Harcourt, 1995. Hare tricks lazy Bear by wheeling and dealing in the tops and bottoms of vegetables. Picture book. Ages five through eight.

Stevens, Janet, and Susan Stevens Crummel. *The Great Fuzz Frenzy*. Illustrated by Janet Stevens. New York: Harcourt, 2005. A tennis ball that lands in the middle of a prairie dog town causes quite a commotion. Picture book. Ages five through nine.

Teague, Mark. *Dear Mrs. LaRue: Letters from Obedience School*. New York: Scholastic, 2002. Banished to obedience school, Ike the dog writes a series of letters to his mistress that bend the truth. Picture book. Ages five through eight.

Turnage, Sheila. *Three Times Lucky*. New York: Dial, 2012. To save the only family she has ever known, Moses LoBeau and her best friend set out to solve the murder that has taken place in their small town. Ages ten through twelve.

Van Allsburg, Chris. *The Widow's Broom*. Boston: Houghton Mifflin, 1992. A broom with special powers brings out the prejudices of a widow's neighbors. Picture book. Ages eight through twelve.

Weatherford, Carole Boston. *Moses: When Harriet Tubman Led Her People to Freedom*. Illustrated by Kadir Nelson. New York: Hyperion, 2006. This is the story of Harriet Tubman's heroic efforts to lead slaves to freedom through the Underground Railroad. Picture book. Ages seven and older.

Willems, Mo. *Don't Let the Pigeon Drive the Bus*. New York: Hyperion, 2003. A determined pigeon will try any trick to realize his dream of driving the bus. Picture book. Ages five through eight.

———. *Let's Say Hi to Friends Who Fly!* New York: Balzer and Bray, 2010. A cat meets all sorts of flying friends in this repetitive book. Picture book. Ages five through eight.

———. *That Is Not a Good Idea!* New York: Balzer and Bray, 2013. A hungry fox invites a goose to dinner only to have the tables turned. Picture book. Ages five through eight.

Zelinsky, Paul O. *Z Is for Moose*. New York: Greenwillow, 2012. Moose can't wait for his turn to appear on stage in the alphabet play, but when the time finally arrives, Moose discovers that he has been replaced by Mouse. A monumental (and hilarious) tantrum follows. Picture book. Ages six through nine.

■ BOOKS FOR STORYTELLING

Aardema, Verna. *Why Mosquitoes Buzz in People's Ears*. Illustrated by Leo and Diane Dillon. New York: Dial, 1975. In this African pourquoi tale, an unexpected chain of events explains why mosquitoes buzz in people's ears. Picture book. Ages five through eight.

Erdoes, Richard, and Alfonso Ortiz. *American Indian Myths and Legends*. New York: Pantheon, 1985. A collection of Native American tales and lore written for adults but also good for read-alouds. Ages ten through young adult.

Forest, Heather. *Wonder Tales from around the World*. Atlanta, GA: August House, 1995. An international collection of fairy tales of enchantment. Ages eight through eleven.

Fujita, Hiroko. *Stories to Play With*. Atlanta, GA: August House, 1999. These stories intended for young children come complete with directions for props to be used in telling the tales. Ages five through eight.

Garza, Xavier. *Creepy Creatures and Other Cucuys*. Houston, TX: Arte Publico, 2004. A collection of short stories featuring scary creatures from the folklore of south Texas. Ages eight through twelve.

———. *The Donkey Lady Fights La Llorona and Other Stories*. Houston, TX: Arte Publico, 2015. This is a collection of short stories featuring creepy characters from Mexican and Mexican American folklore. Ages eight through twelve.

Hamilton, Martha. *Scared Witless: Thirteen Eerie Tales to Tell*. Atlanta, GA: August House, 2006. This collection contains tales both funny and scary. Ages nine through twelve.

Hamilton, Martha, and Mitch Weiss. *Noodlehead Stories: World Tales Kids Can Read and Tell.* Atlanta, GA: August House, 2000. This is a collection of humorous knucklehead tales from around the world. Ages seven through twelve.

Hamilton, Virginia. *Her Stories: African American Folktales, Fairy Tales, and True Tales.* Illustrated by Leo and Diane Dillon. New York: Scholastic, 1995. These stories celebrate African American women. Ages nine through young adult.

———. *The People Could Fly: American Black Folktales.* Illustrated by Leo and Diane Dillon. New York: Knopf, 1985. This collection contains favorites such as "Brer Rabbit and the Tar Baby" and "Wiley and the Hairy Man." Ages nine through young adult.

Hayes, Joe. *The Day It Snowed Tortillas/El Día Que Nevaron Tortillas.* El Paso, TX: Cinco Puntos Press, 2003. This is a collection of bilingual folktales from the Southwest. Ages nine through twelve.

———. *El Cucuy: A Bogeyman Cuento in English and Spanish.* El Paso, TX: Cinco Puntos Press, 2003. This is a bilingual retelling of the story of El Cucuy from Hispanic cultures. Picture book. Ages five through eight.

MacDonald, Margaret Read. *Earth Care.* Atlanta, GA: August House, 2005. These tales from around the world share ecological themes. Ages nine through twelve.

———. *Shake-it-up Tales!* Atlanta, GA: August House, 2000. This collection of multicultural tales invites audience participation. It contains riddle stories, singing tales, and others. Ages five through eight.

———. *Three-minute Tales.* Atlanta, GA: August House, 2004. This collection offers tales for all occasions. Ages nine through twelve.

Mourning Dove. *Coyote Stories.* Lincoln: University of Nebraska Press, 1990. Stories of the trickster Coyote, collected in the 1930s by an Okanogan teller. Ages nine through young adult.

Reneaux, J. J. *Cajun Folktales.* Atlanta, GA: August House, 1992. Animal tales, fairy tales, funny folktales, and ghost stories from the Cajun people of the Louisiana bayou country. Ages nine through young adult.

Schwartz, Alvin. *Scary Stories to Tell in the Dark.* New York: HarperCollins, 1986. Stories for middle elementary grade students and older, collected by a serious folklore collector. Ages eight through thirteen.

▪ REFERENCES

Anderson, Richard, Elfrieda Hiebert, Judith Scott, and Ian Wilkinson. *Becoming a Nation of Readers: The Report of the Commission on Reading.* Ann Arbor: University of Michigan Library, 1985.

de Brunvard, Jan. *The Vanishing Hitchhiker and Other Urban Legends.* New York, Norton, 1981.

Colman, Penny. "A New Way to Look at Literature: A Visual Model for Analyzing Fiction and Nonfiction." *Language Arts* 84 (2007): 257–68.

Fielding, Linda G., Paul T. Wilson, and Richard C. Anderson. "A New Focus on Free Reading: The Role of Trade Books in Reading Instruction." In *Contexts of Literacy*, ed. Taffy Raphael and Ralph Reynolds. New York: Longman, 1986.

Fractor, Jann Sorrell, Marjorie Ciruti Woodruff, Miriam G. Martinez, and William H. Teale. "Let's Not Miss Opportunities to Promote Voluntary Reading: Classroom Libraries in the Elementary School." *The Reading Teacher* 46 (1993): 476–84.

Graves, Bonnie, and Lauren A. Liang. "Transitional Chapter Books: An Update." *Book Links* 13 (2004): 12–16.

Hickman, Janet. "A New Perspective on Response to Literature: Research in an Elementary School Setting." *Research in the Teaching of English* 15 (1981): 43–54.

Hoffman, James, Nancy Roser, and Jennifer Battle. "Reading Aloud in Classrooms: From the Modal toward a 'Model.'" *The Reading Teacher* 46 (1993): 496–503.

Krashen, Stephen D. "The (Lack of) Experimental Evidence Supporting the Use of Accelerated Reader." *Journal of Children's Literature* 29 (2003): 9, 16–30.

Lamb, Annette. "Reading Redefined for a Transmedia Universe." *Learning and Leading with Technology* 39 (2011): 3, 12–17.

Linse, Caroline. "Predictable Books in the Children's EFL classroom." *ELT Journal* 6 (2007): 46–54.

MacDonald, Margaret Read. *The Story-teller's Start-up Book.* Atlanta, GA: August House, 1993.

Martinez, Miriam, Nancy Roser, Susan Strecker, and Phil Gough. "Classroom Libraries and Children's Book Selections: Redefining 'Access' in Self-selected Reading." In *Inquiries in Literacy and Practice: Forty-sixth Yearbook of the National Reading Conference*, ed. Charles Kinzer and Donald Leu, 265–72. Oak Creek, WI: National Reading Conference, 1997.

Martinez, M., and W. H. Teale. "Reading in a Kindergarten Library Center." *The Reading Teacher* 41 (1988): 568–72.

McKenna, Michael, and Dennis Kear. "Measuring Attitude toward Reading: A New Tool for Teachers." *The Reading Teacher* (May 1990): 626–39.

Miller, Donalyn. *The Book Whisperer: Awakening the Inner Reader in Every Child.* San Francisco: Jossey Bass, 2009.

Morrow, Lesley Mandel. "Relationships between Literature Program, Library Corner Designs, and Children's Use of Literature." *Journal of Educational Research* 75 (1982): 339–44.

National Endowment for the Arts. *Reading at Risk: A Survey of Literary Reading in America.* Research Division Report No. 46. Washington, DC: National Endowment for the Arts, 2004.

National Institute on Media and the Family. *Sixth Annual Video and Computer Report Card.* 2001.

Parsons, Linda T. "Storytelling in Global Children's Literature: Its Role in the Lives of Displaced Child Characters." *Journal of Children's Literature* 42, no. 2 (2016): 19–27.

Pierce, Kathryn Mitchell. "'I Am a Level 3 Reader': Children's Perceptions of Themselves As Readers." *New Advocate* 12, no. 4 (1999): 359–75.

Rogers, Lynn. "Computerized Reading Management Software: An Effective Component of a Successful Reading Program." *Journal of Children's Literature* 29 (2003): 9–15.

Roser, Nancy L., Miriam Martinez, Kathleen McDonnold, and Charles Fuhrken. "Beginning Chapter Books: Their Features and Their Support of Children's Reading." In *53rd Yearbook of the National Reading Conference*, ed. Colleen M. Fairbanks, Jo Worthy, Beth Maloch, James V. Hoffman, and Diane L. Schallert. Oak Creek, WI: National Reading Conference, 2004.

Sims Bishop, Rudine. "Mirrors, Windows, and Sliding Glass Doors." *Perspectives: Choosing and Using Books for the Classroom* 6 (1990): ix–xi.

Sipe, Lawrence R. *Storytime: Young Children's Literary Understanding in the Classroom.* New York: Teachers College Press, 2008.

Springen, Karen. "Virtual Visits." *Publishers Weekly*, December 14, 2012, www.publishersweekly.com/pw/by-topic/childrens/childrens-industry-news/article/55154-virtual-visits.html.

Teale, William H. "Reading Aloud to Young Children As a Classroom Instructional Activity: Insights from Research and Practice." In *On Reading Books to Children: Parents and Teachers*, ed. A. van Kleeck, Steven A. Stahl, and E. Bauer, 114–39. Mahwah, NJ: Lawrence Erlbaum, 2003.

RESOURCES

Giorgis, Cyndi, and Frank Serafini. *Reading Aloud and Beyond.* Portsmouth, NH: Heinemann, 2003.

Hamilton, Martha, and Mitch Weiss. *Children Tell Stories: A Teaching Guide.* Somers, NY: Richard C. Owen, 1990.

Lipke, Barbara. *Figures, Facts, and Fables: Telling Tales in Science and Math.* Portsmouth, NH: Heinemann, 1996.

Lipson, Eden Ross. The New York Times *Parent's Guide to the Best Books for Children.* 3rd ed. New York: Three Rivers Press, 2000.

Martinez, Miriam, and William H. Teale. "Reading in a Kindergarten Library Center." *The Reading Teacher* 41 (1988): 568–72.

McClure, Amy, and Janice V. Kristo. *Adventuring with Books: A Booklist for Pre-K–Grade 6.* 13th ed. Urbana, IL: National Council of Teachers of English, 2002.

Messner, Kate. "Authors Who Skype with Classes and Book Clubs (for Free!). www.katemessner.com/authors-who-skype-with-classes-book-clubs-for-free.

Miller, Donalyn. *The Book Whisperer: Awakening the Inner Reader in Every Child.* San Francisco: Jossey Bass, 2009.

Moller, Karla J., with Lisa Ferguson. "Apps in Literature-based Classroom Instruction: Integrating through Traditional and Digital Media." *Journal of Children's Literature* 41 (2015): 54–60.

Ralston, Marion V. *An Exchange of Gifts: A Storyteller's Handbook.* Ontario: Pippin Publishing, 1993.

Rubright, Lynn. *Beyond the Beanstalk.* Portsmouth, NH: Heinemann, 1996.

Sawyer, Ruth. *The Way of the Storyteller.* New York: Viking, 1942.

Teale, William H., Junko Yokota, and Miriam Martinez. "The Book Matters: Evaluating and Selecting What to Read Aloud to Young Children." In *Effective Early Literacy Practice*, ed. Andrea DeBruin-Parecki, 101–22. Ypsilanti, MI: High Scope, 2008.

Trelease, Jim. *The Read-Aloud Handbook.* 7th ed. New York: Penguin, 2013.

Yokota, Junko, and Miriam Martinez. "Authentic Listening Experiences." *Book Links* 13, no. 3 (2004): 30–34.

WANT TO KNOW MORE?

1. Learning to read aloud is an art that must be cultivated. Many popular books are available on tape. Go to the public library and check out some of your favorites or perhaps one that you would like to learn to read aloud well. Study how the reader modulates his or her voice. At what points in the story does it slow down or speed up, grow quieter or louder? What effect does that have on the reader? Being able to read a story effectively requires practice. Read the book aloud to yourself. Does what you hear resemble what you heard on tape? Tape yourself reading. (Sometimes you must read in a way that seems exaggerated to your own ear, but the listeners only notice an interesting, exciting, and engaging tale.) Now share the story with children and gauge the responsiveness of the listeners. What changes (if any) do you think you should make for future read-alouds?

2. Visit the library centers in two different classrooms of the same grade level. Examine the centers to determine how the books are organized. How would you

describe the organization of each? Are the books organized by genre, topic, reading level, or in some other way? If possible, interview the teacher to find out why he or she chose to organize the center in this way. Then observe children using the library centers. How do the children appear to go about the process of choosing books to read? Does the organizational structure of the library appear to be helpful? Does one library center appear to be easier to maneuver than another? Based on your observations, reflect on how you hope to organize the library center in your own classroom.

CHAPTER 4

Let's Talk about Literature

Tyler looks out the window of his bedroom and can't believe what he is seeing. He rubs his eyes. Still there! Some strange people are coming out of the trailer where the hired help usually stays. They have brown skin and black hair, and although they don't wear feathers or carry tomahawks, they sure look like the American Indians in his history book in fifth grade.

—from *Return to Sender* by Julia Alvarez (2010, 1)

This chapter is a tool kit of ideas for sharing literature with young people—fiction, poetry, and nonfiction books. Sometimes our purpose is to guide children in looking more deeply into works of literature, and sometimes we want to give them strategies they can use over and over to explore and better understand what they read, but always our aim is to help young readers enjoy literature. Here's a note about enjoyment, though. The late Canadian literary critic Northrop Frye observed that one of the main reasons we educate is to expand the range of things—including kinds of literature and other art forms—that children *can* enjoy (Frye, 1964).

In chapter 2 of this book we explored in detail the main features of literary works, and in this chapter we consider ways that you can guide your students' appreciation of those and other features.

EXPLORING SETTINGS

Settings are the stage on which a story plays out. Here we explore several dimensions of settings. An obvious one is where the events of a story happen: the geographical setting. Another is when they happened: the historical dimension. Then there are the people among whom the events play out, or the social dimension. We address the social dimension on two levels: the social setting, wide view, and the social setting, close up. We explain this later in the chapter. Not all of the dimensions of settings presented here will matter in every story, so the teacher must pick and choose among them.

The Historical Setting

The historical setting doesn't matter in the *Frog and Toad* books or *Harry Potter*. The historical setting does feature prominently in books like Christopher Paul Curtis's

The Watsons Go to Birmingham (1995), set in the 1960s amid racial struggles and campaigns for black rights, and in Clare Vanderpool's *Moon over Manifest* (2010), set during the Depression with the Prohibition, illegal bars, and Hoovervilles (camps where hobos lived), with flashbacks to the Great War years (and people's passage from thrilled patriotism to weary and sad disillusionment). Asking how the historical time period influences or even shapes the plot in those books can be a useful exercise. How might the events of *The Watsons Go to Birmingham* have played out in a different time? How about *Moon over Manifest*? How did the time period give a context to or shape events in that book?

Questions about the Historical Setting

To engage students in exploring historical setting, suggest that they read through the assigned pages and lightly write a "T" in the margins beside any details about the time when the story happens that are important to the story—things that they might have seen in that time period and not in another. They can go back and choose three or four important points and enter them in the left-hand column of an organizer like the one in Figure 4.1. Then they should decide how each detail matters in the story. That is, what does that detail cause, make possible, or make impossible?

Figure 4.1 Settings: Time

What are some important details from the *time* of the story?	How do these details matter in the story?

The Geographical Setting

Geography often frames what happens in a book. Deborah Ellis's books present the lives of believable young people living in different trouble spots of the world—Afghanistan, Bolivia, and Malawi. To be sure, there is always a gripping social issue at work in the setting: the oppression of the Taliban that was especially harsh on girls and women in *The Breadwinner* (Ellis, 2001); the conflict between traditional rural coca growers and cocaine traffickers in Bolivia in *I Am a Taxi* (2007); and the AIDS epidemic in East Africa in *The Heaven Shop* (2007). In many children's books, the geographic setting shares the stage with the historical one. *Esperanza Rising* (Ryan, 2000) could have happened just that way only in Mexico and California—and also only during the Depression of the 1930s. *The Watsons Go to Birmingham* (Curtis, 1995) generated its sense of shock by contrasting the life of a black family in the north and the Deep South, but this contrast played out most intensely during the 1960s.

Technology Tip

When a book is set in a place far removed from a reader's own world, the reader may have a difficult time visualizing the book's setting. Marjorie Agostin's *I Lived on Butterfly Hill* (2015), which is set in part in Valparaiso, Chile, is a book that might present such a problem for many readers. Though Agostin gives rich descriptions of the busy streets, steep hills, and colorful cable cars of Valparaiso, readers may benefit from finding actual images of the city on the Internet.

Questions about the Geographical Setting

Like before, suggest that students read through the assigned pages and lightly write a "P" in the margins beside any important details about the place where the story happens—things that they might see in that place but not somewhere else. They can go back and choose three or four important ones that they marked and write a few words about them in the left-hand column of an organizer like the one in Figure 4.2. Next, they should decide how each detail matters in the story. That is, what did it cause to happen or prevent from happening, because of the place the story is set?

Figure 4.2   Settings: Place

What are some important details about the *place* where the story happens?	How do these details matter in the story?

The Social Setting, Wide View

Race and social class can play prominent roles in books for children. In *Shiloh* (Naylor, 1991), Marty's family are country people. They have limited financial means, live close to the land, and are at home in the woods. They follow a social code where neighbors carefully manage their relationships with each other in order to maintain harmony.

Marty's social class explains the grammar he uses, as in "The day Shiloh come. . . ." His membership in this rural, earthy community tacitly explains why Marty must work out his conflict with Judd Travers—the brutish man who mistreats his hunting dog—man to man (or boy to man) instead of simply calling 911, as David Howard (Marty's friend who lives in town) might have done. Social class–bound codes define much of what can happen in *Shiloh*.

The characters in *Shiloh* are all white, but the characters in Rita Williams-Garcia's *One Crazy Summer* (2011) are all African American. The differences among her African American characters create a checkerboard of racial identities that the main character must negotiate. Delphine and her sisters were brought up rather conservatively in Brooklyn with a grandmother from the Deep South who represents traditional stay-in-your-place views of black people's roles in society. When Delphine and her sisters travel to Oakland, California, their deeply troubled mother who had abandoned them years before introduces the girls to members of the nascent Black Panther Party. Delphine and her sisters struggle to define themselves as family members and also as black—not "colored"—girls. And, of course, because it is the 1960s, the porous borders between "liberation" and insanity, racial identity, geography, and history all weave together to create the setting of this fascinating book.

Questions about the Social Setting, Wide View

Social class, race, and gender can be delicate things to talk about in the classroom, even when children's books give them prominent roles. The intention of discussing social class, race, and gender is to explore how groupings and privileges based on race, social class, and gender shape what happens in the story by facilitating or limiting characters' possibilities—just as the historical period or the geographical setting does. Unlike historical or geographic settings, though, the way that people grant or withhold privileges to other people based on social factors are the results of choices people make. Thus, calling attention to the social setting can invite a debate about the injustice of the stratifications and unequal distribution of privileges in society.

You can begin by asking the students to discuss who the main character's "people" are, her or his "group." Using a graphic organizer like the one depicted in Figure 4.3, have students think about characters in the story that come from different social groups. In the left-hand column, write the name of a character who represents each group. Underneath the character's group, write descriptions of each group—the way the characters talk, what they eat and how they get it, where they live, what they do for work, how they spend their leisure time, how much education they have, what they do to stay safe, how they relate to people from their own group and from other groups, and what privileges members of each group do or do not enjoy. In the right-hand column, have students record how each detail matters to the story. You will want to carry out this discussion with sensitivity, of course.

Another way to query social class, race, and gender is to ask how the story or a scene from the story might have played out had the character been of a different social class (and here you should name it), race (and, again, name it), or gender (male or female). For example, the main character in *Wonder* (Palacio, 2012) is Augie, who has a congenitally deformed face. What if Augie's family had been poor and not well off? Or recent immigrants? What if the main character in *Shiloh* had been a girl? Or

Figure 4.3 Settings: Social Groups

What are some key details about the main character's *people* or *group* that matter in the story?	How do these details matter in the story?

Don't Miss . . .
Books with Distinctive Settings

I Lived on Butterfly Hill by Marjorie Agostin

The Underneath by Kathi Appelt

Chasing Redbird by Sharon Creech

The Midwife's Apprentice by Karen Cushman

Listen, Slowly by Thanhha Lai

Hattie Big Sky by Kirby Larson

Sarah, Plain and Tall by Patricia MacLachlan

The Small Adventure of Popeye and Elvis by Barbara O'Connor

Splendors and Glooms by Laura Amy Schlitz

wealthy and privileged? What if the namesake character in *Esperanza Rising* had been poor to begin with?

The Social Setting, Close Up

Characters in books usually are presented in close relationships with others. Those relationships are often troubled; in fact, it's rare for a main character in a children's book simply to get along fine with her or his family members. Note the troubled relationship between Delphine and her sisters and their mother, Cecile, in *One Crazy Summer* or between Abilene Tucker and her estranged father, Gideon, in *Moon over Manifest* or between Opal Buloni and her emotionally absent father in *Because of Winn Dixie* (DiCamillo, 2000).

The relationships among characters in R. J. Palacio's *Wonder* are especially interesting, because the shifts in narrative perspective allow us to see how each character feels about the others. The main character, Augie, born with a face that evokes horror, is fortunate to enjoy loving support from his family as he bravely and sensitively handles the scary challenges of forging relationships with schoolmates. When the narrator's perspective shifts to that of his sister Via, we learn that her brother has absorbed so much attention and concern from their parents that she has essentially raised herself, finding emotional support only in a grandmother, who wisely perceives the girl's need. Via has her moments of self-pity, but she is quickly ashamed of them, since her problems pale in comparison to her brother's. The family setting portrayed in the book reminds us of the ecology of a frog pond, where everything in it affects everything else.

Questions about the Social Setting, Close Up

Here we are looking at the way the main character fits into the setting of the people she or he interacts with day to day, and how the pushes and pulls of those relationships shape the narrative. Those other people are often family members. As Sigmund Freud noted, the family circle is the scene of the most powerful dramas of a person's life, dramas that often lay down patterns that we follow as long as we live.

Some questions to ask about the close setting of a book are then:

- How is this character like the other people closest around her or him? How is the character different? What evidence of both the similarities and differences can you find?
- How does the character feel about the people closest around? How do the others feel about him or her? How do you know?
- How do the expectations of others around the main character influence what she or he does or set limits on his or her actions?
- What does the character perceive or understand (or think she or he perceives or understands) that the others do not and vice versa? How does the author tell us these things?

■ GETTING TO KNOW CHARACTERS

Understanding people, ourselves included, occupies much of everyone's attention every single day. Whether we're watching a reality show on TV; reading *People* magazine; deciding whether to friend someone on Facebook, date someone, or marry someone; whether we're distracted by gossip on the Internet; pondering what motivated people in the news to do something wonderful or awful; weeding through old memories with a therapist seeking to understand why we feel the way we feel and do what we do; or even writing a term paper in history, sociology, anthropology, economics, psychology, women's studies, cultural studies, or educational studies—all of us spend long parts of our days consciously or unconsciously sifting through data to help us shape our working theories of what people are like, and why people act the ways they do, the ways they did, and the ways they will. Stories have always been the most common sources of the knowledge we use for understanding people. Stories have been around for thousands of years longer than any of the academic and professional fields devoted to understanding people, and even today they are what we turn to far more often than any other academic source. We say this because the business of exploring characters in stories is far more serious than simply a school task. It is the essential business of understanding our common humanity. So how do books portray characters?

Through Their Actions

We know characters by their deeds. Opal Buloni in Kate DiCamillo's *Because of Winn Dixie* reaches out and penetrates the shells of people who are trapped by their own secret sufferings and thus keep to themselves. In the process, she creates a community of people who come to appreciate each other. August Pullman, the boy with the genetically rearranged face in R. J. Palacio's *Wonder*, courageously throws himself into one challenging situation after another, rarely giving in to self-pity. His actions lead the readers to conclude that he is courageous and sensitive; he is what we would hope ourselves to be if we were born with his challenges.

Questions about Actions

We can ask students to reflect on ways a character is revealed through their actions by asking them to name the traits they associate with a character and then provide evidence of those traits in the form of that character's actions in the story that reveal those traits.

Through Their "People" and Their Relations with Others

Characters are presented in the context of those immediately around them, and that is usually the family. Earlier when we discussed the setting close up, we named the other people immediately around the main character as part of the story's setting, since the supports the others provide, the obligations they exact, and the misunderstandings and irritations they cause frame the action much as a football stadium frames a sporting event. Other people are also one of the devices writers use to bring characters to life. In *Shiloh*, Marty Preston loves his family and shares most of their interests, but he is far more sensitive and reflective and a much deeper thinker—and those differences make him stand out from the other family members. What makes a character distinctive is both who she is and what she is not—how she is like other people, and how she is unlike them.

Questions about the Character's "People"

Ask students to reflect on ways a character is revealed through their fit with their "people" by asking:

- How is the character like the people closest around him or her? How is she or he different?
- How do those similarities and contrasts help us see and understand the character?
- How might we readers describe ourselves in our similarities to and differences from those around us?

Through Their Sense of Themselves

In children's books, especially those for third-grade readers and higher, authors can have their characters express their inner reflections aloud. In *Return to Sender*, Julia Alvarez uses the device of personal letters and journal entries to share the thoughts of Mari, the Mexican American girl who shares the role of main character with Tyler, her Anglo counterpart:

> It is difficult to be the one different from my sisters. Some boys at my school made fun of me, calling me an "illegal alien." What is illegal about me? Only that I was born on the wrong side of a border? As for "alien," I asked the teacher's helper, and she explained that an alien is a creature from outer space who does not even belong on this earth! So, where am I supposed to go? (Alvarez, 2010, 14)

In Phyllis Reynolds Naylor's *Shiloh*, the protagonist, Marty, often thinks aloud about his situation when pondering the morality of lying to his parents in order to save the dog, Shiloh, which has to be one of the greatest displays of self-awareness in contemporary children's literature. Such expressions are especially striking when you realize how rare it is to hear young people insightfully explain what they are feeling and experiencing ("I'm like, OMG" doesn't count!). Characters' self-reflections in children's books can point the way for actual readers to understand their own emotions and moral struggles. Let's elaborate on that point.

Back in the 1930s, the Russian psychologist Alexandr Luria (1976) wanted to know if reading made a difference in the way people thought about the world and about themselves. He traveled across several time zones to the steppes of Uzbekistan, where he met and interviewed illiterate farmers—women and men who had never learned to read and whose ancestors hadn't, either. When he asked them to describe themselves—to tell him their major traits and foibles—their typical answers were along the lines of, "How can I talk about myself? Ask someone else. They will tell you about me!" But when Luria found and interviewed villagers who had attended night classes and learned to read, sure enough, when asked, one said she was patient, and another said she was impatient; one said he was careful, another admitted to being impulsive, and so on.

How do you explain the differences between nonreaders and readers' self-consciousness? One critic (Postman, 1994) suggested the answer may be because in literature, readers get to look inside the private experience of characters. When we understand how other people experience their lives, we find the way to reflect on our own lives, also. Not all children have language to express their emotions or to understand those of others. Mary Cowhey's *Black Ants and Buddhists* (2006) is a classroom teacher's thoughtful account of how she helped children to think about their own feelings, to become aware of the effects of their actions on others, and to learn empathy.

Try This
Questions about Characters' Sense of Self

A lively way to explore characters' sense of self is to ask students to make up "inner conversations" for characters when the author has not supplied them. One way to ask for an inner conversation is to ask the class, "What do you suppose the character is saying to himself right now?" Another way is to ask students to write imaginary diary entries, such as: "Dear Diary, Today I _____. I did it because _____. When others think of me they may say, '_____.' But when I think of myself I say, '_____.'"

Call attention to examples of characters sharing their inner thoughts when you come across them in a text. Even when those thoughts are not made explicit, invite the students to write "inner conversations" (Shakespeare would call them soliloquies) that characters might have with themselves at critical moments in the story.

Through the Roles They Play in the Story

Another way we understand characters in stories is by the roles they play in the plot. Whether we are watching a closely contested football game or reading fiction, it is normal for us to cheer the hero, boo the rival, and save a warm place in our hearts for the trusty helper. Authors of stories wittingly or unwittingly use these propensities to shape the reader's reactions to characters, assigning one the role of protagonist or main character, another the role of rival or enemy, and another the role of helper.

The French drama critic Etienne Souriau (1955) represents characters' roles by means of zodiac symbols, the first four are common to nearly all stories:

 ♌ : The *hero* is the character whose desire and need drives the story forward.

 ☼ : The *goal* is the hero's main need or desire.

 ♂ : The *rival* is the person who works against the hero and stands between the hero and her or his goal.

 ☾ : The *helper* is a person (or persons) in a story who helps the hero along the way, as he or she works to achieve the goal.

The last two roles appear only occasionally in stories:

 ☌ : The *beneficiary* is the person, people, or some other entity that benefits or is intended to benefit from the main character's actions in the story and receives the goods.

Often, but not always, the beneficiary is the hero her- or himself.

 ♎ : The *judge* is the person or power that decides if the hero or someone else will receive the benefits.

In simple stories, characters may play roles consistently throughout the story. In "Jack and the Beanstalk," Jack is the hero, the Giant is the rival, and the Giant's wife is Jack's reluctant helper. But in more sophisticated literature, characters may go from playing one role to playing another. In *Stone Fox*, John Reynolds Gardiner (1980) shocks his young readers when the rival, Stone Fox, turns into the helper at the last minute. In *Because of Winn Dixie*, Dunlap and Stevie Dewberry and "old pinch-faced" Amanda Wilkinson are Opal's rivals (or at least unfriendly strangers) who become her helpers. In *Wonder*, R. J. Palacio manages to turn several rivals into helpers—all but one key character, that is, and that character offers a clue on the last page that he may come around at some time in the future. The other students—the whole school!—turn out to play the role of the judge (spoiler alert!) when they proclaim Augie a true hero and a wonderful kid at the end of the story. In *Because of Winn Dixie*, the various characters Opal befriends are the beneficiaries of her socializing grace but only after they have played the role of judge, too, and accepted the idea of becoming a community.

Try This
Questions about Characters' Roles

You can use the idea of dramatic roles in several ways to help children think about stories. One way is to ask children to identify characters who are playing the roles of hero, rival, and helper and to discuss their choices with others. These discussions can become lively, because not all role assignments are obvious. Is the helper in "Jack and the Beanstalk" the mysterious old man or the Giant's wife? If it is the Giant's wife (and the Giant is the rival), why should the wife help the person who is striving against her husband? Is Jack's goal to obey his mother, to get money, to satisfy his curiosity, or to prove himself? Or is it all of these things, one after another? Judd Travers, the brutish poacher in *Shiloh*, is clearly the rival through most of the story—but doesn't he become the judge, too, at the end of the book, when he puts Marty through an ordeal to win the dog? And who is the beneficiary in *Shiloh*—the boy or the dog? Or both? Discussing these issues takes students deep into a story, even a supposedly simple one like "Jack and the Beanstalk." Examining roles can be even more interesting in books where characters change roles as events unfold.

Want to Know More?

The late Shelby Wolf's *Interpreting Literature with Children* (2003) examines the approaches taken by several traditions of literary theory in looking deeply into children's books. Especially useful for exploring structuralist theories of literature, including dramatic roles, is Robert Scholes's *Structuralism in Literature* (1975).

Another way of using dramatic roles is to take different perspectives on a story. Take a character who seems to be playing one role and imagine how the story would change if that character played a different role. For example, in "Jack and the Beanstalk," suppose the Giant's wife were the hero; that is, suppose we saw things from her perspective. What is her goal? Who is her rival? Exploring such questions can lead us to think of even seemingly transparent stories in strikingly new ways. As mentioned earlier, R. J. Palacio does exactly this by telling *Wonder* from several perspectives. Have students try retelling stories from new perspectives that haven't already been explored by the authors.

As the Author Describes the Characters

In earlier times, it was common for authors to describe the appearance of their characters in rich detail. Here is how Horatio Alger's narrator describes the rags-to-riches hero of *Ragged Dick* at the opening of the book:

> Dick's appearance as he stood beside the box was rather peculiar. His pants were torn in several places and had apparently belonged in the first instance to a boy two sizes larger than himself. He wore a vest, all the buttons of which were gone except two, out of which peeped a shirt which looked as if it had been worn a month. To complete his costume he wore a coat too long for him, dating back, if one might judge from its general appearance, to remote antiquity. (Alger, 1868)

That description may be vivid, but it may strike you as more elaborate than it needs to be. In contrast, here is how Phyllis Reynolds Naylor's narrator describes Marty in *Shiloh*. (. . .) Got that? Good. Now here is how Kathryn Erskine's narrator describes Caitlin, the main character in *Mockingbird* (Erskine, 2010). (. . .). Right. And here comes Louis Sachar's narrator's description of Stanley Yelnats: "He was overweight" (2000, 7). At last, some kind of description. In Stanley's case, though, being overweight figures in the plot, explaining why he might have had trouble making friends back home and providing a yardstick by which to measure the rigors of forced labor at Camp Green Lake, which melted the pounds away.

As those examples demonstrate, authors rarely throw many words at characters, especially the main ones. The reason may be that describing characters from the narrator's perspective may conflict with how readers imagine those characters. Think about it: you don't need to describe yourself to yourself, do you? Also, many authors believe in showing and not telling: rather than overtly telling us how characters looked or what they were like, they prefer to bring characters to life through their actions, their relations to other people, and their inner thoughts.

When characters *are* described by authors, the descriptions convey more than just appearance. Author Louis Sachar doesn't tell us that the warden at Camp Green Lake, Mr. Sir, was threatening and sadistic, but the reader readily infers those characteristics from the description:

> A man was sitting with his feet up on the desk. . . . Even though he was inside, he wore sun glasses and a cowboy hat. . . . He had a tattoo of a rattlesnake on his arm, and as he signed his name, the snake's rattle appeared to wiggle. (1998, 12)

In *Turtle in Paradise* (Holm, 2010), Turtle provides some description of herself, but the effect is to explain something of her world view as much as to describe her appearance—and to contrast both with her dreamy mother and the cousin she sees for the first time and has taken an instant, self-protective dislike to:

> Folks have always told me that I look like Mama. My hair's brown, same as hers, but it's cut short in a bob with bangs, like a soup bowl turned upside down. Mama keeps hers long as a good dream, because that's the way Archie likes it.
>
> Our eyes are different, though. I think the color of a person's eyes says a lot about them. Mama has soft blue eyes, and all she sees is kittens and roses. My eyes are grey as soot, and I see things for what they are. The mean boy on the porch has green eyes. Probably from all the snot in his nose. (17)

The authors of both these books, *Holes* and *Turtle in Paradise*, are economical in their descriptions and very efficient. In the hands of skilled writers, descriptions of characters, when supplied at all, convey more information than simply what characters look like.

Characters Who Remind Us of Other Characters

Characters in literature often occupy stock roles, so that a story might be recast as "This is what happens when a character like X gets into a situation like Y." For example, Jack in "Jack and the Beanstalk" is the plucky, young, underestimated hero who overcomes a much more powerful foe. The character of Jack reminds us of other plucky, underestimated heroes who face powerful foes, such as David in the story of David and Goliath or Tweety in the Tweety and Sylvester cartoons. In contemporary literature, the character of Augie in *Wonder* overcomes huge challenges to win the appreciation of his peers and even to inspire them. The character of Junie B. Jones is an updated (and brasher) version of Ramona Quimby. Both are examples of children with strong opinions whose intellect is sometimes underestimated by adults (and they often bristle at being misunderstood by adults and treated as less mature than they are)—but are also sometimes *over*estimated by the girls themselves (so they also do foolish things, like Ramona crowning herself with a ring of burdocks in *Ramona and Her Father*). And in that, they are like their readers, too.

■ EXPLORING PLOTS

In chapter 2 we noted that plots revolve around four varieties of conflicts: conflict between characters, conflict within a character, conflict between a character and nature, or conflict between a character and society. We also noted that stories have predictable structures. In chapter 2 we shared the structure of introduction (or exposition), complication, rising action, falling action, and denouement. These steps come from the descriptions of plots that literary scholars use.

Here is another way to describe story structures:

Try This
Questions about Characters Who Are Like Other Characters

You can ask children to compare characters from one book with those in another. Ask them to think of characters in different books that play similar roles when compared to other characters, such as Augie versus his classmates in *Wonder* and Caitlin versus her classmates in *Mockingbird*. They can slot the characters into a graphic organizer as on page 117 and then list descriptive words under each character. It may work even better for them to choose characters who are in an important relationship to each other—conflict or support—and to list two characters from each book in the columns in a graphic organizer as shown on page 125. You might also ask them to make comparisons between characters in books and people in real life—even ourselves.

Figure 4.4   Comparing Characters to Others

Character 1	Other book characters like character 1	Real people who are like that	Character 2	Other book characters like character 2	Real people who are like that

- There is an introduction of the character or characters in a setting.
- The character has a problem and sets a goal.
- The character attempts to reach the goal.
- There is an outcome of that attempt.
- There may be several attempts, each followed by an outcome. If so, these clusters of attempts-plus-outcomes are "episodes."
- Finally, there is a resolution of the original problem: the main character achieves her goal or she doesn't.

There is a consequence to all of the actions: the character has usually reached a different state of affairs from the one in which she started.

The description of story structure we just shared has been assembled from the work of cognitive psychologists and educators (Stein and Glenn, 1979). It seems to

Don't Miss . . .
Picture Books with Problem-solution Structures

Journey by Aaron Becker

Click, Clack, Moo: Cows That Type by Doreen Cronin

Strega Nona by Tomie dePaola

Lilly's Purple Plastic Purse by Kevin Henkes

The Mysterious Tadpole by Steven Kellogg

Doctor De Soto by William Steig

The Gardener by Sarah Stewart

A Chair for My Mother by Vera B. Williams

Hey, Al! by Arthur Yorinks

fit the way many stories work in real life, too. If a friend asks you, "How did you get your new puppy?" or "When did you become such a passionate environmentalist?" it is likely that the story you tell will have most of the above elements in it and in roughly the same order.

Many children perceive the structures of stories in this way intuitively without being taught. You can see that when they make accurate predictions of what will happen in stories, sometimes with no more than the first page or even the cover illustration to go on. But it is still worth presenting the elements to children—both to make sure that all of the students can use them to follow stories, and also because using the elements of the story structure can be an interesting way of discussing what is happening. Being conscious of story structure can help children when they are writing stories, too.

Teaching Story Structure

One popular way of teaching story structure is to have children fill out a "story map" such as the one shown in Figure 4.5. The class can do this collectively, discussing entries for each box, agreeing on an answer, and letting the teacher write their responses in each box.

One way to proceed is to have the students suggest ways to fill out different parts of the story map as they read a book as a class. Early on they can decide on who the main character is and the setting. Then they can fill in each episode—each unit of attempts and outcomes—as they come across them in the book.

Another way to approach the story map is to do so dynamically. That is, the class can make predictions early on as to what the resolution and the consequence will be, revising those predictions as they read more. For example, in *Because of Winn Dixie*, we know early on that Opal is lonely. At first we think the solution will be to have a closer and warmer relationship with her father. We also learn that she sadly misses her mother, and readers may hope that the solution will be for her mother to return before the story ends. Then we are introduced to one quirky character after another, all of whom are suffering from isolation. Finally, the solution becomes evident that

Opal will craft a community—a surrogate family—from this cast of strangers. That solution does address the problem readers were aware of in the beginning, yet readers will not have anticipated it until the end of the book approaches, even though that solution was hiding in plain sight. The story map in Figure 4.5 has space for the class to predict what they think the resolution and the consequence will be before both are finally revealed.

Figure 4.5   Story Map

Who's the story about?	Where does the story take place?	How is the character doing in the beginning? What's the character's problem, or what does she or he need?	Who or what is standing in the character's way?	What does the character do to solve his or her problem?	How is the character doing in the end?

Kinds of Plots

Stories come with different kinds of plots, as we saw in chapter 2. Traditional tales include hero stories, numbskull tales, tall tales, legends, cumulative tales, pourquoi stories, or animal stories. Contemporary children's chapter books and novels, though, include hero or adventure stories, bildungsroman or coming-of-age stories, journey tales, layered stories, moralistic or didactic tales, fantasy, and mystery stories. Some stories fit more than one category. Also, each of these plot types may be developed differently as historical novels, books featuring foreign settings, and multicultural books or books featuring children from parallel cultures.

Here are more descriptions, along with some questions teachers might ask about stories with each kind of plot.

Bildungsroman or Coming-of-Age Stories

The plots of *Shiloh*, *Because of Winn Dixie*, and *Holes* are all good examples of the bildungsroman, which a combination of two German words that literally mean "education" and "novel." Bildungsroman, therefore, refers to a novel about the growth or maturation of the main character. In each aforementioned book, the child protagonist begins in a relatively innocent state and goes through trials that lead the character to mature. The last two sentences of *Shiloh* demonstrate what we mean: "But the good part is I saved Shiloh and opened my eyes some. Now that ain't bad for eleven" (Naylor, 1991, 144).

To guide students thinking about a coming of age story, we might ask questions such as those in Figure 4.6.

Figure 4.6   Coming of Age Questions

What are some words that describe the character in the beginning?	What are the major events that helped the character grow?	What did the character learn from each event?	What are some words that describe the character at the end?
What are some examples that support those words?			What are some examples that support those words?

Journey Stories

Since the story of *Huckleberry Finn* and before that *Pilgrim's Progress*, people have enjoyed stories whose plots are built around journeys from one place to another. Tales like Guadalupe Garcia McCall's *Summer of the Mariposas* (2012), Beverley Naidoo's *Journey to Jo'burg* (1985), Frances Temple's *Grab Hands and Run* (1995) and *The Ramsay Scallop* (1994), and Deborah Ellis's *Parvana's Journey* (2002) keep interest alive by presenting new scenes, new people, and new challenges at each new setting along the way. There is usually a thread of character development that runs through each book. In *Grab Hands and Run*, the family of Salvadoran refugees gradually comes to accept the loss of the father who has been "disappeared" and to recognize their need to rely upon each other. In *The Ramsay Scallop*, set in the year 1300, a young girl betrothed to a returned Crusader who is suffering from something like posttraumatic stress disorder comes to love him and look forward to their life together as woman and man, husband and wife. There are often growing insights into the setting, too. In *Journey to Jo'burg*, Naledi, age thirteen, and her younger brother make a desperate trip across South Africa during apartheid to save the life of a younger sister and discover along the way the inhumanity of the racial divide as well as the occasional kindness of strangers. In *Summer of the Mariposas*, Mexican American Odilia and her sisters go on a quest that begins with returning a dead man to his family and morphs into a quest to find their grandmother and learn why their father abandoned them a year before. On the way, they (and the readers) become acquainted with characters from Mexican folklore and Aztec mythology.

Students might draw maps of the journeys of the main characters in such books and label them with notes about major events and resulting insights that occur in each place. They could also draw maps of their own life experiences showing where they began, where they have gone, and what has happened to them along the way.

The teacher can also distribute unlined index cards, and the students can create postcards, drawing pictures of a location on one side and writing another (possibly made-up) character on the other, describing what the main character has just experienced and how he or she feels about it. After writing several cards, students should write a card from the character at the beginning of the story describing her or his expectations and misgivings about the journey and another card from the character at the end of the journey, relating what she or he has learned and the ways in which she or he has been changed by the experience. To launch the activity, Vera and Jennifer Williams's *Stringbean's Trip to the Shining Sea* (1988) might be shared with the class as a great example of homemade postcards.

Stories within Stories

Many stories contain flashbacks—brief sections that tell of events that happened in the past that shed light on the present state of affairs. Kathryn Erskine's *Mockingbird* begins with the narrator, Caitlin Smith, describing a scene of mourning. We gradually learn, through a narration challenged and complicated by Caitlin's Asperger's syndrome, that her brother Devon has been murdered in a senseless mass killing. Flashbacks fill in what happened to him, but the narration stays almost entirely in the fictional present.

In contrast, Louis Sachar has woven a mystery novel, *Holes*, with robust strands of past histories bubbling up into the fictional present through metaphorical mineshafts of memory. Similarly, *Moon over Manifest* opens with the protagonist, Abilene Tucker, rolling out of a train car and into the depressed town of Manifest, Kansas. (The year is 1936, after all, so the whole country is amid the Depression.) She knows this town has much to do with her absent father's past, but it will take exploring several strands of incomplete and often mysterious narratives before a coherent story emerges.

Stories like *Holes* are fascinating but challenging for some students. To support students' reading, ask them to keep reading journals, noting major questions on each two-page spread about the characters and how they fit into the story. They can enter answers as they read through the book. When they have finished reading the book, ask them to retell the story in each strand that was revealed bit by bit in the narration (see Figure 4.7).

Moralistic or Didactic Tales

A hundred years ago, most published works for children were heavily moralistic. In many countries of the world and in a fair number of communities in America they still are. In fact, there is a thriving religious publishing industry in America. Religious books are rarely distributed to public schools, though, because of concerns regarding the separation of church and state, but they do find a sizable market in religious private schools, among parents who homeschool their children because they object to public schools on religious grounds, and also among other parents who want their

Figure 4.7 *Holes* **Map**

Characters	What Happened to Them?	How They Figure in the Plot
Stanley Yelnats		
Elya Yelnats		
Kate Barlow and Onion Sam		
Zero		
Clyde Livingston		

children to read either religious literature or literature that they consider safe and wholesome. Here we are not talking about religious books.

Contemporary children's books published in North America tend to avoid "preaching," as many authors would put it. Rather, they tell engaging stories, often putting characters into moral dilemmas, and leave it to readers to draw their own lessons. Judy Blume's *Blubber* (1974) and *Forever* (1975) would not be purchased by the parents who are fans of religious books, and neither would *Harriet the Spy* (Fitzhugh, 1964), since those books have young people behaving in ways many parents would not condone. Yet those books do teach moral lessons by showing young readers the undesirable consequences of behavior that is unkind or dangerous but also commonplace among many young people. Eleanor Estes's *The Hundred Dresses* (1944), a "nicer" book than those just mentioned, also points to moral lessons through the regret the protagonists experience because they missed opportunities to show kindness when it would have mattered.

Echoing children's books from earlier eras, psychologist Trudy Ludwig's books such as *Sorry!* (2006) are more deliberately didactic than most contemporary children's books from mainstream publishers. They typically present a child who is having a social problem with another child and then bring in a wise adult who proposes a solution to the problem. The suffering child tries the solution, and, lo and behold, it works.

What Do *You* Think?

Thousands of books for children are published each year in the United States, and for each one published, hundreds more are rejected. There is tremendous pressure on authors and illustrators to produce books that will sell. Guides for authors such as *The Giblin Guide to Writing for Children* (Giblin, 2006) and *How to Write a Children's Book and Get It Published* (Seuling, 2004) frankly advise would-be writers to tell good stories rather than to moralize or hold back too much on graphic details in books for children. They urge writers to look at what is being published today for children. We knew and respected both of these writers, but we have to ask: When it comes to the moral influence of children's books on children, should the tone really be set by market forces? If not entirely, is there an alternative? What do *you* think?

How do we lead students in exploring the moral lessons of stories? One way is to fill in a graphic organizer such as the one in Figure 4.8. Ask students to name a character then to list that character's most important deeds, what happened to the character seemingly as a result of those deeds, and finally, the conclusions the reader draws from all of that.

Figure 4.8 Exercise in Exploring Morals

Characters	What is she or he like?	What does she or he do?	Why?	What does she or he get?	Why?	What do we learn from the consequences?

■ EXPLORING THEMES

A theme is a central insight or truth that is clearly conveyed by a text or inferred by a reader. A theme is somewhere between a topic and a message. A theme is usually

> **Reaching *All* Students**
>
> So far we have spoken about plot structures as if they applied equally well to all children's books. But that is not so. Children's books from other parts of the world, especially from countries influenced by France or Spain, may be more spontaneously fanciful and far less predictable in their structures than children's books that are popular in the United States, so students from other countries may not be so quick to recognize the familiar plot structures we have just described.
>
> Moreover, we should bear in mind that outside of the United States, Canada, Europe, Japan, Argentina, and a few other places, books for children are quite rare. Even in those countries that have their own children's books, they may be old classics meant to be revered as icons of a local cultural heritage rather than as entertainment. And they are almost never meant to inspire young people to discuss issues relevant to their lives.
>
> Children who grew up in cultures outside of the United States may need more scaffolding so that they may adjust to and appreciate the benefits and expectations that come with American children's literature.

demonstrated by example rather than stated outright, and it is often suggested on several planes via statements, actions, and symbols.

Of all the elements of literature we might discuss with children, themes are the most challenging for several reasons. One is that considering themes requires abstract thinking that does not come naturally to children. Another is that contemporary children's literature shies away from conveying messages; authors strive to tell a good story and let readers draw their own conclusions rather than to teach. Third, contemporary approaches to literary criticism—at least until the advent of the Common Core state standards—allowed and even emphasized the reader's role in constructing meaning and acknowledged that the meaning of a work could vary with the reader's background and concerns. All of these points make exploring themes a challenging enterprise.

Let's address the cognitive challenge first. Saying what the theme is in a work of literature is essentially an act of translation. The author told a story, but by stating the theme we are restating the story as a precept (to borrow a term from Mr. Greene in R. J. Palacio's *Wonder*) or an epigram—a statement of truth. That act of translation requires a kind of abstract thinking that is challenging even for many adults, much less children. But let's try to do it anyway.

Finding a Theme in a Statement from the Work

Sometimes authors have characters state aloud what might be taken as a central truth or theme of a work. In *Shiloh*, Marty's bedroom soliloquy and prayer is a good example:

> "Jesus," I whisper finally, "Which do you want me to do? Be one hundred percent honest and carry that dog back to Judd so that one of your creatures can be kicked and starved all over again, or keep him here and fatten him up to glorify your creation?"
>
> The question seemed to answer itself, and I'm pretty proud of that prayer. (Naylor, 1991, 57)

Marty's words here might suggest a theme of the book: the validity of doing the right thing even if it means not following rules.

Finding the Theme in Actions in the Work

Sometimes a set of actions in a book can take on symbolic meaning and possibly represent a theme. In *Moon over Manifest*, Miss Sadie, the diviner, is the character who reveals the past bit by bit and connects it to the present, eventually helping Abilene reunite with her father. The diviner is the go-between who links two time periods and shows the influence of the past on the fictional present, demonstrating, in the words of William Faulkner, that "The past is never dead. It's not even past" (1951, 73).

Finding the Theme in an Image in the Work

Sometimes objects or images might symbolize a core meaning or theme of a work. Often a thematic symbol is found in the title of a book. For example, the dog whose name appears in the title, *Because of Winn Dixie*, is not the main character. The real hero who builds community in the story is Opal, but the ever-present Winn Dixie reminds readers that a catalyst is necessary to make good things happen, and that idea could serve as a theme.

The title of the book, *Holes*, might remind readers that if we dig down into the history that lies beneath the present, we may understand the meanings of present circumstances and events. That seems like a central idea or theme of the book, *Holes*, too.

If these attempts to identify themes seem debatable, it's because they are. We know of many cases where authors, including ourselves, have been amused by and disagreed with interpretations of works, including statements of purported themes. As Sigmund Freud once said, sometimes a cigar is just a cigar. And sometimes a good story is just a good story.

Questions about Themes

Some of the best questions about themes are indirect ones.

Draw a Picture of an Important Moment

Ask students to draw a picture of the most important moment in the story and to be ready to explain why they consider it the most important one. Or, before they interpret the picture themselves, ask other students to interpret the picture and explain why it is important to the story.

Find the Most Important Paragraph

After the students have read a chapter, several chapters, or the entire book, ask them to look back through what they have read and identify the most important scene, paragraph, sentence or even word. Have them explain why it is important and how it relates to what the book is about.

Role Play the Author

Have the students read several chapters or the entire book. Then ask a student volunteer to play the author of the book and other students to interview the author. Write the following questions on slips of paper and give them to different students.

- "Why did you write this book?"
- "What was an important idea that you were trying to get across?"
- "What were you trying to tell us by writing this book?"
- "What do you think is most important about this book?"
- "What would you want us to do, now that we've read your book?"

Students can take turns being the author. To introduce the activity, it is a good idea for the teacher to take the role of the author and demonstrate to the students how they might answer a couple of questions.

▪ ADOPTING A POINT OF VIEW

The point of view is the perspective from which the events in a story are narrated. The choices of point of view are almost always either first person (in which one of the characters in the work narrates the story, using the first-person pronoun "I") or third person (in which a narrator outside the story relates events that happened to those in it, using the third-person pronouns "she," "he," and "they"). When the author's knowledge of events shifts freely among different characters' points of view and the author describes events no one character could have known, he or she is writing from the point of view known as third-person omniscient ("all-knowing"). Occasionally books are written in second person. Judy Allen's Backyard Books series, which includes titles such as *Are You a Spider?* (2003), engage their readers by addressing them directly (the pronoun "you" signals second-person narration).

First-person Narration

Shiloh, Moon over Manifest, and *Because of Winn Dixie* are all narrated from the point of view of the first person. So is *Wonder,* though, interestingly, different chapters are narrated from the points of view of different characters, though always in first person. Narration in first person lends immediacy to the action and lets readers know what the character is feeling. But it also limits readers to that character's perspective. There may be things going on that the character who is speaking doesn't fully appreciate, and when the reader understands things that the narrating character doesn't, a sense of irony is introduced: that is, the character describes things one way, and the reader knows they are another. Here is an example from *Shiloh* where Marty describes what he sees from the hill above his house:

> One morning I saw three kinds of animals, not counting cats, dogs, frogs, cows, and horses. Saw a groundhog. Saw a doe with two fawns, and saw a

grey fox with a reddish head. Bet his daddy was a grey fox and his ma was a red one. (Naylor, 1991, 13)

He'd lose that bet, and many readers would know that red and grey foxes do not interbreed.

Kathryn Erskine's narration of *Mockingbird* from Caitlin's perspective has a powerful effect on the reader. Caitlin has Asperger's syndrome, and Erskine's first-person portrayal of Caitlin's most commonplace social interactions shows readers how challenging they are for Caitlin to negotiate.

Third-person Narration

Sometimes authors describe the action as if it were happening to someone else. This is third-person narration. Pam Muñoz Ryan narrates *Esperanza Rising* in third person. Though she did not narrate the story from Esperanza's voice, she did stick strictly to Esperanza's point of view: Ryan never tells us anything that Esperanza herself did not know.

Esperanza Rising
(Scholastc)

Third-person Omniscient Narration

Sometimes authors tell stories through the voice of a narrator who knows more than any one character could. Louis Sachar narrated *Holes* in the third-person omniscient voice, enabling him to tell different stories from different time periods that only later come together as a whole.

Writing in third person gives the author a broad range of choices regarding what to show the reader, but skilled writers usually narrate events in a scene through the eyes of one character at a time. For example, in the first Harry Potter book, *Harry Potter and the Sorcerer's Stone* (1998), J. K. Rowling shows the opening scene from the point of view of Mr. Dursley, who sees Dumbledore and his colleagues lurking outside his home but is only mildly puzzled by them, because it is not his nature to be curious or observant. When the scene shifts to the Dursleys' kitchen, Mr. and Mrs. Dursley and their son, Dudley, are described from Harry Potter's point of view, and readers see through his eyes how repulsive the Dursleys are.

Are there reasons behind the author's choices of point of view? Usually there are. As we said earlier, narrating in first person can seem more intimate and can draw the reader into identifying with the character. But note that Jerry Spinelli made just the opposite choice in writing *Maniac Magee* (1990). Spinelli chose third-person omniscient, presumably because he wanted to portray Maniac, the homeless boy who brings together a segregated community, as a legendary character, someone appearing larger than life and beyond most people's direct experiences. It would have ruined the effect to write the book in the first person.

Taking the Role of the Implied Reader

Rudine Sims Bishop (1990) taught us that books about young people from specific cultures can serve as "windows" and "mirrors": windows into that culture for the readers who do not share it (and want to know about it) and reflections of themselves for those readers who do (and want to recognize themselves). When readers are drawn into a story to identify with characters who are unlike themselves, the windows and mirrors effect can be especially powerful.

For example, consider an early scene in Mildred Taylor's *Roll of Thunder, Hear My Cry* (1976). In a segregated rural community in Mississippi in the 1930s, black children begin school weeks later than white children. Black children walk to school; white children ride a public school bus. The Logan children, who are black, are walking to school along a muddy road when the white children's school bus drives into deep puddle, deliberately splashing them with thick red mud. The white children laugh and jeer as the bus speeds away.

By the time this bus scene is reached, readers have already identified with Cassie Logan, because Taylor anchors the narration from her perspective. Cassie Logan is black. It is likely that readers of any background will feel angry and vicariously victimized. For white readers, the experience is especially unsettling: they feel anger that is directed at people like themselves, and they identify with those who have suffered injustice, who are unlike themselves.

Another example is presented by Julia Alvarez's *Return to Sender* (2010). Readers come to identify and sympathize with Mexican American fifth grader Mari Cruz, whose family is working on a farm in Vermont. We share her indignity when two mindless bullies in her class tell her she has no right to be in the United States. Readers vicariously hunker down with Mari and her family in fear of the *Migra*, the immigration law enforcers sent to catch and deport people who are in the United States without legal papers.

The "implied reader" (Iser, 1978) is a term used to describe the stance that the author of a work hopes the reader will take toward characters and events in a book. Authors present details in books in such a way that the reader may conclude that some characters are sympathetic and laudable, some are not; some events deserve approval, and some don't. Readers may be led to identify with a certain character or characters, and then vicariously experience (and tacitly approve of) what that character experiences and does. At the same time, readers may be coaxed to feel animosity toward other characters and afford them less sympathy or even disapproval.

With multicultural books, when readers read about a culture of which they are not members, the device of the implied reader can help them to take the perspective of people from the other group (or gender) and feel empathy with them. But the implied reader can also be at work in a traditional fairy tale that makes us uneasy, such as "Sleeping Beauty," with its passive heroine with no discernible talents or personality who is nonetheless sought by the Prince, or "Jack and the Beanstalk," with its larcenous and homicidal young hero whom we are expected to cheer. The implied reader may work in more negative ways, of course, such as when we hear a somewhat racist or sexist joke and are expected to laugh with others: do we laugh or do we stand up and chastise the teller? History is full of terrible examples of what happens when people "just went along."

One way to explore the effects of the implied reader with students is to read alternative versions of the same story. A fine resource here is Jon Scieszka's *The True Story of the Three Little Pigs* (1996). Students can make up their own alternative versions of familiar stories. Be sure to ask them to explain what led readers to have different attitudes toward the characters and their actions in the alternative version.

Another way to explore the effects of the implied reader is simply to ask students, "How do you feel right now about what happened or about this character? What did the author write to make you feel that way?" You might also ask, "What character do you think the author wants you to identify with/agree with/cheer on? Why? What did the author say or how did the author portray events to make you feel that way?"

■ READING FOR THE PLOT

Learning plots comes naturally to children who hear many stories from an early age. That is, they intuitively understand the way that stories are organized in their culture. That was an interesting finding in cognitive psychology during the 1970s (Stein and Glenn, 1979; Mandler and Johnson, 1977). But not all children are as sensitive as they might be to the structures of plots, or story structure, as it has come to be called. Also, stories can be told in different ways in different cultures, something that is important to remember given the increasing diversity of student populations in today's schools.

In this section we share several strategies for calling children's attention to plot structure. The thinking behind all of them is that teachers are deliberately working themselves out of a job: we do these activities only to the point at which children internalize the idea of story structures and no longer need us around to remind them of it.

The Directed Reading Activity: Story Elements

In this activity, the teacher divides the text to be read during the period into smaller sections and, before the reading, asks questions that the students will answer after they have read each section.

What questions? The questions should lead the students to pay attention to important elements of a story. As we suggested in chapter 2, the elements that are common to most stories are:

- setting
- characters (main character and others)
- problem

- efforts to solve the problem
- resolution (how the problem is or is not solved)
- consequence (the state of affairs at the end of the story that resulted from the actions)

Of course, there are questions to ask within each question, but let's begin with the questions about the main elements. Here are the steps that you might use if the story is short enough to read in one class session.

Step 1: The teacher examines the text and decides on its main elements and where each one is revealed. If it is a story, as we just noted, the teacher looks for:

- the setting and the characters: the section that tells where the story takes place and who the main characters are;
- the problem and the goal: the section that tells what the problem is, what the main character wants or needs, or whatever action starts the story moving along;
- the attempts to solve the problem: the part that tells about what the character or characters do to meet their needs and who or what they must strive against;
- the resolution: the part where it is revealed what the solution to the problem is; and
- the consequence: the section that describes the situation at the end of the story.

Step 2: The teacher plans questions to ask the students before they read each section. The questions should guide the students' attention to the main points in each section as they read. A question before the first section could be, "Read this page to yourselves and find out where the story takes place and who the character or characters are—the people the story will be about. I will ask you what you found out after everyone has finished reading."

Step 3: The teacher explains the procedure to the students. Before they read each section, they should listen to the question. Then they should read the assigned part of the text—the teacher being careful to tell them where to stop reading—to find the answer to the question.

Step 4: The students read the assigned section of the text.

Step 5: After waiting for students to read the assigned section, the teacher reminds them of the question and invites them to answer it. Note that for more interaction, the teacher may ask the students to share their responses with partners before sharing them with the whole class.

This directed reading activity can be done with a whole class of students, but if some children in the class read more slowly than others—and when isn't that the case?—it may be best to introduce this activity by reading the sections of the story aloud. That way everyone has an equal chance to participate and no one feels rushed. Once the students have practiced the activity by reading the story aloud, the students can read it on their own. Then they will have a better idea about how it is supposed to work—and they will understand that it's more enjoyable if they wait for each other to read and not read ahead.

The Directed Reading-thinking Activity: Predictions

The directed reading-thinking activity with predictions, or DRTA/P, is used to meet the following goals:

- to teach students to follow a narrative text, especially one with a suspenseful plot;
- to encourage students to read carefully;
- to build reading comprehension; and
- to have students carefully read a text that they will discuss in depth later.

In this activity, students read a story and make predictions about what will come next. They are asked to confirm their predictions from time to time with information from the text and to make new predictions. DRTA/P requires that all students have access to a text—either books in front of them or legible text on a chalkboard.

This activity may be done with groups ranging from about six to thirty or more students. More than thirty students will limit everyone's participation, but it can still be effective.

Texts for DRTA/P work best when they are stories with predictable plots: where there is a problem and a sequence of actions moving toward a conclusion. The time needed for the activity depends on the length of the story and how closely the teacher decides to have students consider it. It should not be longer than about thirty minutes. DRTA/P follows these steps:

Step 1: The teacher chooses a predicable story for sharing with the class.

Step 2: The teacher chooses stopping points—places just before something is about to happen or significant new information about the characters or plot is about to be revealed. There should be around five of these—more will break up the flow of the story and reduce momentum (and interest).

Step 3: The teacher may begin by having students read just the title, explaining the genre of the story (folktale, realistic fiction, fable, myth, etc.) and asking students what things they think might happen in it. The teacher presses the students to make the most specific predictions they can and quickly records them on the board for reference. After the predictions have been made, the teacher challenges students to decide which predictions they think will most likely happen in the story (even if someone else made them) and then to read carefully to see what will happen.

Step 4: The students read the first section of the story, and the teacher asks which predictions are coming true and what makes students think so. Then students are asked to make more predictions and read the next section. The prediction and confirmation cycle continues until the story is finished.

Step 5: After the story is finished, students are asked to reflect on their predictions. Which predictions turned out to be accurate? How were they able to make them?

How did their awareness of the genre, plot, or theme of the story help them predict what would come next? What advice would they give other students for making accurate predictions?

Terms in Advance: Another Way to Encourage Prediction

Terms in advance is an enjoyable strategy that can entice students to make predictions about a story when they otherwise might be inclined to say "I don't know." This is how it works:

Step 1: Prepare in advance a list of five or six key terms or phrases from the text that will be read and discussed. These should be the most important words that, taken together, provide a "skeleton" of the work. You can also choose unfamiliar words, as long as they are important in the work and you explain their meaning.

Step 2: Display the words on a whiteboard or smartboard. Take time to discuss each term and make sure everyone understands what they mean.

Step 3: Explain to the students that each term either appears in or explains something that is going to happen or be important in the passage they are going to read and discuss.

Step 4: Have students hypothesize about ways in which the terms might be related in the story. Individuals or pairs of students can also write down their predictions before sharing them with the class. Accept all hypotheses or predictions encouragingly.

Step 5: Tell the students to make up their own story, making sure to incorporate those terms into the story. Then challenge them to compare their own story with the one they are going to read as they read or listen to the part you want them to consider. Then have them listen to or read the assigned pages.

Step 6: After they have listened to or read the story, ask the students to compare the story they heard or read to their initial predictions.

Close Reading

The Common Core state standards ushered in the expectation that even in the primary grades, children should be able to ferret out fine details of a literary work. Some of those details have been discussed earlier in this chapter, but a few others, such as the effect of word choices in the narration, are new.

To make these careful analyses, children need to read short pieces of a work several times, very closely. Close reading is an intense examination of a short piece of text with the aim of unearthing the meaning of the text and all the parts that work together to convey that meaning. Until recently, close reading was reserved for high school and college classes. But if it is conducted as a lively intellectual exercise, close reading can be enjoyable.

Five Close Readings

Below we sketch how you might conduct five readings of one passage. Of course, depending on your purpose, it may be best skip or combine some of these readings or even substitute some.

First reading: Get the gist. Ask students to retell the passage in their own words, answering the questions who, what, where, when, and why.

Second reading: Get the details. This time ask students to look more deeply into the passage. It can help to guide the students' inquiry by reminding them of the means that authors use to develop characters, settings, and plots, as shown earlier in this chapter.

Third reading: Get the words. What does the word choice say about the narrator's social class? What does it say about the author's tone? What does the word choice say about the speaker's feelings, attitudes, and mood or about the author's intentions? Where are the ellipses—things that are not said but implied?

Fourth reading: See where it fits. Judging from this passage, what kind of plot is the work shaping up to be? How does the passage function in the plot? Remember the plot elements we discussed earlier—introduction of the characters; the elements of the setting; the character's problem, goal, and attempts to reach the goal; outcomes of each attempt; and the resolution of the action and consequence. Which of these might explain what the passage is doing in the work? What might have come before this passage? What is likely to come after it?

Fifth reading: Get the style. Is the text meant to be humorous, exciting, mysterious, intimately revealing, magical, matter-of-fact, or something else? How do we know? What effect does the author seem to be striving for? How does she or he achieve the effect? If the author was advising us about how to write a passage like this one, what would he or she say? What is the perspective of the narration?

In Figure 4.9 we will apply the five readings to the opening paragraphs of Phyllis Reynolds Naylor's *Shiloh*. First, here is the passage:

The day Shiloh come, we're having us a big Sunday dinner. Dara Lynn's dipping bread in her cold tea, the way she likes, and Becky pushes her beans up over the edge of her plate in her rush to get 'em down. . . . It isn't that I don't like fried rabbit. Like it fine. I just don't want to bite down on buckshot, is all, and I'm checking each piece.

"I looked that rabbit over good, Marty, and you won't find a piece of buckshot in that thigh," Dad says, buttering his bread. "I shot him in the neck." "Did it die right off?" I ask, knowing I can't eat at all unless it had. "Soon enough."

"You shoot its head clean off?" Dara Lynn asks. She's like that.

Dad chews real slow before he answers. "Not quite," he says, and goes on eating.

Which is when I leave the table. (Naylor, 1991, 11–12)

■ ENCOURAGING RESPONSES TO LITERATURE

One of the greatest values that literature offers all of us, students included, is stimulating material to talk about. Literature has a way of capturing, framing, and condensing events that might happen in real life and giving them purpose and meaning. Literature

Figure 4.9 Closely Reading a Passage from *Shiloh*

Get the Gist	Marty and his father, mother, and sisters are eating fried rabbit for Sunday dinner. Marty finds out that when his father shot the rabbit, the rabbit's head came most of the way off. Marty is repulsed by the news and leaves the table.
Get the Details	The first sentence says someone or something named "Shiloh" came, but unless the cover of the book gave it away, the reader doesn't know who that is yet. The author has opened with a mystery. The geographical setting hasn't been revealed yet, either. Neither has the larger social setting. The social setting, close up, is Marty's family. Marty is shown to be more sensitive than the others, because he leaves the table when killing the rabbit on his plate comes up. The fact that the family's Sunday dinner consists of bread, beans, and a hunted rabbit suggests the family has limited means. That Marty knows to be careful to avoid biting down on buckshot suggests the family eats wild game often. Dara Lynn's table manners—dipping bread in her cold tea—are a little crude for Sunday dinner, too; it's striking that the mother doesn't correct her. The fact that the father continues eating while he describes blowing a rabbit's head mostly off displays his utter lack of squeamishness. And Dara Lynn's question about the rabbit's head shows her morbid curiosity and lack of sensitivity. A reader with hunting experience might question whether the father would really shoot a rabbit with buckshot (that might utterly destroy the rabbit).
Get the Words	The book opens with the phrase "The day Shiloh come." The name "Shiloh" has Southern associations—Shiloh, Tennessee, was the site of one of the bloodiest battles of the Civil War. The name also carries the connotations of "shy" and "low,"—which, we soon learn, accurately describes the dog's initial behavior. The wording and even the author's punctuation of the opening phrase introduce Marty as a boy from a modest social class, Southern and probably white. The comma calls for a pause after the opening phrase, and it would be voiced with a rising inflection, like a question—a feature of Southern speech. Marty's speech is slightly ungrammatical—saying "come" for "came," and "real slow" instead of "really slowly." Those grammatical aberrations mark Marty as a member of an undereducated family. Marty's sentence, "Which is when I leave the table" follows an ellipsis (a gap) where the reader infers that Marty couldn't take any more; he was repulsed by the conversation, the way the rabbit died, or both.
See where it fits	So far we seem to have a work of realistic fiction on our hands. The setting could be contemporary. This passage introduces Marty as the narrator and also presumably the main character in the social setting of his rural family. The geographic setting is not disclosed yet (we soon learn it is in the mountains of West Virginia). What does this passage suggest will happen in the rest of the story? A main problem hasn't been introduced yet, but it's likely that Marty's sensitivity and concern for animals—and also his love for and yet differences from other members of his family—promise to figure in the plot.
Get the Style	The narrative so far is entirely in the first person from Marty, with his casual ungrammatical speech and all. It appears that Marty will be the hero or protagonist of this story. He is introduced through his thoughts and actions and is not otherwise described. The style of the writing promises to take us deep inside Marty's thoughts. This passage is already almost embarrassingly revealing—in the very opening lines of the book, Marty is fully displaying his family in an unflattering light and showing that he sometimes can't cope with their ways. The book promises not only to tell a story, but to intimately reveal the boy's feelings and reactions to events.

may teach lessons, but it is also valuable even when it does *not* always lead to an obvious conclusion or teach one obvious truth. In those cases, we can ask students to interpret the text and defend their reasoning and also to listen to other interpretations and learn to agree or disagree politely.

In this section we share several teaching strategies that can be used to promote lively discussions and give students practice interpreting what they read.

Shared Inquiry Discussion

The Great Books Foundation developed the shared inquiry method to accompany its literature discussion program, which has been conducted in thousands of schools and libraries for more than half a century. Shared inquiry is a procedure by which someone leads a deep discussion into a story. It is best done with a group of eight to ten people—few enough for everyone to participate but large enough for a good mix of ideas. It goes like this:

Before the discussion, choose a story or a section of a story worth discussing. Such a story should lend itself to more than one interpretation (not all stories do this well) and raise interesting issues. Folktales often meet these criteria very well.

Prepare four or five discussion questions. These should be what the Great Books Foundation calls "interpretive questions," and which have three criteria:

- They are real questions; the sort of question one might ask friends following a provocative film.
- They have more than one defensible answer. (This criterion guarantees a debate. If it is not met, the discussion won't be a discussion but a read-my-mind exercise where the teacher already knows the "right" answer.)
- They must lead the discussion into the text. (A question such as "Why was the Giant's wife kinder to Jack than his own mother was?" leads the children to talk about what is in the text first, even though they might then comment on what they know from experience. A question such as "Have you ever done anything as brave as Jack?" leads the discussion away from the text and out into twenty-five different directions.)

Have the students read the story. They should all have a good grasp of the story because the emphasis of this activity is on interpreting it rather than figuring out what happened in it. If the story is to be read as a class, it can help to stop and ask for predictions and comments along the way and also to "think out loud" yourself—you want students to be engaged in the story and to follow it closely.

After everyone has read the story and presumably understood it, put a question to the class for discussion. The the question can be written on the board, signaling that the students will stay with it for a while. But in a less formal setting, just say, "I wonder about _____," and leave time for the question to sink in. (The point is, we're not in a hurry. Thinking takes time.) Ask students to think about the question. Ask older students to jot down their answers. Allow some time for this.

As you invite students to share their ideas, invite reluctant speakers to read what they wrote, as well. Encourage debate among students, pointing out differences in what they say and asking them to expand on the differences. Remind students to support their ideas by drawing on the story or from their own experiences. Give them time to restate ideas more clearly, but avoid correcting anyone or suggesting that any student's answer is right or wrong. If you want to offer your own answer to the question, make sure the conversation already has momentum so that you don't come across as the "expert."

Keep a seating chart with the students' names and brief notes about what each one says. When the discussion of a question seems to have run its course, read from your notes, summarize what students have said so far, and ask whether anyone has anything to add.

Once the discussion gets going, follow the students' lead and continue to discuss the issues they raise.

Even when they don't use the whole approach, many teachers use aspects of the shared inquiry procedure in conducting book discussions. For example, they might ask students to write down ideas to bring to a discussion, they might take notes during the discussion, or they take care to draw out the students' ideas and not dominate the discussion themselves.

Corners

Corners is a group discussion activity that is used after students have heard a story to invite them to choose and defend different positions on an issue raised in that story. Corners requires a story that raises an issue that has three or four defensible responses. (If the story doesn't have at least two plausible responses, choose another story or another discussion strategy.)

After choosing the question and teasing out three or four likely responses, explain to the students that they are going to think about a question, choose a position, and support it.

Once the issue has been raised, have the students rank the answers from the most to least preferred. For that, it is necessary to state the responses and assign a number to each one.

Next, have all of the students who preferred the first response go to one corner, all those in favor of the second go to another corner, and so on. (Note: one corner can be for those who are undecided.)

Next, have the students in each corner share their views with each other. What are their reasons for taking the position they have chosen?

Now call for a debate by inviting one corner to state succinctly its position and the main reasons the group has for supporting their view. Ask each group, in turn, to do the same.

Once the formal debate has been presented by the spokesperson for each group, all other students in each group should be encouraged to participate in the conversation. If the groups need prodding to begin this discussion portion, then ask some probing questions such as: "Why should those of you in group A not accept the opinion of group B? Where do you disagree with what group B has to say?" or "What about the undecided group? What have you heard that moves you toward a clearer opinion?" or "Why are those of you in group B not convinced by what group A has said?"

Explain now that some students may have changed their minds by what they have heard. If that is the case, they should feel free to change groups at any time. To do so, they simply leave the group they are in and join the group they now support. In fact, encourage students to move as their opinion shifts. Also encourage the remaining members of the groups to try to persuade those who are leaving with arguments for staying with their group. This puts the burden on the group members within each group to be persuasive enough to keep their group members or draw more supporters. It is also wise for students to take some notes regarding their thinking as they listen and discuss. This will help them later when they have to write down their position on the issue and defend it.

Finally, once the discussion has ended and everyone has moved to their final group, ask each group to summarize its position and reasons that support it.

Discussion Web

The discussion web is a cooperative learning activity that involves all students in deep discussions of readings. The discussion web proceeds with the following steps:

The teacher prepares a thoughtful binary question—a question that can be answered "yes" or "no" with support. For example, in discussing "Jack and the Beanstalk," a binary discussion question might be "Was Jack right to steal from the Giant?"

Ask pairs of students to prepare a discussion web chart that looks like the one shown in Figure 4.10. The pairs of students take four or five minutes to come up with three reasons each that support both sides of the argument.

Next, each pair joins another pair of students. They review the answers they had on both sides of the issue and add to each other's lists. Then they argue the issue through until they reach a conclusion; that is, a position they agree on, with a list of reasons that support it.

At the conclusion of the lesson, call on several groups of four students to give brief reports of their position and the reasons that support it. Perhaps invite groups to debate each other if they took different sides of the argument.

Academic Controversy

Academic controversy is another cooperative learning activity from Spencer Kagan (1990) that will come naturally to those who enjoy the discussion web. The method helps students practice the art of thinking critically—in this case, taking a position and producing reasons to support arguments. It also can help them to practice debating politely, using arguments and reasons, especially if you remind them to do so.

To begin, assign students to groups of four and give them a question to discuss. As with the discussion web, it needs to be a binary question: it should have a "yes" or "no," "this" or "that" answer so that there are one of two sides that students can take.

Figure 4.10   A Discussion Web

Question: Was Jack right to steal from the Giant?	
Yes! Here's why:	No! Here's why not:
Conclusion:	

Students should begin by discussing the question in their groups of four in order to reach a common understanding of what the question means and why it matters. This shouldn't take more than three minutes.

Then have students count off within their group, 1, 2, 3, and 4 (if there are five students in any group, then there will be two students with the number 1). Tell students with numbers 1 and 2 that they should prepare to argue for one point of view; students with numbers 3 and 4 should prepare to argue the other.

Now direct both pairs of students within each group to go off by themselves, taking paper and pens with them, and spend five minutes listing reasons to support their position, whichever one it is.

Here is an interesting step: after four or five minutes, call time. Now tell all the students preparing to argue the "no" side of the issue to remain seated while the "yes" students stand. Tell the "yes" students to make eye contact with another "yes" student, but not his or her original partner. Then have the "yes" students sit down and invite the "no" students to stand and similarly find a new partner. Give the signal for the students to meet for three minutes with their new partners and share with each other the reasons they found for holding their "yes" or "no" positions. After three minutes, give the signal for the students to return to their original partners and compile all the reasons they now have that support their positions.

They should think carefully about all of the reasons listed and identify the best reasons that support their position. They should prepare to debate the other pair within their group of four. In order to debate, they should come up with a sentence stating their position and two or three good reasons for their position.

When they are ready to debate (after about four more minutes), tell the pairs of students to join the other pairs in their group and begin the debate. One side states its position with the reasons for it, and the other does the same. Then they debate each other's reasons and conclusions. That is, students from one side may say why they believe their reasons are more compelling than those of students on the other side and thus should lead them to conclude whatever their position is.

Here comes another interesting twist. Let the debate continue for six or seven minutes. Then tell students in each group that they are now free to drop their assigned positions and argue for whatever position they personally believe. (Usually a collective groan of relief goes up at this point.) Invite groups to come up with a consensus position: that is, a position with which everyone agrees and reasons to support that position.

After four or five more minutes, call on a member of each group to give a statement of the group's conclusions from their debate.

Value Line

The value line is best suited for discussing questions with yes or no answers, but it might invite a range of conviction along a continuum. Here are the steps to the value line:

Pose a question to students. For example, after telling "Jack and the Beanstalk," the teacher might ask, "Do you think we should consider Jack a hero? Why or why not?"

Give students three minutes to consider the question alone and write down their answers.

Now the teacher stands on one side of the room and announces that she represents one pole, or extreme position, on the argument. She might say, "Yes, I believe Jack was an outstanding hero, and someone we should emulate. We would be great people if we were like Jack." Invite a student to stand at the other end of the room to represent the other pole of the argument. The student might say, "No, I don't think Jack is a hero. Not at all. We should never try to be like Jack. We would be terrible people if we did."

Now invite students to line up between the two of you in places along the imaginary value line between the two poles of the argument. Each stands at a point in the line that reflects his or her position on the question.

Next, ask students to compare their views with those of students immediately around them to make sure they are all standing in the right spots. After hearing others' answers, some students might elect to move one way or another along the value line. Students may continue to discuss their responses with those on either side of them until they feel they are standing with a group that shares their views.

Identify three or four clusters of students who seem to represent different positions on the question. Invite them to come up with a statement of their position. After a minute, invite a spokesperson from each cluster of three or four students to share their position and their reason for it with the whole group. Encourage debate among the groups, and invite students to move from one group to another if they feel persuaded.

This exercise can be followed with a writing opportunity in which students write down what they think about the issue and why.

"Save the Last Word for Me"

"Save the Last Word for Me" (Short, Harste, and Burke, 1996) provides a framework for a small-group or whole-class discussion of a text. The procedure is especially good for encouraging children to take the lead in discussing their reading. The steps of the strategy are as follows:

After being assigned a reading to do independently, students are given note cards and asked to find three or four quotations that they consider particularly interesting or worthy of comment. Students write the quotations they have found on the note cards.

On the other side of the card, students write comments about their chosen quotations. That is, they say what the quotations made them think about, what is surprising about the quotations, and why they chose them.

Students bring their quotation cards to discussion groups. The teacher calls on someone to read a card aloud. After reading the quotation on his or her card, the student invites other students to comment on that quotation. (The teacher might need to help keep comments focused on the subject of the quotation.) Also, the teacher may choose to comment on the quotation. Once others have had their say about the quotation, the student who chose it reads his or her comments aloud. Then there is no further discussion. The student who chose it gets the last word.

That student can now call on another student to share his or her quotation and begin the process all over again. Not all students will be able to share their quotations if the whole class takes part in the activity, so the teacher will need to keep track of who shared quotes and make sure other students get chances to share their quotes the next time.

■ DRAMATIZING A STORY

Dramatizing a story allows students to take a closer look at a story by getting a real feel for the action. The procedure for dramatizing a story is adapted from the works of Spolin (1986) and Heathcote (Wagner, 1999).

Immerse Students in Story

Before the dramatic activity begins, it is important to ensure that students get the story on a literal level—that they know what happened. This might mean reading the story to them or asking them to reread the part they will be dramatizing.

Choose Critical Moments

It can be particularly useful to dramatize just a few choice scenes from a story, especially the turning points when the most is at stake. In "Jack and the Beanstalk," such a scene might be when Jack first approaches the Giant's castle, knocks on the door, and is greeted by the Giant's wife.

Segment the Situation

Now assign students to take each of these roles. Invite other students to join them as they think about the situation from each character's point of view. What must be on Jack's mind when he approaches the huge door? What do the door and the walls of the castle look like? How large are they in proportion to Jack? What does Jack hear around the place? What does he smell? How does the place make him feel? What makes him pound his fist on the door? What is at stake for him? What are his choices? What will he do if he *doesn't* knock on the door? Why does he decide to do it?

Do the same for the Giant's wife. How does the knocking sound to her—thunderous or puny? What does she think when she sees the small but plucky boy at her door? What thoughts go through her mind, knowing what she knows about her husband? What are her feelings as she looks down at Jack? Ask the actors to focus their minds on a few of these considerations as they prepare to act out the scene.

Dramatize the Scene

Use minimal props and minimal costumes to help students think their way into their roles. Ask the other students to watch carefully and see what the actors make them think of.

Side Coach

As the director, the teacher should not be passive, but take opportunities to make suggestions from the sidelines that will help students act more expressively. She might ask, "Jack, do you feel scared now or brave? How can you show us what you're feeling?"

Invite Reflection

Ask the other students what they saw. What did they think was on the characters' minds? It is worthwhile to invite several groups of students to dramatize the same scene and have the class discuss the aspects of the situation that each performance brings to light.

▪ WRITING IN RESPONSE TO FICTIONAL WORK

There are several reasons to have students write in response to their reading. The first reason is to keep track of the quantity and variety of students' reading. Putting on our pedagogical hats for a moment, we can point out that simply reading a lot is hugely important. Without intervention from the teacher, the least avid readers in the primary grades will need two lifetimes to read as many words as their more avid classmates will read in one year. That's not an exaggeration. Look up Anderson, Wilson, and Fielding's study (1988) of the differences in the amounts of independent reading by fifth graders in the references at the end of this chapter.

Reading thousands upon thousands of words in a year benefits children tremendously. Reading builds their vocabulary, and that in turn literally makes them smarter in the sense that it gives them greater capacity to store old knowledge and also to gain new knowledge (as psychologists have been telling us for years, you can perceive and understand only what you can name [Brown, 1958]). It also makes them more fluent readers, because well-oiled machinery, including reading skill, works a lot better with practice. It boosts their comprehension, as well, because vocabulary plus fluency adds up to just that.

Related to the goal of boosting the quantity of children's reading, writing (a log, for example) in response to reading is a way of keeping parents in the loop about their children's reading.

One caveat: simply requiring a lot of reading apparently has less effect on students' growth as readers than requiring some kind of response to what they read, so declared the National Reading Panel in 2000. So it makes sense to ask students to write something meaningful in response to the books they read in addition to the number of pages read.

The second reason for having students write in response to their reading is to evoke personal responses to their reading. Reader response theorists such as Louise Rosenblatt (1978) and David Bleich (1982) argue that the meaning of a work, especially a work of fiction or poetry, is constructed through a transaction between each reader's personal store of meanings and the suggestions provided by the text. That view implies that the meaning each reader takes away from a text is somewhat different for each reader and that teachers should encourage students to constantly ask what a text means to them as they construct the meaning.

There is a social dimension of reader response criticism, too. To prevent students from spinning off into loopy relativism with everyone firmly believing her or his own truth, teachers also have the task of asking students to explain their interpretations and to compare them with those of others in an attempt to construct meaning together. This social dimension of reader response criticism extends beyond literature. If a work of literature evokes different responses and is interpreted differently by different readers, then how about the daily news? Or the state of the nation's economy? Or what constitutes racial fairness and social justice? Or how to define family values or sexual mores? In fact, as we are reminded daily, people disagree widely and sometimes even violently on these issues—often with no middle ground to support a civil debate. A classroom run to some extent on reader response principles can be a relatively safe laboratory, what David Bleich (1975) called an "interpretive community" where students can learn to venture and support their own interpretation, listen politely to each other's interpretations, and work toward consensus.

If one's goal is to encourage personal responses to writing, then ask students to write down what they notice in a text, what it made them think of, and how it made them feel. Be sure to welcome diverse answers and take time to have students share their written responses with each other, both so the students will be motivated to justify their responses to their classmates and so their classmates will understand that people can interpret the same data differently according to their backgrounds and dispositions.

A third reason to have students write in response to reading is to have them notice and work with the features of literary works that we emphasize in this chapter. If you want to make sure that students get main ideas, make inferences, follow plots, visualize details, understand the dimensions and effects of settings, make sense of characterizations, and infer themes, then ask more focused questions in the writing assignments.

English Language Learners' Responses to Literature

Reader response criticism as a conception of understanding literature stresses the role of a reader's background knowledge in constructing the meaning of the work. It is important, though, to be sensitive to students' backgrounds. Learners who come to our schools from other parts of the world and other cultures may lack the background knowledge that is needed to make sense of a particular story. They may not know what a mall is, or a lawn mower, or a baby sitter, or a retirement home, or shopping as a pastime, or even typical adolescent rebellion. Moreover, they may have different associations for the same referents. For example, students who grew up in the United States usually think of a wedding as a happy occasion, but in some parts of India, a wedding is a source of considerable stress, a matter of bargaining over the relative prestige of the two families, an occasion where a bride may be bartered away by her parents into a miserable subservient role in a family of strangers. In the United States, going out to a restaurant is typically considered a pleasure, but it is not always so in some parts of Morocco, where going out to eat brings scorn on a family since it is assumed that the wife is too lazy to cook. Be careful to look for places in texts where culture-based background knowledge may be essential to readers' understanding, and explain that knowledge as needed.

Dual-entry Diaries

A dual-entry diary (Berthoff, 1981) is an open-ended way of having students decide which are the most moving or puzzling passages in a text and commenting on them. Students above third grade can be asked to choose a specific number of passages to cite out of a certain number of pages. After they have read, they bring their diaries to class and share them with the class. The "Save the Last Word for Me" strategy (see page 148) works well as a format for sharing. An example of a dual-entry diary is found in Figure 4.11.

Figure 4.11   Dual-entry Diary

Quotations from the Book	Student Comments (what each quote made you think of, why you think it's important, what it makes you wonder about)
"He was holding up a rope strung with four severed hands, like beads on a necklace" (122).	Oh no! This was the worst thing I ever read! I can't believe Parvana has to live among creeps like this. What makes people so awful? And how can Parvana be so brave as to go about among them?

Complete five entries in a dual-entry diary on *The Breadwinner* (Ellis, 1981). Below is an example of what a dual-entry diary looks like.

Creative Writing Prompts

Imitation is the sincerest form of flattery. It's also a good way to learn the writer's craft. Here follow a series of writing prompts to exercise skills that professional writers regularly draw upon.

Writing to Dramatic Roles

Have students brainstorm a historical and geographical setting. It may be an area that they are studying in social studies or read about in a book the class is reading. Have them brainstorm a set of at least eight characters who might live in such a setting, specifying their ages, gender, who they hang out with, and what they do. Write the name of each character on one side of a index card. Then have the students brainstorm goals that people who live in that setting might have for themselves or others. Goals could be material things: wealth, clothes, food, a pet. They could be circumstances: freedom, recognition, privacy, pride, forgiveness, a spirit of community. They could be relational, too: winning a competition, friendship, or love from someone else. Write each of these on an index card, too.

Have four students come forward. Ask one to draw a card from the character cards. This will be the hero. Have another student draw one card from the goals. This will be the goal that the hero strives for. Discuss for a minute why the hero might want such a goal and for whom he or she might want it. Now remind the students that a good story needs tension, and tension requires a rival. Ask the next student to draw a character card for the rival. Discuss how the rival would work against the hero and why. Then remind the students that heroes in stories usually have helpers. And have the last student draw a character card for the helper. How might this character help the hero and why?

Finally, invite the students, individually or in pairs, to write a rough draft of a story in which that hero wants that goal, but is opposed by the rival. Fortunately, the hero has that helper.

■ EXPLORING POETRY

As we saw in chapter 2, poems serve us in many ways. With their snappy or bouncy or calming rhythms, with their crunchy, punchy, or soothing sounds, with their humor, irony, and occasional sass, they can appeal to our senses as well as our senses of humor. But poetry serves us in another way, too. Think of poetry as a car wash for our perceptions and an oil change for our language. Poetry refreshes and sharpens our capacity to notice, and it restores and reinforces our ability to name what we try to perceive, feel, and understand.

There is a distinction to be made between enjoying and benefitting from poetry and studying it. So much of what has been called "interpreting" poetry is restating a poem as an essay, which begs the question: why didn't the poet just write an essay to begin with?

So let's share poems with young people every chance we get, enjoy them, remark on them, perform them, and write them.

Sharing Poetry

We recommend reading poems to children every day, if possible, and if daily isn't possible, try Sylvia Vardell and Janet Wong's "Poetry Friday" idea—an event at the end of each week when the teacher shares a delightful poem (2015). Having a scheduled time set aside is a way to make sure children regularly get to experience poetry, a time to which they can look forward.

The poems might be related to topics that engage the students at the moment—a change in seasons, a holiday, the introduction of a new unit of study in science, history, literature, art, or music. But they don't have to be. Sometimes we bring in poems because they are fresh, funny, beautiful, or insightful, and we know the children will enjoy them. However, we offer a word of warning for those who may want to use poems topically: be careful not to force it. There is no reason to introduce a saccharine or trite poem just because it snowed last night. There are some great collections of poems arranged topically to have on hand. Many collections are listed in the box below.

For younger children, read a poem as part of circle time at the beginning of the day, after recess, or after lunch. Perhaps invite children to put their heads down or close their eyes and let the poem wash over them and sink in. Some days one might ask the children to listen to a certain outstanding feature of the poem—its use of rhythms, sounds, or fresh images, for instance. If the poem makes a striking observation, ask the students if they have ever noticed anything similar or thought about it that way.

There are collections of poems addressing a surprising range of topics—from weather patterns to geometric shapes in nature to insects to mammals to sports to features and traditions of cultures—that can be shared, along with a lesson, for a class period or longer. Some of them should be written on newsprint and put up on the wall for students to revisit. Keep refreshing them, though, at least once a week.

Performing Poetry

Reading poetry aloud is a good way to boost young people's enjoyment of it. And it's also a good way to develop reading fluency, as well as skill at interpretation. After all, to figure out how a poem should sound, students must first understand what it means and how the narrator was feeling about it.

Poems can be read aloud in voice choirs—groups of readers who rehearse and refine their performances just as singing choirs do. What are the possible variations of sound? Texts may be read

- by the whole chorus, by individuals, by pairs, or by two alternating sections;
- in loud or soft voices;
- rapidly or slowly;
- melodiously, angrily, giggling, or seriously.

Voices in Unison

When children chorally read a poem in unison, the teacher should prepare them by talking about the context in which the lines could be said. For example, a good poem to read in unison—that is, everyone reads all lines together—is "The Grand Old Duke of York." The poem has the rhythm of marching soldiers, so invite the children to imagine that they are villagers hearing the approach of a platoon of soldiers from a single vantage point along the road. While they are still far off, the soldiers sound very quiet, then louder as they approach, then very loud when they are passing right in front of the class, then quieter and quieter as they move along down the road. Have students practice reading the poem in unison, with their readings imitating the sound of marching soldiers going from very quiet, to a little louder, to very loud, to a little quieter, and then very quiet at the end.

"The Grand Old Duke of York" (Traditional)

The Grand Old Duke of York
He had ten thousand men.
He always marched them up the hill
Then he marched them down again.
And when they were up they were up.
And when they were down they were down.
And when they were only halfway up
They were neither up nor down.

Poems in Two Parts

Reading poems in two parts, or antiphonally, allows a sort of call-and-response or dialogue pattern. It is challenging for two groups of children to read different lines of the same poem while keeping the rhythm intact, and the challenge leads naturally to many repeated readings as the children work to perfect their reading. The repeated reading is desirable, of course, because the practice builds fluency.

"Come Play Catch?" by Bucksnort Trout can be read by two individual children or by two groups. The groups will read alternate lines with the indented lines serving as a sort of chorus, like Greek tragedies, or more recently, 1950s groups like Diana Ross and the Supremes or Dickey Doo and the Don'ts. The children should practice reading the poem—it's a bit of a tongue twister—until they can maintain the rhythm perfectly. Have them practice reading it with different emotions, too. They can read it once as if it were a dare, then again as if it's a secret invitation, uttered in the middle of the night, but they can shout the last verse.

"Come Play Catch?"

Hey, Cousin Kenny, can you come play catch?
    Can you catch come, come? Can you come play catch?
Whatcha say, Cousin Kenny, can you come play catch?
    Can you come catch, come play catch—huh?
Hey, Aunt Jody, can you come jump rope?
    Can you rope jump, jump? Can you come jump rope?
Whatcha say, Aunt Jody, can you come jump rope?

Can you rope jump, come jump rope—huh?
Hey, Uncle Harry, can you come hopscotch?
Can you scotch hop, hop? Can you come hop scotch?
Whatcha say, Uncle Harry, can you come hop scotch?
Can you scotch hop, come hop scotch—huh?
Hey, gorilla, will you put me down?
Will you down, put, put? Pretty please, down, down?
Whatcha say, gorilla, will you put me down?
Will you down put, put me down—huh?

Poems in Rounds

Everyone knows "Row, Row, Row Your Boat." It's a song, of course, but its form is a round. *Rounds* are poems that are sung or read with the lines divided among two or three groups who begin reading at different times so the words overlap. Reading poems in rounds is a lot of fun, and it requires students to pay close attention to each other so everyone can keep the timing just right.

The traditional Appalachian poem, "Can You Dig That Crazy Music?" can be performed as a round with up to three parts. When the students are performing the poem, have each group begin reading right after the group before it completes the first line. Have each group read the poem through two times fully, going straight without a pause from the last line on the first reading to the first line on the second reading. The second time through, the first group repeats the last line while the second group reads it, and then the first and second group repeats the last line as the third group reads it. It helps if someone claps to keep time. (It makes sense once you do it!)

"Can You Dig That Crazy Music?"

Can you dig it, can you dig it, can you dig it, can you dig it?
Can you dig that crazy music?
Can you dig it, can you dig it, can you dig it, can you dig it?
Oh, look. Here's a chicken come struttin' down the road.
Now, now. There's another on a barbed wire fence.
Maaaaaa-ma! Maaaaaa-ma!
Get that son-of-a-gun off my porch!

More evocative poems can be arranged for choral reading, too. Take, for example, this poem, "Is The Moon Tired?" by the nineteenth-century English poet Christina Rossetti (1830–1894):

Is the Moon Tired?

Is the moon tired? she looks so pale
Within her misty veil:
She scales the sky from east to west,
And takes no rest.

Before the coming of the night
The moon shows papery white;
Before the dawning of the day
She fades away.

[One voice, with a rising, questioning tone] Is the moon tired?
[A chorus] she looks so pale
Within her misty veil:
[One different voice] She scales the sky from east to west,
[A chorus of voices, sounding sleepy] And takes no rest.

[A different voice, softly] Before the coming of the night
[Two voices, a little louder] The moon shows papery white;
[Three voices, louder still] Before the dawning of the day
[Another voice pauses, then quietly stretching out the word fades]
    She fades away.

There are many variations that can be done with voice choirs: high voices and low voices; loud and soft; fast and slow; assigning lines, phrases, and individual words to different readers.

With practice, any poem can be performed to sound charming or powerful or both. Once the class has worked up a poem, take it on the road to other classes. Perform it with morning announcements over the intercom, at a school assembly, or for parents' night.

Teaching Aspects of Poetry

In chapter 2 we highlighted several aspects of poetry that make up a poet's tool kit. They include sound (rhythm, rhyme, alliteration), imagery, and comparisons (similes, metaphors, and personification). We add one more feature here: insight, the surprise of noticing and naming something that might not have been put into words.

Calling out Features of Poetry in Daily or Weekly Readings

If you are reading poems to the class once a week or more frequently, call students' attention to a poetic feature every third poem. For example, before reading "The Grand Old Duke of York" for the first time, tell the students to listen for the rhythm: doesn't it sound just like a military parade? Before reading Christina Rossetti's "Is the Moon Tired?" ask the students to listen for the ways she talks about the moon as if it were a person. To call attention to rhyme, challenge the students to identify the rhyming words in Robert Service's "The Cremation of Sam McGee."

"The Cremation of Sam McGee"

There are strange things *done* in the midnight *sun*
    By the men who moil for *gold*;

The Arctic *trails* have their secret *tales*
    That would make your blood run *cold*;
The Northern *Lights* have seen queer *sights*,
    But the queerest they ever did *see*
Was that night on the *marge* of Le*barge*
    I cremated Sam Mc*Gee*.

To call attention to rhythm, go back to the same poem and have students clap their hands on the stressed syllables.

For insights, read Robert Louis Stevenson's "Bed in Summer" and ask the students if they have ever had the same complaint.

"Bed in Summer"

In winter I get up at night
And dress by yellow candle-light.
In summer quite the other way,
I have to go to bed by day.

I have to go to bed and see
The birds still hopping on the tree,
Or hear the grown-up people's feet
Still going past me in the street.

And does it not seem hard to you,
When all the sky is clear and blue,
And I should like so much to play,
To have to go to bed by day?

It can be helpful to explain to the students that Scotland, where Stevenson lived, was located very far in the north, and in summer, sunset could be as late as 10:00 p.m.! Also, Stevenson was writing in the 1800s, when many houses still lacked electricity.

Similes and metaphors are both ways of making comparisons. Similes come right out and use "like" or "as" between the things being compared, whereas metaphors speak of one thing as if it were another.

To call attention to similes, challenge the students to listen to the things compared—that is, what is compared with what—in the following poem. The clue is to listen for the words "like" or "as."

"Morning in Buffalo"

The dawn broke grey as a party no one came to.
As I rolled from my bed like a log off a truck
My feet touched the floor, cold as railroad tracks in winter
So I flew down to the kitchen like a zinging hockey puck.

To call attention to metaphors, challenge students to find the things being compared in this poem by Emily Dickinson.

"Hope Is the Thing with Feathers"

"Hope" is the thing with feathers—
That perches in the soul—
And sings the tune without the words—
And never stops—at all—

And sweetest—in the Gale—is heard—
And sore must be the storm—
That could abash the little Bird
That kept so many warm—

I've heard it in the chillest land—
And on the strangest Sea—
Yet—never—in Extremity,
It asked a crumb—of me.

To further explore similes, students might enjoy Loreen Leedy's *Crazy Like a Fox: A Simile Story* (2009), an exciting story told largely through similes.

▪ NONFICTION

As noted in chapter 2, nonfiction is an umbrella term—a beach umbrella term—that stretches and strains to cover every work of literature that isn't a story, poem, or play. The Common Core standards argued for scooping far more nonfiction into children's reading diets than has heretofore been provided—50 percent by grade four and more thereafter. There are good reasons for that recommendation. Most adults read nonfiction far more than fiction. Nonfiction is structured differently and uses different vocabulary than fiction, so being taught to read fiction is not adequate preparation for much of reading people do as adults. Nonfiction also provides more "world knowledge" than fiction, and world knowledge forms the background of concepts with which we comprehend texts. And as we noted in chapter 2, reading nonfiction—especially contemporary nonfiction for children—can be really interesting.

Nonetheless, we have a long way to go to hit the new targets. Renaissance Learning (2015) has tallied the twenty-five most-read books in first through twelfth grades between the years 2012 and 2013, 2013 and 2014, and 2014 and 2015. Of the three hundred most-read titles each year, how many were nonfiction? Zero. True, the data was obtained from accelerated readers, which may not be representative of students' reading. And the many titles in a few book series—notably the Biscuit, Wimpy Kid, and Fly Guy series—accounted for many entries in some grade levels. But the study suggests we have work to do if we are going to seriously increase

What Does the Expert Say?
Why I'm a Fan of Nonfiction

Wendy Saul
Professor of education and international studies

About ten years ago I offered a pretty good workshop on using nonfiction with children. In this case we observed spiders at work and jotted down participants' questions as they occurred: What

are their webs actually made of? How long do spiders live? Mating habits? Food preferences? My job as a literacy educator was to gather together books about the creatures (providing the requisite bibliography) and encourage folks to search for answers to their questions in these books. The information would be recorded on chart paper, and, if time permitted, they would write a nonfiction piece of their own.

Today, the landscape of children's nonfiction and the tools we have available for information seeking have changed radically. To answer basic questions about a plant, animal, historical event, or sports hero, students go to the Web. It is an efficient and relatively reliable way to gather or check facts. So why bother with children's nonfiction at all? Wouldn't time and money be better

Wendy Saul

spent on the purchase of computers? "Not so" comes the unequivocal response. Here are just a few of the many benefits of nonfiction literature.

1. Although facts are interesting, my favorite children's informational books are coherent. They tell a story—not necessarily a story with a plot—but they do have an arc. They engage the reader from the beginning and continue to weave and complicate and sort through the information presented. They serve as the basis for further question posing. They make the strange familiar and the familiar strange. In this way they also serve as models of good writing. How did the author grab me in one spot and lose me in another? A good science or social studies book—less conceptually dense and designed to offer pleasure—differs markedly from a textbook or a Wikipedia entry.

2. Speaking of pleasure, good nonfiction offers aesthetic delights. For beautiful and well-made books, look at yearly recommended book lists from the National Association of Science Teachers or the National Council of Social Studies. Look closely at metaphors that science authors use: Seymour Simon tells us that if the Earth were the size of a basketball, the sun is approximately the size of the basketball court!

3. I love to consider the different treatments of a single topic proposed by talented writers. Consider, for example, different treatments of the Civil War. How are issues related to slavery addressed?

4. Comparing examples from within a genre is also fascinating. Before asking students to write their own question-and-answer book about an assigned topic, take a bunch of question-and-answer books on different topics into the classroom. What makes certain ones so much better than others? What layouts work most effectively? How are the questions ordered? Similar comparisons can be made of biographies. Are these "dawn to dusk" treatments or are they organized differently? Do they introduce the character's achievements and then move back to childhood details? What incidents are highlighted? Approaching text in this comparative way invites readers to learn information while simultaneously attending to conceptual and aesthetic decisions made by the author and responded to by the reader.

5. The Common Core standards are pushing nonfiction near the front of the literacy line, arguing that much of the reading that career and college-ready adults—young and old—do is informational. Attending to nonfiction presents an opportunity for teachers to share some of

(continues)

What Does the Expert Say? (cont.)

their favorite titles and to help students understand the satisfactions found in a great work of reality-based presentation of information.

Wendy, what do you do these days professionally, and why do you choose to do that?

I serve as professor of education and international studies at the University of Missouri, St. Louis, and in that role I support the teaching of active learning and critical thinking through work with educators in the United States and abroad. What could be better than learning, teaching, traveling, and making new friends, all at the same time?

What is one children's book that you hope everybody reads, and why you think so?

Tuck Everlasting by Natalie Babbitt helps me, as well as younger people, to put issues of life and death in perspective, both personally and in terms of world issues.

children's reading of nonfiction books and help them to form the habit of reading such books on their own.

Helping Children Negotiate Nonfiction

Children's nonfiction books have exploded in number and quality during the past decade. Visit the new book displays at any literacy or library convention, and you are likely to see far more nonfiction titles than any other genre. But there is work to do to help children engage with and get the most from informational books.

Nonfiction books take many forms. Many are brilliantly designed by their authors, illustrators, and book designers to virtually teach themselves. Others require a little more ingenuity on the part of teachers to help children get the most of them.

Following the Scripts of Contemporary Nonfiction

Writers of nonfiction books for children use many rhetorical and design devices to hook young readers' interest and pull them into their books. As a result, many nonfiction books for children are designed to practically teach themselves.

Question-and-Answer Books

Some informational books are designed to raise questions and invite children to seek answers. Steve Jenkins's books—*What Do You Do with a Tail Like This?* (Jenkins and Page, 2008), *What Do You Do When Something Wants to Eat You?* (Jenkins, 2001), and others—are keenly focused on select features of animals. Text and illustrations interplay nicely to rouse curiosity and suspense and create satisfaction. In *What Do You Do When Something Wants to Eat You?* and *What Do You Do with a Tail Like This?* a question is posed on one page accompanied by a partial illustration, and the answer is given on the next page along with the complete illustration. It's natural to stop and ask children to guess the answers before turning the page and finding out.

Other books that follow a question-and-answer format are the Scholastic Books series on historical subjects with titles such as *If You Lived at the Time of the Great San Francisco Earthquake* (Levine, 1992). These books, created by various authors and illustrators, are divided into sections, each introduced by questions such as "What did San Francisco look like after the earthquake?" "Who was up at the time of the quake?" and "How many people died?" Scholastic also publishes a question-and-answer series about animals and nature with titles like *Can It Rain Cats and Dogs?* (Berger and Berger, 1999). These, too, have sections organized around child friendly questions.

Can It Rain Cats and Dogs?
(Scholastic)

A natural way to share such books with children is to show the cover, ask the question on the cover, and invite children to guess the answer. You can also ask the students to predict correct answers to the other questions in the books and then read each section and discuss the answers as they are revealed. Later, you can conduct quiz show–like games to challenge the students to remember what they learned from the books.

Judy Allen's Backyard Books mentioned earlier in this chapter have outlandish questions for their titles, such as *Are You a Spider?* Of course, these are tongue-in-cheek questions, but the books detail the lives of the creatures named in the titles as if readers *are* the creatures. To effectively guide students through these books, it is necessary to preview them ahead of time and devise questions to ask before turning to the dramatic spread by the illustrator Tudor Humphries.

The patterns of such books lend themselves wonderfully to creative writing. Following the pattern of Judy Allen's Backyard Books, have students think of an insect or other animal to write about.

Other Patterns for Presenting Information

Sensationalism sells, so why not use it to hook young readers' attention to informational books? Franklin Watts has a series of books called Wicked History for readers in the upper primary grades. These books feature historical figures such as Genghis Khan, Julius Caesar, Grigory Rasputin, Henry VII, Vlad the Impaler, and Hitler. Each book has a portrait of its namesake on the cover with a colorful adjective spray painted graffiti-style across it—"Barbaric," "Lethal," "Persecutor," "Ruthless," "Heartless"— to inspire curiosity of a certain kind (mostly boyish and mostly preadolescent). The books are remarkably full of information, both historical and often geographical, with text, historical illustrations, maps, timelines, and glossaries. They are made accessible and engaging by their short chapters, illustrations or graphics on every other page, and cliffhanger chapter endings.

Grosset and Dunlap offers a series of historical titles that focus on events and people that young people might be assumed to know about but possibly don't. Some of the topics include the Super Bowl, Michael Jackson, Malala Yousafzai, Blackbeard, and even Jesus. The titles in this series make clear the focus of the book. For example, one title is *Who Is Malala Yousafzai?* (Brown and Thompson, 2015). The books have a large print illustration on every page and an uncomplicated writing style, so they can work well for readers whose age has advanced beyond their reading levels.

Instructional Strategies for Use with Nonfiction

To guide students' appreciation, in a group setting, of books like those mentioned, we recommend the following strategies.

Preparing the Text

To be prepared to guide students' interaction with a work of nonfiction, it is important to first read the book carefully. Note the valuable knowledge the book contains. Note, too, what students will need to know about the historical period, geography, culture (such as relations between groups; relations between men, women, and children; technology; and other topics that are important for the students to know and understand in order to appreciate the book). Be sure to carefully consider the book's contents: is it going to be too troubling for some students or their parents, especially if they hear about it secondhand? If you think it might, plan to send an explanatory letter home or perhaps even choose another book.

As you peruse the book in preparation of putting it in the hands of students, make note of any features that students might need help using, such as the table of contents, timelines, graphics, the glossary, the index, and the bibliography. Remember, too, that learning about these devices will be useful to the students beyond that particular book.

You should also collect any resources that can help provide context for understanding the book. These can include maps, short stories, or a mini-lecture about the topic to share with the students.

Be sure and identify any challenging words in the book (you can do this before reading each chapter). Remember to note not only specialized terms related to the topic, but also words of general use that may not yet be in the working vocabularies of many of the students.

Finally, locate and prepare to explain any challenging uses of grammar and text structure, which appear often in nonfiction text but not as often in fiction.

As You Read the Text Together

As students prepare to read the book, begin by explaining why you chose the book and what students can expect to learn from reading it together. Remember to explain both the content goals (the knowledge they will gain) and the pedagogical goals (how they will grow their reading skills and their ability to read new kinds of texts).

As part of the introduction, show the cover, read the title, and discuss the topic of the book. Tell stories or give any accounts you can to help the students understand its importance and what is interesting about it. More than likely, it will be possible to work several of the new terms from the book into the talk and explain what they mean. This gives students the opportunity to hear them used in a meaningful context.

Before students read each chapter, tell them what information they should look for in the reading. If the chapter introduces the geographic setting and the time period, ask them to try to find out about those things.

Consider using the "think-aloud" strategy. Read aloud any especially important or challenging parts of the chapter. Say aloud what you think it means and what it makes you think of. Invite student comments.

Consider asking teams of students to look for different things as they read. Some can keep track of what happened, others can keep track of where it happened, still others can follow who was involved, and others can think about how the events followed from what happened before. Invite the students to share their answers, first within small groups made up of students assigned to answer each question, and then with the whole class. Later, the class can be asked to predict what will happen next in the book.

It is important to call students' attention to any illustrations or other graphics in the text. Think out loud as you interpret the feature and point out what it means. Also, point to any challenging vocabulary items. If terms are explained in the glossary, demonstrate how the glossary can help readers understand the terms. If the words are not in the glossary, discuss informally what they mean.

After Reading the Book
A good place to start after the students have read the chapter is by reviewing the answers to the questions that the students discovered. Clarify details as needed.

It is particularly effective to engage students in a creative activity based on what they have read. For example, students might produce and record a news show. The show can follow the following format with different students starring in each part.

- Start with a headline. What happened? Who, what, where, and when?
- Offer background information. What led up to the events?
- Provide two or three eyewitness interviews. The witnesses can have different perspectives about what happened.
- Interview an expert. Why did this event matter?
- Provide a conclusion. Repeat what happened and what we expect will happen next.

The students should write out notes about what they are going to say and rehearse their parts.

As an alternative to videotaping, students might do a news story in the form of a newspaper article. Students may work alone, or teams of students can work on sections of the article and put them all together when finished.

Students might also respond to nonfiction by creating a mural depicting what they read. Tape a long strip of butcher paper to the wall of the classroom or in the hallway. Draw a time line on the bottom of the paper with notations for time intervals spread well apart. Assign small groups to illustrate the events on the mural.

A final suggestion for having students respond to nonfiction is to ask them to write "RAFT" papers. RAFT is an acronym that stands for role, audience, format, and topic. To carry out the RAFT procedure, tell the students to choose a topic to write about, which would be an event in the book they read. Then they should choose a role—if they could be anyone who participated in, observed, or knew about the event, who would they be? Then they choose the audience to whom they are writing. Finally, they choose a format: will they write a personal letter, a newspaper story, a poem, a letter of complaint?

In this chapter we looked at a host of instructional strategies that can be used to engage students with works of fiction, poetry, and nonfiction. In the next chapter we explore the goals and organization of literary units and literature-based content units. The strategies featured in this chapter are the ones you will want to use in the units you develop for use with students.

▪ RECOMMENDED BOOKS

Agostin, Marjorie. *I Lived on Butterfly Hill.* New York: Atheneum, 2015. Told through the eyes of a young girl, this is the story of a brutal dictatorship that overwhelmed Chile. Ages eleven through twelve.

Allen, Judy. *Are You a Spider?* Illustrated by Tudor Humphries. New York: Kingfisher, 2003. Like the other Backyard Books series by Allen and Humphries, this one addresses the reader with a facetious question and then spells out all the features that would be true of the reader if she or he *were* a spider. Picture book. Ages six through ten. Other books in this series include *Are You a Snail?* (2000) and *Are You a Ladybug?* (2000).

Alvarez, Julia. *Return to Sender.* New York: Yearling, 2010. Fifth-grader Tyler Paquette's family is in danger of losing their farm in Vermont, so they hire the Cruz family from Mexico to help out. Narrated from the point of view of Tyler and Mari Cruz, also a fifth grader, the book explores the human side of immigration issues and the meaning of patriotism in America. Winner of the Pura Belpré Award. Ages ten through twelve.

Appelt, Kathi. *The Underneath.* New York: Atheneum, 2008. This fantasy set in distinctly different time periods tells the stories of lonely creatures seeking the comfort and security found in others. Ages ten through twelve.

Babbitt, Natalie. *Tuck Everlasting.* New York: Farrar, 1975. Winnie discovers that the Tuck family drank from a spring that has given them eternal life. When the Tucks reveal their feelings about having eternal life, an enterprising man overhears the secret and attempts to capitalize on it by selling the water. Ages nine through twelve.

Becker, Aaron. *Journey.* Somerville, MA: Candlewick, 2013. A young girl confronts evil in this wordless adventure. Picture book. Ages eight through twelve.

Berger, Melvin, and Gilda Berger. *Can It Rain Cats and Dogs?* New York: Scholastic, 1999. One of a series of books that raises questions about nature and then provides answers. Ages seven through eleven. Other titles in this series include *Do Whales Have Belly Buttons?* (1999) and *Do Tornadoes Really Twist?*

Boynton, Sandra. *Happy Hippo, Angry Duck.* New York: Little Simon, 2011. This is a light-hearted book about moods. Picture book. Ages five through eight.

Brown, Dinah, and Andrew Thompson. *Who Is Malala Yousafzai?* New York: Grossett and Dunlap, 2015. One of a series of books about famous people or events that young readers may seek more information about, this one about a brave Pakistani girl who was shot in the face for the crime of going to school. Ages nine through twelve.

Creech, Sharon. *Chasing Redbird*. New York: HarperCollins, 1997. When Zinnia sets out to uncover a lost path, she uncovers even more than she expected. Ages ten through twelve.

Cronin, Doreen. *Click, Clack, Moo: Cows That Type*. Illustrated by Betsy Lewin. New York: Simon, 2000. Farmer Brown's cows want electric blankets and decide to use an old typewriter to negotiate their demands. Picture book. Ages six through nine.

Curtis, Christopher Paul. *The Watsons Go to Birmingham, 1963*. New York: Delacorte, 1995. An African American family from Detroit visits Birmingham in 1963, the summer of the fateful church bombing that set the civil rights movement into high gear. Ages ten through twelve.

Cushman, Karen. *The Midwife's Apprentice*. New York: Clarion, 1995. The world opens up for a homeless child living in medieval England when she is given the opportunity to become a midwife's apprentice. Ages ten through twelve.

dePaola, Tomie. *Strega Nona*. New York: Simon & Schuster, 1979. To impress the townspeople, Big Anthony makes Strega Nona's magic pasta pot work, but he doesn't know how to stop it. Picture book. Preschool through age seven.

DiCamillo, Kate. *Because of Winn Dixie*. Somerville, MA: Candlewick, 2000. Her newly adopted dog, Winn Dixie, becomes the means by which Opal connects to others in her small town and thereby comes to terms with her mother's leaving. Ages nine through twelve.

Edwards, Pamela D. *Some Smug Slug*. New York: Katherine Tegen Books, 1998. In a book filled with alliteration, slug unfortunately ignores the advice of his friends. Picture book. Ages six through ten.

Ellis, Deborah. *The Breadwinner*. Toronto: Groundwood Books, 2001. During the Taliban's rule in Afghanistan, only males are allowed to earn money. The only way for her family to survive is by eleven-year-old Parvana transforming herself into a boy and working to earn a living. Ages ten through twelve.

———. *The Heaven Shop*. Markham, Ontario: Fitzhenry & Whiteside, 2007. When her parents become victims of the AIDS epidemic in Malawi, Binti and her brother are sent to live with relatives who treat them as lowly servants. Ages ten through twelve.

———. *I Am a Taxi*. Toronto: Groundwood, 2008. Though Diego lives with his parents in a Bolivian prison, he is allowed to attend school, go to the market, and run errands for the prisoners. However, his desperate situation leads him to involvement in the illegal cocaine trade. Ages ten through twelve.

———. *My Name Is Parvana*. Toronto: Groundwood Books, 2012. In this sequel to *Breadwinner*, Parvana remembers the past four years of her life after being reunited with her mother and sisters in war-torn Afghanistan. Ages ten through twelve.

———. *Parvana's Journey*. Toronto: Groundwood Books, 2002. Amid a war raging in Afghanistan, Parvana sets out on a perilous journey to find her missing mother and siblings. Ages ten through twelve.

Erskine, Kathryn. *Mockingbird*. New York: Philomel, 2010. When Caitlin, a fifth grader with Asperger's syndrome, loses her brother to shooting violence, she struggles to find a place in the world without the beloved brother who her helped her make connections. Ages ten through twelve.

Estes, Eleanor. *The Hundred Dresses*. Illustrated by Louis Slobodkin. New York: Harcourt, Brace, 1944. When Wanda is ridiculed by her classmates for wearing the same faded dress every day, she claims she has a hundred dresses at home. Ages eight through eleven.

Gardiner, John Reynolds. *Stone Fox*. New York: Harper & Row, 1980. Though determined to win the national dogsled race to save his grandfather's farm, Little Willy seems to face insurmountable odds. Ages nine through twelve.

Henkes, Kevin. *Lilly's Purple Plastic Purse*. New York: Greenwillow, 1996. When Lilly disrupts class to show off her new purple plastic purse, she is devastated when Mr. Slinger, her teacher, confiscates the purse. Picture book. Ages five through eight.

Holm, Jennifer. *Turtle in Paradise*. New York: Random House, 2010. A new world opens up for Turtle when she is sent to Key West to live with relatives during the Depression. Ages nine through twelve.

Jenkins, Steve. *What Do You Do When Something Wants to Eat You?* Boston: Houghton Mifflin Harcourt, 2001. Jenkins explores the unique defense mechanisms of various animals. Picture book. Ages five through eight.

Jenkins, Steve, and Robin Page. *What Do You Do with a Tail Like This?* Boston: Houghton Mifflin, 2008. In this interactive picture book, readers discover some of the wonderful things animals can do. Picture book. Ages five through nine.

Kellogg, Steven. *The Mysterious Tadpole*. New York: Puffin, 2004. Louis loves the tadpole his uncle gave him and is determined to find a home for it when the creature mysteriously outgrows the family bathtub. Picture book. Ages five through eight.

Lai, Thanhha. *Listen, Slowly*. New York: HarperCollins, 2015. When a young girl unwillingly accompanies her grandmother to Vietnam, she makes important discoveries about her roots. Ages ten through twelve.

Larson, Kirby. *Hattie Big Sky*. New York: Delacorte, 2006. In the early 1900s, Hattie travels alone to Montana to homestead the land inherited from her uncle. Ages eleven and twelve.

Leedy, Loreen. *Crazy Like a Fox: A Simile Story*. New York: Holiday House, 2009. This exciting story is told largely through similes. Picture book. Ages six through nine.

Levine, Ellen. *If You Lived at the Time of the Great San Francisco Earthquake*. Illustrated by Pat Grant. New York: Scholastic, 1992. In this work of nonfiction, the author poses questions readers are likely to have about this historical event and provides the answers. Ages seven through ten. Another title in this series is *If You Traveled on the Underground Railroad* (1993).

Lewis, J. Patrick, ed. *National Geographic Book of Nature Poetry: More Than 200 Poems with Photographs That Float, Zoom, and Bloom!* Washington, DC: National Geographic Children's Books, 2015. Poems about nature by contemporary and classic poets, paired with the stunning nature photography that *National Geographic* is known for. Ages five through nine.

Ludwig, Trudy. *Sorry!* Illustrated by Adam Gustafson. New York: Knopf, 2006. This is a story about the importance of meaning you are sorry when you say you are. Picture book. Ages six through nine. Other books in the series include *Better Than You* (2011) and *My Secret Bully* (2015).

MacLachlan, Patricia. *Sarah, Plain and Tall*. New York: Harper, 1985. Siblings hope that Sarah will choose to stay on the prairie and become their mother. Ages nine through twelve.

McCall, Guadalupe Garcia. *Summer of the Mariposas*. New York: Tu Books, 2012. Odilia and her sisters, Mexican Americans from Eagle Pass, Texas, find a corpse floating in the Rio Grande and embark on an odyssey to return the body to its family in Mexico, encountering enchantments along the way that derive from Aztec mythology. Ages nine through twelve.

Naidoo, Beverley. *Journey to Jo'burg: A South African Story*. New York: HarperCollins, 1985. When they journey to Johannesburg to find their mother, a brother and sister are caught up in the cruelty of apartheid. Ages ten through twelve.

Naylor, Phyllis Reynolds. *Shiloh*. New York: Atheneum, 1991. When Marty's desire to own a dog results in his hiding an abused dog from his rightful owner, he soon faces moral decisions about his actions. Ages nine through twelve.

O'Connor, Barbara. *The Small Adventure of Popeye and Elvis*. New York: Farrar, Straus and Giroux, 2009. Popeye is convinced that life in rural South Carolina is too boring—until Elvis appears in his world. Ages eight through eleven.

Palacio, R. J. *Wonder*. New York: Knopf, 2012. Augie likes the same things other kids like, but when he goes to public school for the first time, his major facial distortion poses challenges. Ages nine through twelve.

Prelutsky, Jack, ed. *The Random House Book of Poetry for Children*. Illustrated by Arnold Lobel. New York: Random House, 1983. A time-honored collection of classic and contemporary (as of the 1980s) poems edited by the Children's Poet Laureate and illustrated by the beloved creator of the Frog and Toad books. Ages five through twelve.

———. *The 20th Century Children's Poetry Treasury*. Illustrated by Meilo So. New York: Knopf, 1999. An updated collection by Prelutsky, tilting toward more contemporary children's poets than his previous collection, *The Random House Book of Poetry for Children*. Ages five through twelve.

Rowling, J. K. *Harry Potter and the Sorcerer's Stone*. New York: Scholastic, 1998. An orphaned boy discovers that he is the most famous wizard alive and begins his education at Hogwarts School of Witchcraft and Wizardry. Ages nine through fourteen. Other titles in the series include: *Harry Potter and the Chamber of Secrets* (1999), *Harry Potter and the Prisoner of Azkaban* (1999), *Harry Potter and the Goblet of Fire* (2000), *Harry Potter and the Order of the Phoenix* (2003), *Harry Potter and the Half-blood Prince* (2005), and *Harry Potter and the Deathly Hallows* (2007).

Ryan, Pamela Muñoz. *The Dreamer*. Illustrated by Peter Sis. New York: Scholastic, 2012. A fictional biography of the Chilean poet Pablo Neruda written in lyrical prose and poetry with evocative illustrations to excite and inspire readers' imaginations. Winner of the Pura Belpré Award. Ages ten through fourteen.

———. *Esperanza Rising*. New York: Scholastic, 2000. Amidst the Great Depression, Esperanza and her mother must flee Mexico and go to California, leaving behind their lands and wealth. Living in a Mexican farm labor camp, Esperanza learns to relinquish her past and embrace the future in her new community. Ages eleven and older.

Sachar, Louis. *Holes*. New York: Farrar, 1998. When Stanley Yelnats is sent to a juvenile detention center for a crime he didn't commit, he is sure it is just another instance of the family curse, but his stay at Camp Green Lake presents him with the opportunity to finally break that curse. Ages ten and older.

Schlitz, Laura Amy. *Splendors and Glooms*. Somerville, MA: Candlewick, 2012. In Victorian London, the lives of two orphaned puppeteers, their evil master, and a powerful witch consumed by greed and regret become intertwined with the life of Clara, a child of a wealthy family. Ages ten through twelve.

Schmidt, Gary D. *Poetry for Young People: Robert Frost*. Illustrated by Henri Sorenson. New York: Sterling, 2008. A collection of 25 of Frost's poems with notes and suggestions by the Newbery-winning author of *The Wednesday Wars* and other books for late elementary and middle school readers. Ages nine through twelve.

Scieszka, Jon. *The True Story of the Three Little Pigs*. Illustrated by Lane Smith. New York: Puffin, 1996. The wolf tells *his* version of what happened to the three little pigs. Picture book. Ages six through ten.

Spinelli, Jerry. *Maniac Magee*. New York: Little, Brown. 1990. A homeless boy brings together a segregated community and in the process becomes a legend. Ages nine through twelve.

Steig, William. *Doctor De Soto*. New York: Farrar, 1982. When a fox with a toothache threatens to eat Dr. De Soto and his wife, the mouse dentist must come up with a plan to outfox the fox. Picture book. Ages six through nine.

Stewart, Sarah. *The Gardener*. Illustrated by David Small. New York: Farrar, 1997. When sent to live in an unfamiliar city with an uncle she doesn't know, Lydia seeks a way to bring joy into her life. Picture book. Ages six through nine.

Taylor, Mildred. *Roll of Thunder, Hear My Cry*. New York: Puffin, 1976. The Logan family are African American farmers in Mississippi in the 1930s doing their best to survive the Depression and the racist injustices of the white-dominated system. Winner of the Newbery Medal. Ages ten through thirteen.

Temple, Frances. *Grab Hands and Run*. New York: Orchard, 1995. This is the story about the flight of a Salvadoran refugee family from their homeland through the United States to Canada. Ages ten through thirteen.

———. *The Ramsay Scallop*. New York: Orchard, 1994. When a young couple joins a pilgrimage from England to Spain, their views of the world and each other are transformed. Ages eleven to young adult.

Vanderpool, Clare. *Moon over Manifest*. New York: Delacorte, 2010. Only as she gradually learns of events from 1917 and 1918 does Abilene come to understand why her father has sent her to live in the town of his youth while he travels the country seeking work during the Great Depression. Ages ten through twelve.

Vardell, Sylvia, and Janet Wong, eds. *The Poetry Friday Anthology for Celebrations (Children's Edition): Holiday Poems for the Whole Year in English and Spanish*. Princeton, NJ: Pomelo Books, 2015. Vardell, a children's literature expert, and Wong, a noted children's poet, offer this volume as one of several in their well-received initiative to help teachers find a regular place for poetry in the school week. Ages five through ten.

———. *The Poetry of Science: The Poetry Friday Anthology for Science for Kids*. Princeton, NJ: Pomelo Books, 2015. A collection of poems by a variety of poets about wide-ranging science topics. Ages six and older.

Williams, Vera B. *A Chair for My Mother*. New York: Greenwillow, 1982. When a fire destroys everything a family owns, a little girl saves money to buy her mother a special chair. Picture book. Preschool through age eight.

Williams, Vera, and Jennifer Williams. *Stringbean's Trip to the Shining Sea*. New York: Greenwillow, 1988. Stringbean and his brother send postcards home during a summer trip across the country. Picture book. Ages six through nine.

Williams-Garcia, Rita. *One Crazy Summer*. New York: Amistad/HarperCollins, 2010. Delphine and her sisters travel to Oakland to spend the summer with a mother who does not welcome them and sends them to a summer camp run by the Black Panthers. Ages ten through twelve.

Yorinks, Arthur. *Hey, Al!* Illustrated by Richard Egielski. New York: Farrar, 1986. Al and his dog Eddie live a humdrum life in the big city. When a giant bird offers them a chance for what they think will be a better life, they jump at the opportunity. Picture book. Ages seven through ten.

▪ REFERENCES

Alger, Horatio. *Ragged Dick; or, Street Life in New York with the Boot Blacks*. New York: A. K. Loring, 1868.

Anderson, Richard C., Paul T. Wilson, and Linda G. Fielding. "Growth in Reading and How Children Spend Their Time Outside of School." *Reading Research Quarterly* 23, no. 3 (1988): 285–303.

Berthoff, Ann E. *The Making of Meaning*. Portsmouth: Heinemann, 1981.

Bishop, Rudine Sims. "Mirrors, Windows, and Sliding Glass Doors." *Perspectives* 6, no. 3 (1990): ix–xi.

Bleich, David. *Readers and Feelings*. Urbana, IL: National Council of Teachers of English, 1975.

———. *Subjective Criticism.* Baltimore: Johns Hopkins University Press, 1982.

Blume, Judy. *Blubber.* New York: Bradbury, 1974.

———. *Forever.* New York: Bradbury, 1975.

Brown, Roger. *Words and Things.* Garden City, NY: Basic Books, 1958.

Cleary, Beverly. *Ramona and Her Father.* New York: William Morrow, 1977.

Cowhey, Mary. *Black Ants and Buddhists.* Portland, ME: Stenhouse, 2006.

Faulkner, William. *Requiem for a Nun.* New York: Vintage, 1951.

Fitzhugh, Louise. *Harriet the Spy.* New York: Harper and Row, 1964.

Freud, Sigmund. *New Introductory Lectures on Psychoanalysis.* New York: Norton, 1933.

Frye, Northrop. *The Educated Imagination.* Bloomington: Indiana University Press, 1964.

Giblin, James. C. *The Giblin Guide to Writing for Children.* West Redding, CT: Writers' Institute Publications, 2006.

Iser, Wolfgang. *The Implied Reader: Patterns of Communication in Prose Fiction from Bunyan to Beckett.* Baltimore: Johns Hopkins University Press, 1978.

Kagan, Spencer. *Cooperative Learning Resources for Teachers.* San Juan Capistrano, CA: Kagan Cooperative Learning, 1990.

Luria, Alexandr. R. *Cognitive Development.* Cambridge, MA: MIT Press, 1976.

Mandler, Jean M., and Nancy S. Johnson. "Remembrance of Things Parsed: Story Structure and Recall." *Cognitive Psychology* 35 (1977): 111–51.

National Reading Panel. *Teaching Children to Read: An Evidence-Based Assessment of the Scientific Research Literature on Reading and Its Implications for Reading Instruction: Reports of the Subgroups.* Washington, DC: National Institute of Child Health and Human Development, National Institutes of Health, 2000.

Postman, Neil. *The Disappearance of Childhood.* New York: Vintage, 1994.

Renaissance Learning. *What Kids Are Reading and the Path to College and Careers.* Wisconsin Rapids, WI: Renaissance Learning. Digital. Accessed December 26, 2015.

Rosenblatt, Louise. *The Reader, the Text, and the Poem.* Carbondale: Southern Illinois University Press, 1978.

Scholes, Robert. *Structuralism in Literature.* New Haven, CT: Yale University Press, 1975.

Seuling, Barbara. *How to Write a Children's Book and Get It Published.* Hoboken, NJ: Wiley, 2004.

Short, Katherine G., Jerome Harste, and Carolyn Burke. *Creating Classrooms for Authors and Inquirers.* Portsmouth: Heinemann, 1996.

Souriau, Etienne, 1955. *Les Deux Cent Milles Situations Dramatiques.* Paris: Flammarion, 1955.

Spolin, Viola. *Theater Games for the Classroom: A Teacher's Handbook.* Chicago: Northwestern University Press, 1986.

Stein, Nancy L., and Christine G. Glenn. "An Analysis of Story Comprehension in Elementary School Children." In *New Directions in Discourse Processing,* ed. Roy Freedle. Norwood, NJ: Ablex, 1979.

Wagner, Betty Jane. *Dorothy Heathcote: Drama As a Learning Medium.* Portland, ME: Calendar Islands Publishers, 1999.

▪ RESOURCES

Beers, Kylene, and Robert E. Probst. *Notice & Note: Strategies for Close Reading.* Portsmouth, NH: Heinemann.

Buehl, Doug. *Classroom Strategies for Interactive Learning.* 4th ed. Newark, DE: International Literacy Association, 2013.

Crawford, Alan N., E. Wendy Saul, Sam Mathews, and James MaKinster. *Teaching and Learning Strategies for the Thinking Classroom.* New York: International Debate Education Association/Open Society Institute, 2005.

ReadWriteThink. International Literacy Association and National Council of Teachers of English. April 1, 2016. www.readwritethink.org.

Temple, Charles, Donna Ogle, Alan Crawford, and Codruta Temple. *All Children Read.* 5th ed. New York: Pearson, 2017.

Temple, Charles, Miriam Martinez, and Junko Yokota. *Children's Books in Children's Hands.* 5th ed. New York: Pearson, 2014.

Wolf, Shelby A. *Interpreting Literature with Children.* New York: Routledge, 2003.

CHAPTER 5

Literary and Content Units

Once upon a time, in a land far away . . .

So begin many old stories and a few contemporary ones, as well. Jane Yolen (1977) once observed that "stories lean on stories." Certainly such "leaning" is evident in old tales handed down from past generations. It is also evident in contemporary spin-offs such as *The True Story of the Three Little Pigs* (Scieszka, 1996), a story in which author Jon Scieszka leaned squarely on the folktale "The Three Little Pigs."

In chapter 1, we discussed intertextuality, the process of bringing knowledge of one text to make meaning of another. This is something mature readers do, and students should also be encouraged to read one story in light of another. Literature units are especially effective vehicles for encouraging students to make these kinds of literary connections. In this chapter we explore ways of devising units centered around children's literature to achieve this goal, as well as other important literary and content area goals.

In the first part of the chapter we discuss the creation of literary units—units designed to achieve literary goals. In the second part, we explore ways of using literature in content units—units that are concerned primarily with achieving goals related to social studies, science, math, and other curricular areas. There are some commonalities in the ways in which the two types of units are organized and in some of the instructional activities used in each type. What sets literary units and content units apart are their goals. In developing and implementing literary units, teachers are focused primarily on literary goals. That is, through the study of literature, teachers intend for their students to learn more about literature—about literary elements and devices, characteristics of genres and formats, authors and illustrators, and themes explored through literature—and about how to engage in literary meaning making. In contrast, teachers organize content units to help students learn more about a particular content topic. For example, a fifth-grade teacher might develop a content unit incorporating children's literature to help children understand issues related to slavery. In a unit of this type, children may learn about the topic *through* literature (as well as other resources), but the primary goal is not to learn *about* literature.

■ LITERARY UNITS

We begin with literary units, recognizing that the literature curriculum has been ne-glected in elementary schools for too long. This isn't to say that children's books are ignored, but all too often trade books are used primarily as tools to teach reading or to achieve content goals. The time has come to broaden our goals to include literary ones as well.

In this section, we focus on the goals of literary units and ways of organizing such units. As you read about literary units (and later as you develop your own), you will want to draw on the information found in chapter 2—information about literary ele-ments, the ways in which picture books and chapter books work, particular children's authors and illustrators, and different genres of literature.

The Power of Literary Units

Teachers frequently have students read or listen to individual stories, and oftentimes this is the best route to follow in order to achieve particular goals, but there are also reasons for bringing together sets of related books. Ralph Peterson and Maryann Eeds (1990) present evidence of the quality of responses that can be evoked when litera-ture is presented in units. They relate the story of a kindergarten teacher who read aloud three of Maurice Sendak's fantasies: *Where the Wild Things Are* (1963), *In the Night Kitchen* (1970), and *Outside over There* (1981). In the first book, *Where the Wild Things Are*, Max sails away from his home on a magic boat to "the land where the Wild Things are," where he proceeds to become the "king of all Wild Things." Soon, though, Max grows lonesome and chooses to sail back home. Mickey, the protago-nist of *In the Night Kitchen*, wakes up one night to the clamorous noise of the night kitchen. Falling out of his bed and into the magical night kitchen, Mickey becomes a hero when he fashions an airplane out of bread dough to fly over the Milky Way to procure milk needed by the bakers in the night kitchen. Mickey's adventure concludes as he tumbles back into bed. In the final fantasy, *Outside over There*, young Ida, having discovered that her baby sister has been stolen by goblins, determines to go "outside over there," where she outwits the goblins to bring her baby sister safely home.

After sharing these three stories with her kindergartners, the teacher invited the children to talk about the commonalities they saw in the stories. This is what the children observed:

- Each book is circular.
- Each book is about a child who makes a trip to an unusual place.
- Each book portrays a powerful child.
- Each book shows a brave child.
- Each book portrays magic moves.
- Each book is scary. (Peterson and Eeds, 1990, 26)

These children did impressive thinking in response to their teacher's invitation to compare Sendak's three stories. Would they have made such perceptive comments if they had listened to only one of the stories? We don't think so. We believe that it is the power of the literature unit that yielded such insightful commentary by kindergartners. Researchers offer confirmation that children sometimes read books in light of other books they have read, and Sipe (2000) argued that these intertextual connections help children interpret narrative elements and make generalizations about story structure and genre. Perhaps the best way of encouraging children to make such connections across books is by intentionally having them read (or listen to) and talk about books that are linked in one way or another.

Educators have recommended author study, genre study, and thematic study as approaches that encourage students to engage in higher levels of thinking in response to literature (Martinez and Roser, 2003). Anecdotal evidence suggests that a unit approach to literature study is indeed effective. For example, Joy Moss includes in her descriptions of "focus units" examples of rich student talk that reveals children's "growing store of literary ideas" (1978, 485).

Nancy Roser, James Hoffman, and Cindy Farest (1990) moved beyond anecdotal evidence in documenting the effectiveness of their Language to Literacy program, which provided books organized into literature units focusing on author, theme, topic, or genre. Teachers in seventy-eight classrooms read unit books aloud to approximately 2,500 primary-aged children whose first language was Spanish. The teachers modeled and encouraged children's responses; they then collected those responses on language charts designed to help the children discover connections among the books. Roser and her colleagues reported significant changes in language arts scores, as well as in the range of literary connections recorded on the charts (Roser, Hoffman, Farest, and Labbo, 1992).

Planning and Organizing Literary Units

In planning literary units, we recommend the use of the curriculum design elements put forth by Jay McTighe and Grant Wiggins (2013): essential questions, backward design, and recursive planning. "Essential questions" are formulated based on important literary concepts and are open ended and thought provoking. These essential questions are about big-picture understandings, and they drive the ways in which students explore the books included in the unit. For a literary unit focused on the genre of science fiction, essential questions might include the following:

- What is the futuristic world like?
- How does the author make this world believable?
- In what ways is this world different than (and similar to) our own world?
- What problems and issues do the characters confront?
- Might this futuristic world become our own world? What makes you believe this?

Once goals are identified, "backward design" (Wiggins and McTighe, 1998) calls on the teacher to plan "backward" to determine how those goals can be achieved. A recursive cycle of assessment and planning occurs throughout teaching and learning.

The following questions can be used to guide the planning process:

- What goals are there for student learning outcome?
- How will you help students achieve their goals?
- What kind of learning experiences are needed?
- What kind of instruction is needed?
- What materials and other resources are needed?

Developing Different Types of Literary Units

Well-designed literary units provide rich contexts for children's literary learning. In this section, we discuss different types of literature units: genre units, author/illustrator units, literary element (or literary device) units, visual craft units, and thematic units. The distinctive, overarching goals of each type of unit are listed in Table 5.1.

Genre Units

One way to link books for literary study is by grouping them by genre. When students compare and contrast stories in the same genre, they can discover what is distinctive about the focus genre—what sets it apart from other genres. This is important knowledge that readers can draw on as they move into and through a book (Galda and Liang, 2003). For example, in a traditional literature unit centering on trickster tales, students might discover the following (among other things):

- Trickster tales have been told around the world.
- There are often clearly differentiated "good guys" and "bad guys" in trickster tales.
- In trickster tales, the character who sets out to do the tricking is often the one who is tricked.
- Trickster tales are typically filled with unexpected twists and humorous turns of events.

When students develop this type of knowledge about a particular genre, it affects the way they approach stories. Knowledgeable readers who are told that a story is a fantasy will have very different expectations for that story than they would for a work of contemporary realistic or historical fiction. These genre-based expectations are critically important and guide readers in the process of constructing meaning.

Table 5.1 Goals of Different Types of Literature Units

Type of Unit	Goal of Unit
Genre	To explore the features of the focus genre that set it apart from other genres
Author/illustrator	To discover what is distinctive about the craft of the focus author and/or illustrator
Literary element	To explore how authors develop and use literary elements or devices
Visual device	To explore how illustrators use visual devices to convey meaning
Thematic	To build a deeper understanding of the human experience as revealed through thematically linked books

Don't Miss . . .
Books to Include in a Unit about Trickster Tales

Borreguita and the Coyote by Verna Aardema

The Monkey and the Crocodile: A Jataka Tale from India by Paul Galdone

Anansi Goes Fishing by Janet Stevens

Coyote: A Trickster Tale from the American Southwest by Gerald McDermott

Zomo the Rabbit: A Trickster Tale from West Africa by Gerald McDermott

Flossie and the Fox by Patricia McKissack

Mrs. Chicken and the Hungry Crocodile by Won-Ldy Paye and Margaret H. Lippert

The Leopard's Drum: An Asante Tale from West Africa by Jessica Souhami

Tops and Bottoms by Janet Stevens

In developing genre units, it is first necessary to determine the particular focus of the unit. This is an especially important step in creating a genre unit because of the diversity of books that may fall within a genre. For example, as we discussed in chapter 2, traditional literature includes myths, legends, various types of folktales, tall tales, and ballads. If you simply selected a story representing each of these subtypes, your unit would contain such a hodgepodge of stories that children would not be able to make any discoveries about the genre. Instead, a unit must have a more cohesive focus. We explore what this means by discussing some of the types of units you might build around two different genres.

Because of its diversity, traditional literature lends itself to a host of engaging ways of organizing literature study. Any of the subtypes of traditional literature explored in chapter 2 can provide the underlying link for the study of traditional literature: trickster tales, pourquoi tales, tall tales, legends, cumulative tales, fairy tales, fables, hero tales, or humorous tales. For example, if students read and compare a variety of fairy tales, they are likely to discover that tales such as "Cinderella," "Snow White and the Seven Dwarfs," and "Rumpelstiltskin" involve magic and that the magic often functions to reward ordinary people for their goodness and steadfastness.

Culture is yet another basis for organizing traditional literature units. As you have learned, the traditional literature from a particular culture frequently shares common features. Through literature study, students can discover some of these distinctive features. For example, in a study of Scandinavian folklore, students might discover the trolls, giants, witches, and hags that frequently appear in tales from this region. A collection such as Lise Lunge-Larsen's *The Troll with No Heart in His Body and Other Tales of Trolls from Norway* (1999) contains a host of Scandinavian tales that can be used in such a unit. Similarly, through a unit devised around African folklore, students could discover that the trickster takes a variety of forms in African folklore; sometimes he is the spider, whereas in other tales he appears as the turtle or the hare.

Chapter 2 offers useful information for teachers who want to build units designed to help children discover some of the distinctive features of modern fantasy. Any of the subcategories of fantasy can provide an undergirding link for a unit about this genre. For young children, you might devise a unit featuring personified animals or personified toys. Older students could be invited to delve into a unit structured around Jon Scieszka's time-slip stories. Or, by grouping books that feature outlandish characters or situations, such as Jon Agee's *It's Only Stanley* (2015) and Philip Stead's *Special Delivery* (2015), students could explore the use of exaggeration in modern fantasy. Yet another possibility is exploring how literary elements are often crafted in fantasy—the use of dual settings linked by a special portal or characters that set off on a quest.

Don't Miss . . .
Books Featuring Exaggeration and Outlandish Situations

It's Only Stanley by Jon Agee
Special Delivery by Philip Stead
Cloudy with a Chance of Meatballs by Judi Barrett
A Million Fish . . . More or Less by Patricia McKissack
Thunder Rose by Jerdine Nolen
Raising Sweetness by Diane Stanley
Saving Sweetness by Diane Stanley

Special Delivery
(Roaring Brook Press/Macmillan)

Children benefit when they develop a well-defined sense of how one genre differs from another. This understanding influences their expectations for particular genres, which in turn affects the ways in which they read and write within the genres. Organizing literature study on the basis of genres helps them to develop these understandings.

Author/Illustrator Units

When mature readers have a favorite author, they are typically on the lookout for that writer's next book and might not even wait for the paperback version to be published before buying it. Further, readers who are about to begin a new book by a familiar writer have expectations that help them to step into the writer's story world and, when reading, to make connections across books written by the author. Understanding what sets the work of particular writers apart from others often influences mature readers' book choices and expectations. Children too can be encouraged to develop a sense of author (or illustrator). Those who discover the rich character relationships found in the books of Kate DiCamillo might seek out other books by this award-winning author. Or readers who are fascinated with the vivid colors and lively (and often unexpected) plot twists of Yuyi Morales's books know just what to look for in new books created by this author/illustrator. Author and illustrator units are designed to help students make such discoveries. In an author unit, students explore a number of works written by one author in order to discover what is distinctive about that individual's work. In parallel fashion, in an illustrator unit, readers study books illustrated by the featured artist in order to discover what characterizes that person's artwork.

Patricia Bloem and Anthony Manna (1999) engaged second and fourth graders in a study of Patricia Polacco's books to help them discover what Polacco does as a writer and illustrator that makes them think and feel the way they do. The researchers read aloud stories by Polacco, modeled questions they had about the author's work, invited the children to share their own questions, and finally had the children conduct an author interview by telephone. Bloem and Manna found that the students responded aesthetically in rich and diverse ways, and over the course of the unit, they found a shift in children's questions from being text based to revealing connections they were making with Polacco and with her books. The children "delighted in the nuances of the texts, and found great pleasure, at the end of the project, in learning ways that the texts reflected Polacco's history and recorded her family stories" (1999, 806).

To develop an author or illustrator unit, a teacher needs to first discover what is distinctive about the work of the individual who will be featured. These insights provide the basis for posing the essential questions for the unit. The best way of doing this is to study various works written or illustrated by the person. For example, those who immerse themselves in the books of Mac Barnett are likely to discover stories characterized by quirky plot twists and characters in outlandish situations. Figure 5.1 features a language chart designed to guide children's explorations of books written by this author.

The Skunk
(Roaring Brook Press/Macmillan)

One can also gain insights into the distinctive nature of an author's work by hearing what the individual says about his or her own work. Visiting author and illustrator Web sites, as well as Internet sites like TeachingBooks.net, is likely to yield interesting insights. Videos of many authors and illustrators talking about their work can also be found on YouTube.

It is relatively easy to characterize the work of some authors or illustrators because they consistently work in the same genre, repeatedly explore particular types of themes, or write in a relatively consistent style. However, others may have a large and diverse body of work. In organizing literature study of a writer whose works vary widely, it may be helpful to narrow the focus of study. For example, a writer such as Tomie dePaola has published many books in widely diverse genres including fantasy, folktales and legends, informational books, realistic fiction, and wordless picture books. Although you may choose to introduce children to the range of dePaola's work in a literature unit, it would make sense to group his works for exploration within the unit. For example,

Figure 5.1   Author Language Chart: Mac Barnett

	This story was about . . .	One of the really funny things that happened was . . .	Something that really surprised us was . . .
Sam and Dave Dig a Hole			
Extra Yarn			
Billy Twitters and His Blue Whale Problem			
The Skunk			
Oh No! Not Again! (Or How I Built a Time Machine to Save History) (Or at Least My History Grade)			

Technology Tip

Many authors and illustrators use technology on Web sites and social media to share their craft in multimedia ways. For example, visit the following YouTube site to hear about how David Wiesner crafted his picture book, *Art and Max*: www.youtube.com/watch?v=ZuIsAIKiNgY.

What insights does Wiesner share about his work? How might you use this information in developing a literature unit focused on the picture books of David Wiesner?

TeachingBooks.net is a subscription-based site that serves as a hub for organizing and accessing a wide range of original author and illustrator interviews, as well as for pointing to other Web-based resources by book creators or teachers.

a literature unit might start with an investigation of some of his realistic stories that draw heavily on his own experiences as a child: *Nana Upstairs & Nana Downstairs* (1998), *Watch out for the Chicken Feet in Your Soup* (1985), *Tom* (1993), and *The Art Lesson* (1989). The unit could then move on to explore dePaola's fantasies featuring Strega Nona and Big Anthony before again moving on to some of the folktales and legends retold by this author and illustrator.

Units Focused on Literary Elements and Devices

Teachers can link books in such a way as to help students make discoveries about particular literary elements or literary and visual devices. For example, a teacher might create a unit featuring stories such as Arthur Yorinks's *Hey, Al!* (1986), Chris Van Allsburg's *The Polar Express* (1985), Melinda Long's *How I Became a Pirate* (2003), and Maurice Sendak's *Where the Wild Things Are* (1963), all of which feature characters who take enchanted journeys—a device that is frequently used by fantasy writers. To explore stock characterization, a teacher might link books about foxes such as William Steig's *Doctor De Soto* (1982), Keiko Kasza's *My Lucky Day* (2005), and Mo Willems's *That Is Not a Good Idea!* (2013).

Units Focused on Visual Devices

In chapter 2 we discussed the ways in which illustrators use visual elements in telling stories, and literary units can be crafted to guide children to better understand these visual elements. For example, illustrators sometimes use shifts in color to convey information about character emotions, to signal character revelations, or to indicate a surprising turn of events or story complication.

Literary units might also be organized around the peritextual features of picture books. For example, illustrators sometimes use the beginning and final endpapers in interesting ways in telling stories. Sometimes important character clues can be found in the endpapers. Still other illustrators actually begin stories on the initial endpapers and/or conclude the stories on the final endpapers. When literature units focus on picture book endpapers, children become attuned to the importance of attending to this component of picture books. Figure 5.2 features a language chart designed to explore endpapers in picture books.

Thematic Units

Because literature is about life, units organized around literary themes have great potential to help students understand the human experience. As Joy Moss has observed, "literary transactions enable readers to enter into the lives of others, to live through their experiences, to see the world through their eyes. In the process, readers have opportunities to gain insights about human experience and to learn about feelings and motivation and relationships" (1994, 5). Literary themes such as "celebrations," "memories," "journeys," "imagination," "courage," "making a difference," and "hopes and dreams" offer rich potential for literary study. Such literary themes cut across literary genres and encompass many authors and illustrators.

After participating in a thematic study, students are likely to emerge with a richer understanding of the unit's central idea. A thematic study focused on the theme of

Figure 5.2   Visual Device Language Chart: Endpapers

	The book was written and illustrated by . . .	In the beginning endpapers we see . . .	Based on these clues, we think . . .	In the final endpapers we see . . .	This is important because it tells us . . .
The Odd Egg					
We're Going on a Bear Hunt					
Suddenly!					
A Beasty Story					
Don't Let the Pigeon Drive the Bus!					

"making a difference" could address important social justice issues. A teacher might choose to include books such as Diana Cohn's *¡Sí, Se Puede!/Yes, We Can!* (2005), the story of Carlitos and his classmates who join a janitors' strike to ensure that Carlitos's mother and other janitors could earn a living wage. Companion books might include Duncan Tonatiuh's *Separate Is Never Equal* (2014) about the Mendez family's fight to integrate California schools in 1944 and Kathleen Krull's *Harvesting Hope: The Story of Cesar Chavez* (2003), the story of the labor leader who led the struggle for fair working conditions for Mexican American farmworkers.

Organizing Literary Units

Once you have decided on the goals of a literary unit, the next tasks are to select books and to organize the unit.

Selecting Unit Books

Literature units can include poetry, picture books, chapter books, or some combination of these. When selecting books, it is critical that you find the right ones—that is, books that are clearly connected to the undergirding goals of the unit. The lists of recommended books in this text can serve as one source for locating unit books. Colleagues and your school librarian might be able to provide further suggestions. At times you may need to rely on various book selection aids to locate connected books. These aids include books such as *Subject Guide to Children's Books in Print* (2012) and journals such as *Book Links*. Internet sites like TeachingBooks.net are also helpful guides for finding related titles.

Technology Tip
Selecting Unit Books

Suggestions for books to include in a literature study can be found online on numerous Web sites dedicated to children's literature. Little time need be spent searching for book titles and connections when you use Internet resources, although it is easy to lose track of time as you surf from link to link reading creative ideas and learning about new titles that quickly seem indispensable. Carol Hurst's Web site is a popular one (www.carolhurst.com). Another especially helpful site is https://sundaycummins.wordpress.com, which provides teaching strategies that build on good literature. There are as many sites as you have the patience to browse.

Reaching All Students

In many communities, there are large populations of immigrant children. To ensure that these children can connect with the books included in literary units, be sure to include at least some books that reflect the children's cultural experiences. For example, if the unit focus is "making the world a better place," books like *The Girl Who Buried Her Dreams in a Can* (Trent, 2015) and *Wangari's Trees of Peace* (Winter, 2008) are likely to resonate with children from Africa. Each of these books features strong individuals—one from Zimbabwe and the other from Kenya—who worked hard to change their communities for the better.

Unit Structure

Although we describe various ways of organizing units, there really is no one best way. Rather, it is important to organize your units in a way that meets your students' needs. When you are planning your own literary units, you might use variations of the ones we describe or create an entirely new structure that enables you to pursue the literary goals of your unit.

Nancy Roser, James Hoffman, and Cindy Farest (1990) devised an easy-to-use organizational structure for picture book units in their Language to Literacy Program. Their units revolve around ten related picture books, one of which is read aloud each day during a two-week period (of course, the length of units can vary). This structure works especially well with younger children who might not yet be reading or who might not yet have the reading skills to read more complex books on their own.

Joy Moss (1984) devised a somewhat different format for picture book units that she terms "focus units." In a focus unit centering on picture books, a daily read-aloud by the teacher is the central activity. However, children also independently read picture books related to the focus of the unit.

In Language to Literacy chapter book units, students are engaged simultaneously with two linked books. One book is read aloud daily by the teacher on a chapter-by-chapter basis. Students read the second book independently, using a pacing guide provided by the teacher or one that they negotiate themselves. At the end of the unit, activities such as a discussion or the completion of a Venn diagram provide students with the opportunity to make connections between the two books.

In a focus unit centering on chapter books, students also engage with more than one book. At the beginning of the unit, the teacher reviews an array of books that are available for independent reading, and each student selects two books to read independently. The teacher reads a chapter book aloud daily on a chapter-by-chapter basis, and students read their two books independently, meeting periodically in small groups to compare the stories they are reading in preparation for a culminating class discussion of all of the unit books.

Unit Activities

In chapter 4, we described a variety of activities to support children's literary learning in the context of literature units. Children can record their personal responses to unit books in literature journals. To give children the opportunity to gather their thoughts in preparation for actively participating in literature discussion, the teacher can invite them to write in their journals immediately following a read-aloud. Journals can also be used with books that the students read independently as part of the unit. Because discussion of these books is not likely to occur daily, students should draw on the ideas they record in their journals when they do meet in small groups or with the entire class.

Literature discussion is an integral part of literature units. The teacher should invite students to join in conversations about unit books that are read aloud, as well as those that they read independently. When teachers participate in these discussions, they can use the discussion tools outlined in chapter 4. Although writing and discussion are widely used as response activities, teachers should invite children to respond through art and drama, as well.

Literature units are designed to help students make connections across a related set of books, and a language chart is the perfect tool to guide students in making connections. Language charts were originally designed for use with related sets of picture books (Roser, Hoffman, and Farest, 1990). These large charts, which are intended to be displayed on a classroom wall, are ruled into a matrix. The titles (and perhaps authors and illustrators) of a set of books are recorded along one axis of the matrix. Questions devised to stimulate connections across the books are recorded along the other axis. These questions might focus attention on particular aspects of the story worlds in the featured books, on themes that emerge from the books, or on the crafting of the stories or illustrations.

In a picture book unit in which the teacher reads a new book each day, the teacher and students can record their thinking regarding how the book relates to the common elements that serve as the foundation of the unit following open-ended discussion of the daily read-aloud. Figure 5.3 presents an example of a language chart designed to guide young students' exploration of a fantasy unit, whereas Figure 5.4 features a chart that can be used in an author/illustrator unit.

Figure 5.3 Example of a Genre Language Chart

	Where does this story start?	Where does the character travel to? How?	Why does the character go there?	What happens in the fantasy world?	How is the character changed?
The Adventures of Beekle: The Unimaginary Friend by Dan Santat	The story starts on an island where imaginary friends are created.	The character goes to the real world and travels there on a boat.	He goes in search of a real child who will choose him and give him a special name.	He searches all over until he finds Alice.	He is able to do the unimaginable by finding his friend.
Journey by Aaron Becker	The story starts in a big city.	The girl goes to a fantasy world by drawing her own opening to the new world.	She's bored with her drab world.	The girl travels around and saves the special purple bird by fighting warriors.	She returns home able to use her new imagination to create adventure and find a friend.
Hey, Al by Arthur Yorinks	The story starts in a dumpy apartment in a city.	The man and his dog are carried by a gigantic bird to an island in the sky.	They go because they are bored.	They begin to like the "good life" until they begin to turn into birds.	They discover that, "Paradise lost is sometimes Heaven found."
The Polar Express by Chris Van Allsburg	The story starts in a little boy's bedroom on Christmas Eve.	The boy goes to the North Pole on a magical train.	He wants to see Santa Claus and the North Pole.	The boy is chosen to receive the first gift of Christmas: a little bell.	The boy believes in Christmas forever, even when he is grown up.
Where the Wild Things Are by Maurice Sendak	The story starts in Max's house.	Max goes to where the Wild Things are on a private boat.	He goes because he is angry with his mother.	He becomes the king of the Wild Things but then he wants to be where someone loves him best.	Max learns that home is the best place of all.

Figure 5.4   Language Chart Exploring the Story Worlds of Chris Van Allsburg

	What was the problem in the story?	How was it solved?	What mysterious things happened in the story?	What was the "twist" at the end of the story?	Where in the pictures did you find the dog?
Jumanji					
The Polar Express					
The Stranger					
The Sweetest Fig					
The Wretched Stone					

A word of warning: some teachers report that language charts can become just a "worksheet on the wall" *if the class begins to complete the chart too soon after reading.* These charts are not meant to replace conversations about books. Rather, teachers and students should turn to the language chart only after discussing a book fully. Teachers who have used language charts in this way report that they can be effective tools for fostering literary understandings. In fact, many teachers change the design of their language charts throughout the school year to help students continue to explore different aspects of literature.

■ LITERATURE ACROSS THE CURRICULUM

Conventional practice has held that the textbook is the primary vehicle through which children learn in the content areas. Indeed, textbooks can play an important role in instruction because they typically provide a broad view of a topic. Yet textbooks should be just one of many instructional resources that innovative teachers employ. Although the writing in textbooks often lacks richness in vocabulary and structure, perhaps the greatest indictment of textbooks relates to the superficial manner in which topics are often treated. One way of offsetting some of these limitations is by using trade books in the classroom. Children's literature is a resource that holds great potential for nurturing children's learning across the curriculum.

The Need for Children's Literature in the Content Areas

Well-written trade books engage children and make them want to keep reading, and when these books open new vistas for children, they encourage young readers to keep learning as well. Literature can be incorporated into content instruction in different ways. A single book can be used to develop a concept, initiate interest in a topic, launch a project, or generate questions about a subject. For example, a teacher can read *The Doorbell Rang* (Hutchins, 1986) by Pat Hutchins to introduce the concept of division. The story begins as two children are getting ready to divvy up twelve cookies their mother has just baked. They are pleased to discover that each one will get six cookies—until the doorbell rings and two more children arrive. As more and more friends appear on the doorstep, each child gets fewer and fewer cookies. Barbara Bash's *Urban Roots* (1990), which focuses on where city birds build their nests, can launch an investigation of the neighborhood surrounding the school, encouraging children to become careful observers of their own environment. Trade books can also serve as valuable companions to textbooks. For example, in a study of ecosystems, textbooks may offer only a broad overview of the topic, whereas trade books can provide detailed examples of ecosystems. Barbara Bash has written a series on trees that offers richly fleshed-out examples of ecosystems. Titles in this series include *Tree of Life* (1989), *Desert Giant* (1990), and *Ancient Ones* (2002).

Literature-based Content Units

Learning within content areas happens in many ways; one way we advocate this is by using literature as the foundation for how content is presented and having students "read to learn." Of course, we intend for content to be presented in as many formats as best suits the learning situation, but a foundation of good books can be critical for students to hone their skills in reading as a basis for acquiring content. This predicates the need for quality literature—that is, literature that presents information in the most engaging and appropriate ways. For nonfiction, there are clearly articulated criteria for evaluating how the information is presented, including analyzing for the ways in which nonfiction is visually organized and presented. The authorial voice in how the information is cast is primarily responsible for the perspective that readers take when reading the material. Evaluating each book for its quality is one step; the other is balancing the range of materials to be presented within the content-based unit.

Planning and Organizing Literature-based Content Units

Although there are numerous ways in which children's literature can be incorporated into the curriculum, in this section we highlight the use of trade books by illustrating the process of selecting books and structuring a literature-based content unit by

What Do the Experts Say?
Literacy Moments: Sharing Poetry across the Curriculum

Sylvia Vardell, professor, and Janet Wong, poet

If you want to grab a literacy moment in any lesson on any subject, there is no faster, easier, more memorable way than to share a poem. Poems offer two distinct advantages over any other literary vehicle: they cover a multitude of subjects and can do so in only a few words shared in a minute or less. For example, read this poem aloud from our recent collaboration, *The Poetry of Science* (2015):

Sylvia Vardell

"Shen Kuo"
(1031–1095)
by *Janet Wong*

Almost a thousand years ago
a Chinese scientist named Shen Kuo,
geologist-cartographer-astronomer-engineer,
discovered fossilized shells
hundreds of miles inland
that made it clear the shoreline had moved.
Petrified bamboo convinced him
that climate change was happening.
But people did not want to hear these things.
Instead he became known for the idea
that true north is not magnetic north.
His magnetic needle compass was worth
spices, gold, jewels—even a giraffe—
as explorers later sailed to Africa and back.

Climate change and the shifting sea:
who would choose such mundane news
over promises of spices, gold, and jewels?

Janet Wong

In just a moment, you've touched on the topic of climate change and the concept of true north, introduced the story of a scientist and his discovery, presented the idea of biography, crossed cultures, time, and place, conveyed the tension between invention and commerce, and emphasized the importance of personal persistence. You can choose which element to emphasize depending on your teaching objective and even share the poem multiple times in various subject areas to highlight different aspects. That's another plus of poetry: kids love hearing a poem over and over again. It doesn't take long to do so and thus reinforces their learning.

Science is probably the easiest content area for infusing poetry because there are so many poetry books available on science-related topics, from animals to weather to space. Recent examples include *Dear Wandering Wildebeest* by Irene Latham (2014), *Dinothesaurus* by Douglas Florian (2009), *Water Sings Blue: Ocean Poems* by Kate Coombs (2012), *Ubiquitous: Celebrating Nature's Survivors* by Joyce Sidman (2010), *Random Body Parts: Gross Anatomy Riddles in Verse* by Leslie Bulion (2015), *Now You See Them, Now You Don't: Poems about Creatures That Hide* by David L. Harrison (2016), and comprehensive anthologies such as *The Tree That Time Built: A Celebration of Nature, Science, and Imagination*, compiled by Mary Ann Hoberman and Linda Wilson (2009), and the *National Geographic Book of Nature Poetry*, compiled by J. Patrick

(continues)

What Do the Experts Say? (cont.)

Lewis (2015). In addition, many children's science-themed magazines and serials—for example, *Ranger Rick, Owl, Chirp, Chickadee, National Geographic Kids*, and *Kids Discover*—regularly feature poems. In fact, magazines are often the first medium in which many new poets get their work published. In our own poetry teaching collection, *The Poetry Friday Anthology for Science* (Vardell and Wong, 2014), a recent "NSTA Recommends" title endorsed by the National Science Teachers Association, we feature 218 poems about solar power and hybrid cars, gears and robots, hurricanes and the human body, video games and glaciers, famous scientists and everyday inventions, and more (along with learning activities for every poem). Using these science poetry resources and many others, it's possible to find a short "poem match" for almost any elementary science topic to provide a moment of learning that is also a fun break in the routine.

In our recent article "The Symbiosis of Science and Poetry," we note, "In less than one minute, a poetry moment can promote incidental science learning, be part of science instruction, offer content-rich poetry lessons in reading and language arts—or simply provide fun Poetry Friday sharing" (Vardell and Wong, 2015). We can also use science poems to lay the groundwork for the research process or as a model for gathering and sharing key facts and vocabulary. You begin by reading widely from science, nature, or animal poems. Encourage students to browse through books and brainstorm possible topics to study. Then lead them to related nonfiction books and help them identify key facts about their topic from these sources. Children can work together to create a collaborative "found" poem using a nonfiction book, a news article, or an encyclopedia entry as source, first underlining or highlighting what they think the most important words in the informational passage are and then arranging those key words to create a poem. We provide more ideas for incorporating science-themed poetry into an established routine in *Book Links* (Vardell, 2013): for example, pairing a science-themed nonfiction or informational book such as *Team Moon: How 400,000 People Landed Apollo 11 on the Moon* by Catherine Thimmesh (2006) with a picture book such as *Moonshot: The Flight of Apollo 11* by Brian Floca (2009). Start the whole program with a short poem such as "The Moon" from *Comets, Stars, the Moon, and Mars* by Douglas Florian (2007) or "Moon Walk: July 21, 1969" by Susan Blackaby from *The Poetry Friday Anthology for Celebrations* (Vardell and Wong, 2015) and "Queen of Night" by Terry Webb Harshman from *The Poetry Friday Anthology for Science for Kids* (Vardell and Wong, 2014) to show children how writers can approach the same topic in very different and distinctive ways. (See PomeloBooks.com and Pinterest.com/PomeloBooks for downloadable images of the Blackaby and Harshman poems.)

In our poetry article for *Science and Children* (Vardell and Wong, 2014), we shared the views of science expert Valarie Akerson (2002) that the "processes of science and literacy learning are similar and may help the development of each discipline" and the "use of language arts to promote literacy and support learning in other content areas is [also] recommended and encouraged by the International Reading Association (IRA) and the National Council of Teachers of English (NCTE)." Jill Castek (2013) recommends "breaking down those instructional silos" of science and literacy to maximize overlap, ensuring that vocabulary exposure is occurring in many contexts for maximum scaffolding. And, of course, that also applies to infusing poetry in instruction in social studies, mathematics, the arts, and even physical education, because there are poems about topics relevant to each of these areas (see recommended titles in Vardell's *The Poetry Teacher's Book of Lists* [2012]). Using poetry across the curriculum is like killing two birds with one stone—or, as poet George Ella Lyon put it, "like hatching two birds from the same egg."

Sylvia, what are you doing professionally these days?

(continues)

What Do the Experts Say? (cont.)

When I'm not teaching courses in children's literature, I'm working with Janet Wong on the Poetry Friday Anthology series, presenting about poetry at conferences, blogging about poetry at Poetry for Children (www.poetryforchildren.blogspot.com) or writing my poetry column for the American Library Association's *Book Links* magazine.

Would you name one children's book that you hope everybody reads and why you think they should?

I urge everyone to follow K. A. Holt's work and read *House Arrest* as soon as possible. This novel in verse is so compelling, honest, and revealing about how one child's serious illness affects another child and the whole family. Plus, it's a great character study of a tween boy growing up and stepping up—under very difficult circumstances. It's angry, hilarious, heartwarming, and real.

Janet, what are you doing professionally these days?

I spend most of my time on The Poetry Friday Anthology series, diverse and inclusive poetry anthologies addressing a wide variety of topics. I also do volunteer work for groups such as the International Literacy Association's Literacy and Social Responsibility special interest group (SIG) and the Children's Literature and Reading SIG.

Would you name one children's book you hope everybody reads and why you think they should?

I hope everybody reads *Cowboy Up! Ride the Navajo Rodeo* by Nancy Bo Flood, a masterful combination of poetry and nonfiction as well as culture and sport, illustrated with photos of contemporary Navajo rodeo participants. We need more books like this—books that blend and blur categories and present new views of underrepresented groups of people.

describing a unit focused on immigration. Literature is an especially powerful tool in social studies because students must gain historical or social empathy in order to develop social studies understandings (Tomlinson, Tunnell, and Richgels, 1993). Children's literature can help students develop such empathy. Linda Levstik has observed that when literature is used in history instruction, students "encounter the complexities of historical events, where facts from the past become living, breathing drama, significant beyond their own time" (1989, 136).

Determining Unit Goals

As is the case with literary units, planning content-based units can be guided by the use of curriculum design elements identified by Jay McTighe and Grant Wiggins (2013). The crucial first step in this model is to identify the essential questions that drive the ways in which students probe the content area. In discussing literature-based content units, we are using an immigration unit as our example. Essential questions for this unit might include the following:

- Why do people choose to leave the land of their birth?
- What is it like to journey to a new land?
- What does it mean build a life in a new land?

Selecting Unit Books

Once the goals have been determined, the next step is to match each reader to the right texts at the right time, as much as is possible. It is also important to provide experiences that create the desire to read and reflect on their own as well as during the instructional experience and to support access to a wide range of potentially interesting books. The right books are interesting, well written, readable, and historically accurate. Further, they stretch and teach, connect to curriculum, show diversity of all kinds, are visually interesting and informative, and (whenever possible) provide opportunities for students to draw on their background knowledge and experiences.

Literature-based content units frequently incorporate literature from diverse genres. In addition, it is important to try and balance different perspectives and different reading levels when selecting unit books. An immigration unit might include historical fiction, contemporary realistic fiction, biography, informational books, poetry, memoirs, and oral history. Reading in any of these genres is likely to stimulate children's questions about immigration, yet books from each diverse genre are likely to make their own special contributions to children's learning. For example, works of historical fiction and contemporary realistic fiction provide the drama of human experience. Hence, these particular genres are especially likely to help children develop historical empathy, especially when the book's protagonist is a child. Oral histories allow

The Arrival (Scholastic)

children to hear the voices of actual immigrants, and informational trade books provide answers to many of the questions students raise about immigration. Shaun Tan has even written a fantasy in graphic novel format entitled *The Arrival* (2006) that explores the immigrant experience. In addition, because immigration stories (particularly contemporary ones) can be found across multiple cultural groups, they can likely provide both windows and mirrors for students to "see" and to "take perspective" and "empathize" with various characters in different immigrant circumstances.

In seeking selections for literature-based content units, you can use the lists of recommended books found in this text. It is likely that you will also need to turn to various book selection aids to locate unit books. *Book Links*, a publication of the American Library Association, is an especially helpful tool for identifying literature for content area units.

There are also Web-based resources that are freely accessible or by subscription. In looking at immigration from a historical perspective, teachers may find it particularly interesting to include primary source materials in their units. Though these materials are increasingly available through digital archives such as the Library of Congress, teachers may have to modify the material for elementary-aged students in order to make it more accessible (Wineburg and Martin, 2009). Of course, immigration is by no means a historical phenomenon. Today the news is filled with real-life stories of refugees and immigrants from around the world, so no immigration unit would be complete without drawing on digital and print news sources as well.

Don't Miss . . .
Books to Include in a Unit on Immigration

Inside Out and Back Again by Thanhhai Lai

Junk Man's Daughter by Sonia Levitin

La Mariposa by Francisco Jiménez

The Matchbox Diary by Paul Fleischman

West of the Moon by Margi Preus

My Name Is Sangoel by Karen Williams

Home of the Brave by Katherine Applegate

Immigrant Kids by Russell Freedman

I Was Dreaming to Come to America by Veronica Lawlor

My Name Is Jorge: On Both Sides of the River by Jane Medina

Unit Structure

One organizational format recommended by educators is literature-based inquiry units. Nancy Roser and Susan Keehn (2002) recommend a plan for developing such units for social studies instruction. The units they describe are organized into three phases, with each phase lasting approximately two weeks, although these times can be modified to accommodate unit goals and students' interests. During phase 1, students are involved in a whole-class read-aloud of a chapter book. In looking at the immigration experience from an historical perspective, a good read-aloud choice might be Karen Hesse's *Letters from Rifka* (1992), the story of a twelve-year-old girl who travels alone from Europe to Ellis Island. Frances Temple's *Grab Hands and Run* (1995) is a more contemporary immigration story about a family attempting to reach Canada in order to escape violence in El Salvador.

During phase 2 of the inquiry unit, students choose to join one of three or four small literature circles to read books that further explore the topic. In an immigration unit, phase 2 could be organized in different ways. All the literature circles might read chapter books that explore immigrants' experiences once they arrive to their new land. The teacher could select books of different difficulty levels to accommodate the varied reading abilities that are likely to be represented in a class. Possible choices for literature circles include Laurence Yep's *Dragon's Gate* (1993), a story of Chinese laborers working to build the transcontinental railroad across the United States. *Return to Sender* (2010) by Julia Alvarez has a contemporary setting. Alvarez's book is told from two perspectives—that of Mari whose father is an undocumented migrant laborer on a Vermont farm, and that of Tyler, the son of the farmer who befriends Mari.

As an alternative, the teacher could form small literature circles that explore different facets of the topic. For example, one group might choose to continue the study of why people choose to leave their homeland. A second literature circle could explore the struggles immigrants so often face as they attempt to journey to a new land, and a third group might explore what it means to be an immigrant in a new land. These groups could read and discuss either a chapter book or various picture books. Literature circles could meet daily or several times a week. Because students read phase 2 books on their own, they can prepare to participate in their literature circle discussions by writing in journals while they are reading. The journal entries can, in turn, be used to launch and support small group discussions.

The purpose of phase 3 is to give students an opportunity to explore questions about the topics of study that emerged during the initial phases of the study. Phase 3 can be launched with students once again meeting as a whole class, this time to pose their questions. An instructional strategy such as K-W-L (Ogle, 1986) can be used at this point. During the first phase of K-W-L (what I *k*now), students brainstorm all that they have learned about the topic at hand (for example, immigration) while the teacher records what students know. During the next phase (what I *w*ant to know), students pose questions they still have about the topic under study, and the teacher records their questions on a chart. The final phase of K-W-L (what I *l*earned) occurs once the students have completed their research.

Inquiry charts can also be used to launch phase 3 of literature-based inquiry units. An inquiry chart lists students' questions in columns with spaces in which they can later record the answers they obtain from different sources (see Figure 5.5). Once students have posed questions that they want to explore, they can join small inquiry groups to research the questions that are of greatest interest to them.

During this final phase of a literature-based inquiry unit, students turn to a variety of sources to find answers to their questions. Certainly informational trade books are likely to be an especially important resource. However, other sources might include the Internet, newspapers, outside experts, and individuals who have personal experience with the topic. Especially when searching for the newest information regarding immigration or when searching for multimedia representations, a well-vetted Internet search can offer links to various sources of information.

Acquiring resources may be the greatest challenge teachers face in developing literature-based content units, and who better to turn to for support with this task than the school librarian? Patti Foerster, a Chicago public school librarian, has created a model for collaboration that involves the librarian not only in acquiring resources for units but also in participating in the planning and coteaching of the unit. Foerster's model appears in Figure 5.6.

Children's literature holds great potential for nurturing children's learning across the curriculum. Writers of diverse genres open the world for children, and as teachers integrate these treasures across the curriculum, they motivate children to explore their world.

Figure 5.5   Inquiry Chart for Recording Students' Questions

	Where do immigrants come from today?	Why do people come to America today?	Where do today's immigrants settle in America?	What work do immigrants do today?	How do immigrants become American citizens?
Immigrants by Martin Sandler					
Immigrant Kids by Russell Freedman					
Denied, Detained, Deported: Stories from the Dark Side of American Immigration by Ann Bausum					
Shutting out the Sky by Deborah Hopkinson					
Graphing Immigration by Andrew Solway					

■ LOOKING BEYOND

There is a wealth of children's literature available in today's market, and these books can be an invaluable resource for knowledgeable teachers. To ensure that teachers are positioned to take full advantage of the best of the world of children's literature as they plan learning experiences and create learning contexts for their students, we have provided foundational information about the nature of books written for children and about ways of connecting children and books. Yet the work of learning about literature for children never really ends. After all, each year publishers put forth thousands

Figure 5.6 APACA (Ask, Plan, Acquire, Co-teach, Assess) Collaborative Model

Ask—The librarian *asks* a colleague teacher to work collaboratively to enhance an existing unit of study.

Plan—The classroom teacher and the librarian *plan* during whatever blocks of time they can find to reformulate the unit to include information literacy components and other learning enhancements. The two also work to identify additional resources that should be added to the library collection to support this unit.

Acquire—The new resources are *acquired* for the school's library.

Co-teach—The collaborative unit is taught by the classroom teacher and the librarian. The *co-teaching* can be done by special arrangement with both individuals together with students, or it can be done in tandem when they each individually have the students in the classroom or the library.

Assess—Student products from the unit are *assessed* and, if possible, compared with products/results from previous years; the collaborative methodology used by the librarian and classroom teacher is also *assessed* for possible improvement.

of new books for children. So we hope that you will view this book as an introduction to the rich world of children's literature and that you will make a commitment to continually seek out books that will enrich children's experiences both in the classroom and beyond.

▪ RECOMMENDED BOOKS

Aardema, Verna. *Borreguita and the Coyote.* Illustrated by Petra Mathers. New York: Knopf, 1991. Coyote is determined to have Borreguita for lunch, but the little lamb proves too clever for Coyote. Picture book. Ages five through nine.

Agee, Jon. *It's Only Stanley.* New York: Dial, 2015. When the Wimbledon family is repeatedly awakened by their dog Stanley, they think he is merely doing necessary repairs around the house. Little do they know that Stanley is preparing for an interplanetary trip. Picture book. Ages five through eight.

Alvarez, Julia. *Return to Sender.* New York: Yearling, 2010. Fifth-grader Tyler Paquette's family is in danger of losing their farm in Vermont, so they hire the Cruz family from Mexico to help out. Narrated from the point of view of Tyler and Mari Cruz, also a fifth grader, the book explores the human side of immigration issues and the meaning of patriotism in America. Winner of the Pura Belpré Award. Ages ten through twelve.

Applegate, Katherine. *Home of the Brave.* New York: Feiwel and Friends, 2007. This novel in verse format features the story of a young Sudanese immigrant struggling to find a place for himself in America. Ages ten and older.

Barnett, Mac. *Billy Twitters and His Blue Whale Problem.* Illustrated by Adam Rex. New York: Disney-Hyperion, 2009. When Billy doesn't do his chores, his punishment—taking care of a blue whale—yields all sorts of complications. Picture book. Ages five through nine.

———. *Extra Yarn.* Illustrated by Jon Klassen. New York: Balzer & Bray, 2012. Annabelle's yarn box produces a seemingly endless supply of yarn, but only for someone willing to share. Picture book. Ages five through nine.

———. *Oh No! Not Again! (Or How I Built a Time Machine to Save History) (Or at Least My History Grade).* Illustrated by Dan Santat. New York: Disney-Hyperion, 2012. An incorrect answer on a history test motivates a young girl to travel back in time to make her answer right. Picture book. Ages six through ten.

———. *Sam and Dave Dig a Hole.* Illustrated by Jon Klassen. Somerville, MA: Candlewick, 2014. When Sam and Dave set out to dig a hole to find something spectacular, they seem to miss opportunity after opportunity—until they fall through the hole they have dug. Picture book. Ages five through eight.

———. *The Skunk.* Illustrated by Patrick McDonnell. New York: Roaring Brook, 2015. A man is desperate to escape the skunk that is stalking him. When he finally succeeds, the man finds himself wondering just what has happened to the skunk—and roles are suddenly reversed. Picture book. Ages six through ten.

Barrett, Judi. *Cloudy with a Chance of Meatballs.* Illustrated by Ron Barrett. New York: Atheneum, 1978. Storms of food fall from the sky in the town of Chew-and-Swallow. Picture book. Ages five through eight.

Bash, Barbara. *Ancient Ones: The World of the Old-Growth Douglas Fir.* Layton, UT: Gibbs Smith, 2002. Another book in Bash's Tree Tales series, the author explores the old-growth forests of the Pacific Northwest. Picture book. Ages six and older.

———. *Desert Giant: The World of the Saguaro Cactus.* San Francisco: Sierra Club, 1990. Bash describes the ecosystem of the saguaro cactus. Picture book. Ages six and older.

———. *Tree of Life: The World of the African Baobab.* San Francisco: Sierra Club, 1989. With lyrical language, the author documents the rich ecosystem of the African baobab tree. Picture book. Ages six and older.

———. *Urban Roosts.* San Francisco: Sierra Club, 1990. The author explores how birds that live in the city have adapted their nest-building habits to their urban environment. Picture book. Ages six and older.

Bausum, Ann. *Denied, Detained, Deported: Stories from the Dark Side of American Immigration.* Washington DC: National Geographic Children's Books, 2009. Bausum tells immigration stories from the darker side of America history. Ages eleven and older.

Becker, Aaron. *Journey.* Somerville, MA: Candlewick, 2013. A young girl confronts evil in this wordless adventure. Picture book. Ages eight through twelve.

Browne, Anthony. *Voices in the Park.* New York: Farrar Straus Giroux, 1998. A visit to a park is told from four perspectives in this postmodern picture book. Picture book. Ages eight through twelve.

Bulion, Leslie. *Random Body Parts: Gross Anatomy Riddles in Verse.* Atlanta, GA: Peachtree, 2015. This collection of witty verses about body parts is accompanied by illustrations. Ages seven through ten.

Cohn, Diana. *¡Sí, Se Puede!/Yes, We Can!* Illustrated by Francisco Delgado. El Paso, TX: Cinco Puntos Press, 2005. To fight for his mother's right to earn a living wage, Carlitos convinces his classmates join him in the janitors' strike. Picture book. Ages eight through twelve.

Coombs, Kate. *Water Sings Blue: Ocean Poems.* San Francisco: Chronicle, 2012. A collection of poems about the seashore. Ages five through eight.

dePaola, Tomie. *The Art Lesson.* New York: Putnam, 1989. Tommy is encouraged by his family to pursue his passion for art, but at school he encounters frustration until an understanding art teacher lends a helping hand. Picture book. Ages five through eight.

———. *Nana Upstairs & Nana Downstairs.* New York: Putnam, 1998. For young Tommy, Sundays were special, for that was when he visited his Nana Upstairs and Nana Downstairs. This is a story about family and remembering family. Picture book. Ages five through nine.

———. *Tom.* New York: Putnam, 1993. Tommy is named after his grandfather Tom, and together the two share memorable times. Picture book. Preschool through age eight.

———. *Watch out for the Chicken Feet in Your Soup.* New York: Little Simon, 1985. His old-fashioned Italian grandmother embarrasses Joey—until he begins to see her through the eyes of his friend. Picture book. Preschool through age eight.

Fleischman, Paul. *The Matchbox Diary*. Illustrated by Bagram Ibatoulline. Somerville, MA: Candlewick, 2013. An Italian American immigrant has stored special objects in matchboxes throughout his life, objects that represent a lifetime of experiences and memories. Picture book. Ages seven through eleven.

Floca, Brian. *Moonshot: The Flight of Apollo 11*. New York: Atheneum, 2009. This is a beautifully illustrated documentation of Apollo 11's historic mission. Picture book. Ages seven through ten.

Flood, Nancy Bo. *Cowboy Up! Ride the Navajo Rodeo*. Illustrated by Jan Sonnemair. Honesdale, PA: Wordsong, 2013. This collection of prose and free verse poetry conveys the sights and sounds of the rodeo. Ages eight through twelve.

Florian, Douglas. *Comets, Stars, the Moon, and Mars*. New York: Houghton, Mifflin, and Harcourt, 2007. Poetry about celestial bodies. Ages six and older.

———. *Dinothesaurus: Prehistoric Poems and Paintings*. New York: Simon & Schuster, 2009. Witty verses about a variety of dinosaurs. Ages six and older.

Freedman, Russell. *Immigrant Kids*. New York: Puffin, 1995. Through photographs and text, this book explores the experiences in America of immigrant children from Europe from the late nineteenth century through the early twentieth century. Ages eight through twelve.

Galdone, Paul. *The Monkey and the Crocodile: A Jataka Tale from India*. Boston: Houghton Mifflin, 1969. Monkey convinces crocodile that he shouldn't eat him until he returns to the tree to get his heart, which is, after all, the tastiest part of him. Picture book. Ages five through eight.

Gravett, Emily. *The Odd Egg*. New York: Simon & Schuster, 2009. All the birds have laid eggs, except for Duck, who *finds* an enormous egg. As their eggs begin to hatch, all the birds are proud mamas, but none is prouder than Duck, whose egg yields quite a surprise. Picture book. Ages five through eight.

Harrison, David L. *Now You See Them, Now You Don't: Poems about Creatures That Hide*. Watertown, MA: Charlesbridge, 2016. A collection of poetry about camouflage in nature. Ages seven through ten.

Hesse, Karen. *Letters from Rifka*. Henry Holt, 1992. Rifka writes about fleeing Russia and having to stay behind in Belgium when her family travels on to the United States. Ages nine through twelve.

Hoberman, Mary Ann, and Linda Winston. *The Tree That Time Built: A Celebration of Nature, Science, and Imagination*. Naperville, IL: Sourcebooks, 2009. A collection of poems about the mysteries of the natural world. Ages nine and older.

Holt, K. A. *House Arrest*. New York: Chronicle, 2016. A novel in verse about a good boy's hard-won path to redemption. Ages ten through fourteen.

Hopkinson, Deborah. *Shutting out the Sky*. New York: Orchard, 2003. This is a historical account of life in the tenements of New York between 1880 and 1924. Ages ten and older.

Hutchins, Pat. *The Doorbell Rang*. New York: Greenwillow, 1986. Two children see their portions of mom's freshly baked cookies dwindle as the doorbell rings and guests continue to arrive. Picture book. Ages five through eight.

Jiménez, Francisco. *La Mariposa*. Illustrated by Simon Silva. New York: Houghton Mifflin Harcourt, 2000. Learning to read in a new language initially seems impossibly challenging for the son of Mexican migrants. Picture book. Ages six through ten.

Kasza, Keiko. *My Lucky Day*. New York: Puffin, 2005. Mr. Fox thinks it is his lucky day when a pig knocks on his door. Picture book. Ages five through eight.

Krull, Kathleen. *Harvesting Hope: The Story of Cesar Chavez*. Illustrated by Yuyi Morales. New York: Houghton Mifflin Harcourt, 2003. This picture book biography tells the story of

César Chavez, who led the struggle for fair working conditions for Mexican American farmworkers. Picture book. Ages eight through twelve.

Lai, Thanhhai. *Inside Out and Back Again*. New York: HarperCollins, 2013. After her father goes missing during the Vietnam War, Hà and her family settle in Alabama where Hà faces the insensitivity of her classmates but finds support from a kind teacher. Ages ten and older.

Latham, Irene. *Dear Wandering Wildebeest: And Other Poems from the Water Hole*. Brookfield, CT: Millbrook/Lerner, 2014. This collection of poetry celebrates animals of the African watering hole. Ages six and older.

Lawlor, Veronica. *I Was Dreaming to Come to America*. New York: Puffin, 1995. This is a collection of excerpts from the oral histories of children and young adults that were collected as part of the Ellis Island Oral History Project. Ages eight through twelve.

Levitin, Sonia. *Junk Man's Daughter*. Illustrated by Guy Porfirio. Ann Arbor, MI: Sleeping Bear Press, 2007. A family finds that building a new life in America is not quite what they dreamed it would be. Picture book. Ages five through nine.

Lewis, J. Patrick, ed. *National Geographic Book of Nature Poetry*. Washington, DC: National Geographic, 2015. A collection of nature poetry. Ages six and older.

Long, Melinda. *How I Became a Pirate*. Illustrated by David Shannon. New York: Harcourt, 2003. When a pirate ship sailed by, Jeremy jumped at the chance to become a pirate, only to discover that it wasn't all that he dreamed it would be. Picture book. Ages four through eight.

Lunge-Larsen, Lise. *The Troll with No Heart in His Body and Other Tales of Trolls from Norway*. Illustrated by Betsy Bowen. Boston: Houghton Mifflin, 1999. This is a collection of troll tales from Norway. Accompanying illustrations are woodcuts. Ages seven through eleven.

Martin, Bill. *A Beasty Story*. Illustrated by Steven Kellogg. San Diego, CA: Harcourt, 1999. Four brave little mice cautiously enter a haunted house in pursuit of what *may* be a scary beast. Picture book. Ages five through seven.

McDermott, Gerald. *Coyote: A Trickster Tale from the American Southwest*. San Diego, CA: Harcourt, 1994. Coyote convinces the crows to teach him how to fly, and the crows agree. But when the crows grow tired of Coyote's boasting, they decide to teach him a lesson. Picture book. Ages five through eight.

————. *Zomo the Rabbit: A Trickster Tale from West Africa*. San Diego, CA: Harcourt, 1992. Zomo the rabbit is portrayed here wearing an African dashiki. Picture book. Ages five through eight.

McKissack, Patricia. *Flossie and the Fox*. Illustrated by Rachel Isadora. New York: Dial, 1986. Flossie turns the tables on Mr. Fox when he tries to get her basket of eggs. Picture book. Ages five through ten.

————. *A Million Fish . . . More or Less*. New York: Dragonfly, 1996. Inspired by the tall tales of his elders, Hugh Thomas embarks on his own outlandish adventure. Picture book. Ages five through eight.

McNaughton, Colin. *Suddenly!* New York: Houghton Mifflin Harcourt, 1998. It seems to be Preston Pig's lucky day as he repeatedly deviates from his plans, inadvertently avoiding the wolf that is stalking him. Picture book. Ages five through eight.

Medina, Jane. *My Name Is Jorge: On Both Sides of the River*. Illustrated by Fabricio Vanden Broeck. Honesdale, PA: Boyds Mill, 1999. These bilingual poems are packed with poignant moments in the life of a Mexican immigrant child. Ages nine through twelve.

Nolen, Jerdine. *Thunder Rose*. Illustrated by Kadir Nelson. New York: Houghton Mifflin Harcourt, 2007. An African American child born on a stormy night, Thunder Rose engages in exploits like facing down tornadoes. Picture book. Ages five through nine.

Paye, Won-Ldy, and Margaret H. Lippert. *Mrs. Chicken and the Hungry Crocodile*. New York: Square Fish, 2014. Illustrated by Julie Paschkis. In this folktale from Liberia, Mrs. Chicken uses her wits to trick Crocodile into freeing her rather than eating her. Picture book. Ages five through eight.

Preus, Margi. *West of the Moon.* New York: Abrams, 2015. This story is a combination of a Norwegian fairy tale and an immigration story set in nineteenth-century Norway. Ages ten and older.

Rosen, Michael. *We're Going on a Bear Hunt.* Illustrated by Helen Oxenbury. New York: Margaret K. McElderry, 1989. A surprise awaits a family that goes on a bear hunt. Picture book. Ages five through eight.

Sandler, Martin W. *Immigrants.* New York: HarperCollins, 1995. Through text and photographs, this book explores immigration to the United States in the late nineteenth century and early twentieth century, with a particular focus on European immigrants. Ages nine through twelve.

Santat, Dan. *The Adventures of Beekle: The Unimaginary Friend.* New York: Little Brown, 2014. Beekle, born on an island for imaginary friends, is waiting for a child to imagine him. When it doesn't happen, he sets off to find such a friend. Picture book. Ages five through eight.

Scieszka, Jon. *The True Story of the Three Little Pigs.* Illustrated by Lane Smith. New York: Puffin, 1996. From behind jailhouse bars, the wolf tells his version of what happened to the three little pigs. Picture book. Ages six through ten.

Sendak, Maurice. *In the Night Kitchen.* New York: Harper, 1970. Mickey awakens to the noise of the night kitchen and embarks on a fantastic trip in which he becomes the hero of the night kitchen. Picture book. Ages five through eight.

———. *Outside over There.* New York: Harper, 1981. When her baby sister is stolen by the goblins, Ida goes "outside over there" to confront the goblins and rescue her sister. Picture book. Ages five through eight.

———. *Where the Wild Things Are.* New York: HarperCollins, 1963. Sent to his room, Max travels to where the Wild Things are and becomes king of all Wild Things. Picture book. Ages five through eight.

Sidman, Joyce. *Ubiquitous: Celebrating Nature's Survivors.* Illustrated by Becky Prange. Boston: Houghton Mifflin, 2010. Each poem about a creature that avoided extinction is accompanied by related prose paragraph. Ages six and older.

Solway, Andrew. *Graphing Immigration.* Chicago: Heinemann Library, 2010. This volume examines the costs and benefits of immigrants to the United States. Ages eleven and older.

Souhami, Jessica. *The Leopard's Drum: An Asante Tale from West Africa.* New York: Little, Brown, 1995. Humble tortoise outwits the boastful leopard to obtain the leopard's drum for the Sky-God. Picture book. Ages five through eight.

Stanley, Diane. *Raising Sweetness.* Illustrated by G. Brian Karas. New York: Putnam, 1999. Sweetness and the other children know that they are lucky to have been adopted by the sheriff. Still, the sheriff's cooking and housekeeping leave something to be desired, so Sweetness sets out to find a solution to their problems. Picture book. Ages five through eight.

———. *Saving Sweetness.* Illustrated by G. Brian Karas. New York: Putnam, 1996. When the orphan Sweetness runs away from the orphanage, the sheriff sets out to save her, but Sweetness doesn't want to have anything to do with being saved. Picture book. Ages five through eight.

Stead, Philip. *Special Delivery.* Illustrated by Matthew Cordell. New York: Roaring Brook, 2015. Sadie tries every imaginable way to deliver an elephant to her aunt, who "could really use the company." Picture book. Ages five through eight.

Steig, William. *Doctor De Soto.* New York: Farrar, 1982. When Doctor De Soto, a mouse dentist, agrees to help a fox with a toothache, the mouse finds he must outfox the fox. Picture book. Ages six through ten.

Stevens, Janet. *Anansi Goes Fishing*. New York: Holiday, 1992. The tables are turned when Anansi sets out to trick his friend into doing all the work. Picture book. Ages five through eight.

———. *Tops and Bottoms*. San Diego, CA: Harcourt, 1995. Industrious and clever, Hare tricks lazy Bear by wheeling and dealing in the tops and bottoms of vegetables. Picture book. Ages five through eight.

Stevens, Janet, and Susan Stevens Crummel. *The Great Fuzz Frenzy*. Illustrated by Janet Stevens. San Diego, CA: Harcourt, 2005. A tennis ball that lands in the middle of a prairie dog town causes quite a commotion. Picture book. Ages five through nine.

Tan, Shaun. *The Arrival*. New York: Scholastic, 2006. This fantasy in graphic novel format explores two facets of the immigration experience—the journey to the new land and experiences in the new land. Ages nine and older.

Teague, Mark. *Dear Mrs. LaRue*. New York: Scholastic, 2002. A dog is sent to an obedience school that seems more like a resort, yet in letters home, he describes it as a prison. Visual elements contrast the implied story against the real. Picture book. Ages five through nine.

Temple, Frances. *Grab Hands and Run*. New York: Orchard, 1995. This is the story about the flight of a Salvadoran refugee family from their homeland through the United States to Canada. Ages ten through thirteen.

Thimmesh, Catherine. *Team Moon: How 400,000 People Landed Apollo 11 on the Moon*. Boston: Houghton Mifflin Harcourt, 2006. This is the behind-the-scenes story of the historic Apollo 11 mission. Ages eight through fourteen.

Tonatiuh, Duncan. *Separate Is Never Equal*. New York: Abrams Books for Young Readers, 2014. Seven years before the *Brown vs. the Board of Education* ruling, the Mendez family successfully fought to desegregate schools in California. Picture book. Ages eight through twelve.

Trent, Tererai. *The Girl Who Buried Her Dreams in a Can*. Illustrated by Jan Spivey Gilchrist. New York: Viking, 2015. This autobiography tells of a young Zimbabwean girl who realized her dream of achieving an education and bringing education to the children in her village. Picture book. Ages eight through twelve.

Van Allsburg, Chris. *Jumanji*. Houghton Mifflin, 1981. When two siblings play a jungle board game, they find themselves swept up in the chaos of a real jungle. Picture book. Ages six through ten.

———. *The Polar Express*. Boston: Houghton Mifflin, 1985. A boy boards a train headed for the North Pole where Santa selects him to receive the first gift of Christmas. Picture book. Ages six through ten.

———. *The Stranger*. Boston: Houghton Mifflin, 1986. Mysterious changes in the weather seem to accompany the stranger who comes to stay on the Bailey's farm. Picture book. Ages seven through eleven.

———. *The Sweetest Fig*. Boston: Houghton Mifflin, 1993. A woman give Monsieur Bibot figs that she promises will make his dreams come true. Picture book. Ages seven through eleven.

———. *The Wretched Stone*. Boston: Houghton Mifflin, 1991. The sailors aboard the *Rita Anne* are transfixed by the mysterious glowing stone and are slowly transformed into apes. Picture book. Ages eight through twelve.

Vardell, Sylvia, and Janet Wong, eds. *The Poetry Friday Anthology for Celebrations (Children's Edition): Holiday Poems for the Whole Year in English and Spanish*. Princeton, NJ: Pomelo Books, 2015. Vardell, a children's literature expert, and Wong, a noted children's poet, offer this volume as one of several in their well-received initiative to help teachers find a regular place for poetry in the school week. Ages five through ten.

————. *The Poetry of Science: The Poetry Friday Anthology for Science for Kids.* Princeton, NJ: Pomelo Books, 2015. A collection of poems by various poets about wide-ranging science topics. Ages six and older.

Wiesner, David. *Max and Art.* New York: Clarion, 2010. Max and Art are both painters, but painters whose styles are quite diverse. Picture book. Ages six through ten.

————. *The Three Pigs.* New York: Clarion, 2001. A postmodern telling of the story of the three little pigs, interweaving various other familiar tales. Picture book. Ages six through ten.

Willems, Mo. *Don't Let the Pigeon Drive the Bus!* New York: Hyperion, 2003. A very persistent pigeon uses a full range of tactics to try and get to drive the bus. Picture book. Ages five through eight.

————. *That Is Not a Good Idea!* New York: Balzer & Bray, 2013. A surprise awaits a hungry fox that invites a goose to dinner. Picture book. Ages six through ten.

Williams, Karen. *My Name Is Sangoel.* Illustrated by Khadra Mohammed. Grand Rapids, MI: Eerdmans, 2009. Sangoel, a refugee from Sudan, comes up with a clever way to ensure that his new classmates in the United States learn to pronounce the name of which he is so proud. Picture book. Ages seven through ten.

Winter, Jeannette. *Wangari's Trees of Peace: A True Story from Africa.* New York: Houghton Mifflin Harcourt, 2008. Upon returning to Kenya from America, Wangari Maathai discovered that the verdant land she remembered from her youth had been stripped of trees. Thus began Wangari's lifetime of work as an environmentalist, work that was recognized internationally when she received a Nobel Prize. Picture book. Ages six through ten.

Yep, Laurence. *Dragon's Gate.* New York: HarperCollins, 1993. In 1837, Chinese men came to the United States and found work digging and dynamiting tunnels through the Sierra Mountains in order to build a railroad to cross the nation. Ages eleven and older.

Yorinks, Arthur. *Hey, Al!* Illustrated by Richard Egielski. New York: Farrar, 1986. Al the janitor and his dog hardly hesitate when offered a better life on a paradise island, but this paradise is not all it promises to be. Picture book. Ages seven through eleven.

▪ REFERENCES

Akerson, Valarie L. "Teaching Science When Your Principal Says, 'Teach Language Arts.'" In *Teaching Teachers: Bringing First-rate Science to the Elementary Classroom.* Arlington, VA: National Science Teachers Association Press, 2002.

Bloem, Patricia L., and Anthony L. Manna. "A Chorus of Questions: Readers Respond to Patricia Polacco." *The Reading Teacher* 52 (1999): 802–8.

Carle, Eric. *The Art of Eric Carle.* New York: Philomel, 1996.

————. *You Can Make a Collage.* New York: Klutz, 1998.

Castek, Jill. "Implementing Dynamic and Interactive Science Instruction to Meet the Common Core." Keynote speech at the Regional National Science Teachers Association conference, Portland, OR, 2013.

Eric Carle: Picture Writer. Directed by Rawn Fulton. Produced by Searchlight Films. New York: Philomel, 1993.

Farest, Cindy, and Carolyn Miller. "Children's Insights into Literature: Using Dialogue Journals to Invite Literary Response." In *Examining Central Issues in Literacy Research, Theory, and Practice*, ed. Donald J. Leu and Charles K. Kinzer, 271–78. Oak Creek, WI: National Reading Conference, 1993.

Galda, Lee, and Lauren Aimonette Liang. "Literature As Experience or Looking for Facts: Stance in the Classroom." *Reading Research Quarterly* 38 (2003): 268–75.

Levstik, Linda. "A Gift of Time: Children's Historical Fiction." In *Children's Literature in the Classroom: Weaving Charlotte's Web*, ed. Janet Hickman and Bernice E. Cullinan, 135–45. Needham Heights, MA: Christopher-Gordon, 1989.

Martinez, Miriam G., and Nancy L. Roser. "Children's Responses to Literature." *Handbook of Research in Teaching the English Language Arts*, eds. James Flood, Diane Lapp, Julie Jensen, and James Squire, 799–813. 2nd ed. Mahwah, NJ: Lawrence Erlbaum, 2003.

McTighe, Jay, and Grant Wiggins. *Essential Questions: Opening Doors to Student Understanding.* Alexandria, VA: Association of Supervision & Curriculum Development, 2013.

Moss, Joy. *Focus Units in Literature: A Handbook for Elementary School Teachers.* Urbana, IL: National Council of Teachers of English, 1984.

———. *Using Literature in the Middle Grades: A Thematic Approach.* Norwood, MA: Christopher-Gordon, 1994.

———. "Using the Focus Unit to Enhance Children's Response to Literature." *Language Arts* 55 (1978): 482–88.

Nakamura, Joyce, ed. *Something about the Author.* Farmington Hills, MI: Gale Group, 1998.

Ogle, Donna. "K-W-L: A Teaching Model That Develops Active Reading of Expository Text." *The Reading Teacher* 39 (1986): 564–70.

Peterson, Ralph, and Maryann Eeds. *Grand Conversations: Literature Groups in Action.* New York: Scholastic-TAB, 1990.

Pinterest.com/PomeloBooks. www.pinterest.com/pomelobooks.

Pomelo Books. http://pomelobooks.com/pocket-poems-cards.

Roser, Nancy, James V. Hoffman, and Cindy Farest. "Language, Literature, and At-risk Children." *The Reading Teacher* 43 (1990): 554–59.

Roser, Nancy L., James V. Hoffman, Cindy Farest, and Linda D. Labbo. "Language Charts: A Record of Story Time Talk." *Language Arts* 69 (1992): 44–52.

Roser, Nancy, and Susan Keehn. "Fostering Thought, Talk, and Inquiry by Linking Literature with Social Studies." *The Reading Teacher* 55 (2002): 416–27.

Short, Kathy G. "Intertextuality: Searching for Patterns That Connect." In *Literacy Research, Theory, and Practice: Views from Many Perspectives: Forty-first Yearbook of the National Reading Conference*, ed. Charles K. Kinzer and Donald J. Leu, 187–97. Oak Creek, WI: National Reading Conference, 1992.

Silvey, Anita, ed. *Children's Books and Their Creators.* Boston: Houghton Mifflin, 1995.

Sipe, L. R. "The Construction of Literary Understanding by First and Second Graders in Oral Response to Picture Storybook Read Alouds." *Reading Research Quarterly* 35 (2000): 252–75.

Sipe, Lawrence R. "Individual Literary Response Styles of First and Second Graders." In *Forty-seventh Yearbook of the National Reading Conference*, ed. Timothy Shanahan and Flora V. Rodriguez-Brown, 76–89. Oak Creek, WI: National Reading Conference, 1998.

Subject Guide to Children's Books in Print: A Subject Index to Books for Children and Young Adults. Amenia, NY: Grey House Publishing, 2012.

Tomlinson, Carl M., Michael O. Tunnell, and Donald J. Richgels. "The Content and Writing in Textbooks and Trade Books." In *The Story of Ourselves: Teaching History through Children's Literature*, ed. Michael O. Tunnell and Richard Ammon, 51–62. Portsmouth, NH: Heinemann, 1993.

Vardell, Sylvia M. "Classroom Connections: Connecting Science and Poetry." *Book Links* 23 (2013): 2.

———. *The Poetry Teacher's Book of Lists.* Princeton, NJ: Pomelo Books, 2012.

Vardell, Sylvia M., and Janet Wong. "Observe, Explain, Connect." *Science and Children* 51 (2014): 31–35.

———. "The Symbiosis of Science and Poetry." *Children and Libraries* 13 (2015): 15–18.

Vardell, Sylvia M., and Janet Wong, eds. *The Poetry Friday Anthology for Science: Poems for the School Year Integrating Science, Reading, and Language Arts.* Princeton, NJ: Pomelo Books, 2014.

Walmsley, Sean A. "Reflections on the State of Elementary Literature Instruction." *Language Arts* 69 (1992): 508–14.

Wiggins, Grant, and Jay McTighe. *Understanding by Design.* Alexandria, VA: Association for Supervision and Curriculum Development, 1998.

Wineburg, Sam, and Daisy Martin. "Tampering with History: Adapting Primary Sources for Struggling Readers." *Social Education,* 73 (2009): 212–16.

Yolen, Jane. "How Basic Is SHAZAM?" *Language Arts* 54 (1977): 645–51.

∎ RESOURCES

Bickford, John H., and Cynthia Rich. "The Historical Representation of Thanksgiving within Primary- and Intermediate-level Children's Literature." *Journal of Children's Literature* 41 (2015): 5–21.

Bickford, John H., and Lieren N. Schuette. "Trade Books Historical Representation of the Black Freedom Movement, Slavery through Civil Rights." *Journal of Children's Literature* 42 (2016): 20–43.

Buss, K., and L. Karnowski. *Reading and Writing Literary Genres.* Newark, NJ: International Reading Association, 2000.

Lattimer, H. *Thinking through Genre: Units of Study in Reading and Writing Workshops 4–12.* Portland, ME: Stenhouse, 2003.

Moss, Joy F. *Using Literature in the Middle Grades: A Thematic Approach.* Norwood, MA: Christopher-Gordon, 1994.

Silva, Cecilia, and Esther L. Delgado-Larocco. "Facilitating Learning through Interconnections: A Concept Approach to Core Literature Units." *Language Arts* 70 (1993): 469–74.

Smith, J. Lea, and Holly Johnson. "Models for Implementing Literature in Content Studies." *The Reading Teacher* 48 (1994): 198–208.

Tunnell, Michael O., and Richard Ammon. *The Story of Ourselves: Teaching History through Children's Literature.* Portsmouth, NH: Heinemann, 1993.

Zarnowski, Myra, and Arlene F. Gallagher. *Children's Literature and Social Studies: Selecting and Using Notable Books in the Classroom.* Dubuque, IA: Kendall/Hunt, 1993.

∎ WANT TO KNOW MORE?

1. Teachers typically initiate literary study with at least some ideas about the types of links that they want children to discover among the books featured in the unit. However, children are very capable of discovering connections on their own—sometimes connections their teachers have not seen. Gather together a set of related books and share them with children. For example, you might choose Cinderella variants such as *Sootface, The Egyptian Cinderella, Cendrillon,* and *Mufaro's Beautiful Daughters.* After reading the books to the children, ask them to

204 ■ CHAPTER 5

brainstorm ways in which the stories are similar and ways in which they are different. In what ways did the children extend your own thinking about the books? Following the literary study of cultural variants of Cinderella, read several versions that parody Cinderella. Humorous versions, like *Bigfoot Cinderrrrrella* and *Cinder Edna* maintain the elements unique to Cinderella—but with a twist.

2. Units in which books are only loosely linked are less likely to evoke children's most insightful thinking. One way of helping to ensure that the books you have selected for a unit are linked in meaningful ways is by creating a language chart that might be used with the books. Working with a group of peers, select a theme that could be explored through literature. Topics such as "celebrations," "journeys," or "courage" offer rich opportunities for thematic study. Gather books that you believe might be appropriate for use in a unit and together design a language chart to use with the books. Are the connections you identified significant ones? Go ahead and complete the chart with your peers. This is a good way of checking to make sure that the questions you posed on the chart are likely to elicit the kinds of responses you envision.

Index

Page numbers in italics refer to images.

Aardema, Verna, 101
Agee, John, 178
Agostin, Marjorie, 115
Alger, Horatio, 123
Allen, Judy, 134, 162
Alvarez, Julia, 136, 192
American Library Association, 191
Anderson, M. T., 42
APACA (Ask, Plan, Acquire, Co-teach, Assess), 195
Applebee, Arthur, 14–15
Are You a Spider? (Allen), 134, 162
Aronson, Marc, 7–8, 54
The Arrival, 191
Art and Max (Wiesner), 64
Ask, Plan, Acquire, Co-teach, Assess. *See* APACA
audiobooks, 89. *See also* digital books
AudioBoom, 93
authors: on characters, 123–24; language chart for, 180; preparation for, 93; role play by, 134; teachers on, 93; visits by, 93–94

Barnett, Mac, 179–80
Barry, Anne, 13
Battle, Jennifer, 94–95
Bear Has a Story to Tell (Stead, P.), 35, *35*, 44–45
Because of Winn Dixie (DiCamillo), 33–35, 118–19, 122, 126–27, 133
Becker, Aaron, 29
Becoming a Nation of Readers, 94
"Bed in Summer" (Stevenson), 158

Beebe, Katy, 79
Berger, Gilda, *162*
Berger, Melvin, *162*
bilingual literature, 18
Bingham, Kelly, 43
Bishop, Nic, 54
Bishop, Rudine Sims, 17–18, 87, 136
Black Ants and Buddhists (Cowhey), 121
Blackout (Rocco), 43
Black Panther Party, 116
Blackwood, Gary, 32
Bloem, Patricia, 179
Blubber (Blume), 130
Blume, Judy, 130
Bomb: The Race to Build—and Steal—the World's Most Dangerous Weapon (Sheinkin), 52
book covers, *69*; of *Freedom in Congo Square,* 68; as introduction, 68
books: animals in, 161; awards for, 84; circular, 174; in classrooms, 1–2; connecting children to, 194–95; devices compared to, 1; gender in, 136–37; immersion in, 31; joke, 83; magic in, 174; multicultural, 136–37; personal connections to, 2–3; post, 164–65; predictable, 86–87; question-and-answer, 161–62; recommendations for, 90, 91–92; settings of, 117; textbooks, 186–87; unit, 175, 182–83. *See also* chapter books; digital books; picture books
bookshelves, 81
Bradley, Kimberly Brubaker, 48
The Breadwinner, 114
Brother Hugo and the Bear (Beebe), 79

Brown Bear, Brown Bear, What Do You See? (Martin), 86
Browne, Anthony, 4, 96
Brown Girl Dreaming (Woodson), 29
Budhos, Marina, 7–8
Burleigh, Robert, 35–36
Buzzeo, Toni, 84
Byrd, Robert, 53

Can It Rain Cats and Dogs? (Berger, G. and Berger, M.), *162*
"Can You Dig That Crazy Music?," 156
cartoons, 124
chapter books, 84; beginning, 87; importance of, 47–48; potential of, 48–49; series of, 84–85; structure of, 48
characters: actions of, 119; authors on, 123–24; comparison of, 125; in fiction, 33–34; goals of, 125; introduction to, 125; in picture books, 46; questions of, 119–20, 121, 122, 125; in read-alouds, 97; relations of, 119–20; resolution for, 125; roles of, 121–23, 124; sense of, 120–21; understanding, 118–24
Chasing Redbird (Creech), 11–12
Chavez, Cesar, 88
Christie, R. Gregory, 69–77
classroom libraries, 80–82; stocking, 83–89
classrooms: books in, 1–2; literature-rich, 79–94; reading promotion in, 90–92; reading workshops in, 90–91
Cleary, Beverly, 48
cliffhanger endings, 162
close reading, 140–41
Cochran-Smith, Marilyn, 12
Colman, Penny, 83–84
"Come Play Catch," 155
coming-of-age stories, 128
Commission on Reading, 94
Common Core State Standards, 2, 13, 140, 159
A Company of Fools (Ellis), 95
constructivist theory, 20
content units, 173, 187, 190
Cowhey, Mary, 121
Crazy Like a Fox: A Simile Story (Leedy), 159
creative writing, 152–53
Creech, Sharon, 11–12

Creepy Carrots! (Reynolds), 92
Creepy Creatures and Other Cucuys (Garza), 100
"The Cremation of Sam McGee" (Service), 157–58
cultural differences. *See* diversity
cultural perspective, 17–20
culture: impact of, 17; in literature, 87, 89; teachers on, 87, 89
curriculum: literature across, 186–94; poetry in, 188–90
Curtis, Christopher Paul, 3–4, 113–15

DEAR (drop everything and read), 90
Dear Mrs. LaRue: Letters from Obedience School (Teague), 42–43, 84, *85*
DeNicolo, Christina, 18
dePaola, Tomie, 41, 179, 181
devices, 1
DiCamillo, Kate, 33–35, 85, 92, 118–19, 122, 126–27, 133
Dickinson, Emily, 159
digital books, 88; e-books, 51; as fiction, 49–51; scanned PDFs, 49–50. *See also* International Children's Digital Library; Overdrive; transmedia storytelling
directed reading: as activity, 137–39; as predictions, 139–40; steps of, 139–40; as thinking activity, 139–40
directed reading-thinking activity with predictions (DRTA/P), 139–40
discussions: academic controversy, 145–47; activities for, 144; calling time during, 147; corners for, 144–45; discussion web, 145, 146; "Save the Last Word for Me," 148; seating charts for, 144; shared, 143–44; for students, 146–47; of text, 163–64; value line of, 147–48
diversity: in children's literature, 18–20; of meaning making, 13–22; in traditional literature, 177
The Donkey Lady Fights La Llorona and Other Stories (Garza), 100
Dragon's Gate (Yep), 192
Draper, Sharon, 64
drop everything and read. *See* DEAR
DRTA/P. *See* directed reading-thinking activity with predictions
dual-entry diaries, 151, 152

Each Little Bird That Sings (Wiles), 65
e-books. *See* digital books
Echo (Ryan), 5
educators, 13–14. *See also* teachers
Electric Ben (Byrd), 53
The Elephant Scientist (O'Connell and Jackson), 51
Ellis, Deborah, 8, 95, 114, 128
English: language learners of, 151; responses to, 151
envisionment, 7–8; going beyond, 10; objectification of, 9–10. *See also* literary responses
Erskine, Kathryn, 123, 129, 135
Esperanza Rising (Ryan), 114–15, 135, *135*
Estes, Eleanor, 130

Farest, Cindy, 175
Feed (Anderson), 42
fiction: chapter books, 47–49; characters in, 33–34; contemporary realistic, 39; digital books, 49–51; fantasy, 40–42; formats of, 42–51; graphic novels, 49; high fantasy, 42; historical, 39–40; literary elements of, 31–36; peritext of, 43–44; picture books, 42–47; plot of, 33; science, 42; settings in, 32; style of, 35–36; subgenres of, 36–42; theme of, 35; traditional literature, 36–39; trickster tales, 41; writing responses to, 150–53
first chapters, 7–8
Fitzhugh, Louise, 130
"five finger rule," 91
Fleming, Candace, 4, 29, 98
Flight (Burleigh), 35–36
Flora and Ulysses (DiCamillo), 84
Foerster, Patti, 193
Forever (Blume), 130
Franklin, Benjamin, 53
Franquiz, Maria, 18
Freedom in Congo Square (Weatherford), 66; book cover of, 68; illustrations of, 67, *69–77*; reading of, 67–68; research of, 67; text of, 67
Freud, Sigmund, 118
Frye, Northrop, 113
Funke, Cornelia, 84

Gardiner, John Reynolds, 122
Garza, Xavier, 100
genre units, 177
Giblin, James C., 131
The Giblin Guide to Writing for Children (Giblin), 131
Giff, Patricia Reilly, 9
Gold, Harry, 52
Gorbachev, Valerie, 88
Grab Hands and Run (Temple), 128
graphic novels, 49
Great Books Foundation, 143
The Great Fuzz Frenzy (Stevens and Crummel), 87
Greenlaw, Jean, 42

Harriet the Spy (Fitzhugh), 130
Harry Potter and the Sorcerer's Stone (J. K. Rowling), 135
Harvesting Hope: The Story of Cesar Chavez (Krull), 87, 88
Heller, Mary, 13
Henderson, Edmund, 99
Hernandez, Moises, 87–88
heroes, 88
Hickman, Janet, 14–15, 79–80, 91
Hoberman, Mary Ann, 87
Hoffman, James, 94–95, 175
Holes (Sachar), 7, 129, 130, 135
Holm, Jennifer, 124
"Hope Is the Thing with Feathers" (Dickinson), 159
Hopkinson, Deborah, 51–52, 54
How to Write a Children's Book and Get It Published (Seuling), 131
Humphries, Tudor, 162
The Hundred Dresses (Estes), 130
Hutchins, Pat, 43

If You Lived at the Time of the Great San Francisco Earthquake (Levine), 162
I Lived on Butterfly Hill (Agostin), 115
illustrations: dancing in, 74; emotions in, 73; of *Freedom in Congo Square*, 67, *69–77*; music in, 76; of slavery, *70–77*; text in, 76–77; tools for, 44
illustrators. *See* authors
Inkheart (Funke), 84
inquiry chart, 194

instructional strategies, 165
International Children's Digital Library, 50
International Reading Association, 85
Interpreting Literature with Children (Wolf), 122
"interpretive community," 150–51
"interpretive questions," 143
intertextuality, 5–6
In the Night Kitchen (Sendak), 174
Into the Unknown: How Great Explorers Found Their Way by Land, Sea, and Air (Ross), 53
"Is The Moon Tired?" (Rossetti), 156–57
It's Only Stanley (Agee), 178
I Want My Hat Back (Klassen), 87

Jackson, Donna, 51
Janeczko, Paul, 55
Jenkins, Steve, 81, 161
Johnson, Jen, 9
Journey (Becker), 29
Journey to Jo'burg (Naidoo), 128

Kagan, Spencer, 145
Kamberelis, George, 12
Kamishibai Man (Say), 99
Kasza, Keiko, 87
Keehn, Susan, 192
Kerley, Barbara, 95
A Kick in the Head (Janeczko), 55
kindergarten: commentary from, 175; reading in, 86–87
King, Coretta Scott, 69
Klassen, Jon, 87
Krull, Kathleen, 87
Kurtz, Jane, 99

Lai, Thanhhà, 9
Langer, Judith, 6–7, 11–12, 29
language arts, 2–3
language charts, 180, 182, 185–86
Language to Literacy program, 175
Last Stop on Market Street (Peña), 96
Leedy, Loreen, 159
Let's Say Hi to Friends Who Fly! (Willem), 86
Levine, Ellen, 162
libraries. *See* classroom libraries
library centers: bookshelves in, 81; characteristics of, 80; designing of, 80–83; materials in, 82; organizational systems in, 82; organization of, 110–11; seating in, 81; selection for, 84; variety in, 82–83. *See also* classroom libraries
Lin, Grace, 96, *97*
The Lincolns: A Scrapbook Look at Abraham and Mary (Fleming), 4
Lindbergh, Charles, 35–36
Listen, Slowly (Lai), 9
literary responses, 11
literary units, 173; activities for, 184, 186; author/illustration units, 178–81; devices of, 181; elements of, 181; genre units, 176–78; goals of, 190–91; organizing, 175–76, 182–86; planning, 175–76; power of, 174–75; selection of, 191–92, 204; structure of, 183–84, 192–94; thematic units of, 181–82; trickster tales, 177; types of, 176, 176–82; visual devices of, 181
Little Bee Books, 69
"Little Red Riding Hood," 36, 39
López-Robertson, Julia, 17
Love, Ruby Lavender (Wiles), 10, 12
Ludwig, Trudy, 130
Lunge-Larsen, Lise, 177
Luria, Alexandr, 120

MacDonald, Margaret Read, 101
MacLachlan, Patricia, 48
magic, 174
making connections, 5–6
Maniac Magee (Spinelli), 135–36
Manna, Anthony, 179
Marino, Gianna, 33
Martin, Bill, Jr., 86
Martínez-Roldán, Carmen, 17–18
Martin's Big Words: The Life of Dr. Martin Luther King, Jr. (Rappaport), 87
The Marvels (Selznick), 1
Maus (Spiegelman), 49
McCall, Guadalupe Garcia, 128–29
McGinley, William, 12
McTighe, Jay, 175, 190–91
meaning making: diversity of, 13–22; literary, 13–22; model of, 6–10; research on, 11–13; social perspective on, 16–17; textual perspective on, 21–22
Miller, Donalyn, 83

Milne, A. A., 94
Mockingbird (Erskine), 123, 129, 135
Moon Over Manifest (Vanderpool), 8, 113–14, 118, 129, 133
morals: exploration of, 131; of students, 131
"Morning in Buffalo" (Stevenson), 158
Morrow, Lesley, 80
Moses: When Harriet Tubman Led Her People to Freedom (Weatherford), 88
Moss, Joy, 175
My Friend Rabbit (Rohmann), *44*
My Name Is Parvana (Ellis), 8
My Name Is Yoon (Recorvits), *10*

Naidoo, Beverley, 128
narration: first-person, 134–35; implied reader, 136–37; third-person, 135; third-person omniscient, 135–36
National Reading Panel, 150
Naylor, Phyllis Reynolds, 115–17, 120, 123, 132–33, 141, 142
Nico y los Lobos Feroces (Gorbachev), 88
Niño Wrestles the World (Macmillan), *86*
nonfiction, 31; benefits of, 160–61; children for, 161; contemporary, 161–63; definition of, 51; devices of, 161; experts on, 160–61; forms of, 161; graphic features of, 53; instructional strategies for, 163–65; organizational patterns in, 52–53; poetry, 54–56; structure of, 52, 159; style of, 52; subgenres of, 54–56; support tools of, 53; visual features of, 53

O'Callahan, Jay, 103
O'Connell, Caitlin, 51
Officer Buckle and Gloria, 42
Oh, No! (Fleming), 29, 98
One Cool Friend (Buzzeo), 84
One Crazy Summer (Williams-Garcia), 116–18
Orbis Pictus Award for Outstanding Nonfiction for Children, 84
organizational systems, 82
Outside over There (Sendak), 174
Overdrive, 89
Oyler, Celia, 13

Page, Robin, 81
Palacio, R. J., 116–19, 122–23, 132

Paley, Vivian, 12–13
Pantaleo, Sylvia, 46–47
Park, Barbara, 48
Parvana's Journey (Ellis), 128
Peña, Matt de la, 96
People, 118
peritext, 43–44, 97
picture books: action heroes in, 85; characters in, 46; development of, 43; as fiction, 42–47; humorous, 85; image of, 46; literary elements in, 43; postmodern, 46; with problem-solution structures, 126
pictures. *See* illustrations
Pictures of Hollis Woods (Giff), 9
Pink and Say (Polacco), 95
plots: exploration of, 124–31; features of, 34; in fiction, 33; reading for, 137–41; structure of, 34; types of, 127–28
poetry, 4, 31; categories of, 55; for children, 154; collections of, 153–54; in curriculum, 188–90; exploration of, 153–59; features of, 157–59; as nonfiction, 54–56; performances of, 154–57; in rounds, 156–57; sharing of, 153–54; teaching of, 157–59; tools for, 55; in two parts, 155–56; types of, 56; voices in unison, 154–55
Polacco, Patricia, 95, 179
Poor Richard's Almanack (Franklin), 53
Potter, Beatrix, 3, 40–41
Pullman, Philip, 94

RAFT (role, audience, format, and topic), 165
Ragged Dick (Alger), 123
The Ramsay Scallop (Temple), 128
Rappaport, Doreen, 87
Rathman, Peggy, 42
read-alouds, 110; after, 98; characters in, 97; introduction in, 97–98; for literary development, 94; preparation for, 96–97; research on, 94–95; selection for, 96; of stories, 98; timing of, 95–96
reader responses: cultural perspective on, 17–20; four perspectives on, 14
reading: benefits of, 150; choice for, 79; comprehension of, 3–4, 31, 94, 133, 150, 203–4; critical, 4; of *Freedom in Congo Square*, 67–68; importance of, 1;

independent, 92; in kindergarten, 86–87; for plots, 137–41; promotion of, 90–92; responses to, 175; rewards of, 94. *See also* close reading
reading areas. *See* library centers
reading level, 86
The Reading Teacher, 85
reading workshops: in classrooms, 90–91; launching of, 91; success of, 91
ReadWriteThink, 32
Recorvits, Helen, *10*
Red Knit Cap Girl (Stoop), *45*
religion, 129–30
Renaissance Learning, 159
research: of *Freedom in Congo Square*, 67; on meaning making, 11–13; by Morrow, 80; on read-alouds, 94–95; on responses, 15–16; by Sipe, 11
responses: evolution of, 16–17; to literature, 141–48. *See also* reader responses
Return to Sender (Alvarez), 136, 192
Revolution (Wiles), 10, *10*
Reynolds, Aaron, 92
Rocco, John, 43
Rohmann, Eric, 44
role, audience, format, and topic. *See* RAFT
Roll of Thunder, Hear My Cry (Taylor), 136
Roser, Nancy, 94–95, 175, 192
Rosie's Walk (Hutchins), 43
Ross, Stewart, 53
Rossetti, Christina, 156–57
Rowling, J. K., 135
Ryan, Pam Muñoz, 5, 114–15, 135, *135*

Sachar, Louis, 7, 123, 129, 130, 135
Sarah, Plain and Tall (MacLachlan), 48
Saul, Wendy, 160–61
"Save the Last Word for Me," 148, 151
Say, Allen, 99
The Scarecrow and His Servant (Pullman), 94
Scary Stories to Tell in the Dark (Schwartz), 100
Schmidt, Gary, 41–42
Scholastic Books, 162
Scholes, Robert, 122
Schwartz, Alvin, 100
Scieszka, Jon, 6, 137, 173
Scotland, 158
Seeds of Change (Johnson), 9

self-consciousness, 120
Selznick, Brian, 1
Sendak, Maurice, 174–75
"sequential art," 49
Service, Robert, 157–58
settings: of books, 117; exploration of, 113; in fiction, 32; geographical, 114–15; historical, 113–14; place for, 116; questions about, 114, 115; social groups, 117; time as, 114. *See also* social settings
The Shakespeare Stealer (Blackwood), 32
Sheinkin, Steve, 52
"Shen Kuo" (Wong), 188
Shiloh (Naylor), 115–17, 120, 123, 132–33, 141, 142
Sibert Informational Book Award, 84
Sipe, Lawrence, 11, 15–16, 47, 175
The Skunk, *179*
Skype, 93, 94
slavery, 68; illustrations of, *70–77*; in literature, 173
Smith, Elizabeth, 17
Smith, Scott, 4
Snakes (Bishop, N.), 54
social dimensions, 150
social justice, 9
social perspective, 16–17
social settings: close ups of, 117–18; questions about, 116–17, 118; wide view of, 115–17
Sorry! (Ludwig), 130
Souriau, Etienne, 121–22
Special Delivery (Stead), *178*
Spiegelman, Art, 49
Spinelli, Jerry, 135–36
Spot (Wiesner), 50
SSR (sustained silent reading), 90
Stead, Phillip, 35, 44–45, *178*
Stead, Rebecca, 6, 29
Stella by Starlight (Draper), 64
Stevenson, Robert Louis, 158
The Stinky Cheese Man and Other Fairly Stupid Tales (Scieszka), 6
Stone Fox (Gardiner), 122
Stoop, Naoko, *45*
stories: bildungsroman, 127–28; clues in, 7; coming-of-age, 127–28; conflict in, 33; critical moments of, 149; didactic tales, 129–31; dramatizing of, 148–49;

exaggeration, 178; family stories, 100; flashbacks in, 129; folktales, 101; friend-of-a-friend stories, 100; immersing students in, 149; immigration, 191–93, *192*; introduction to, 97–98; jokes, 100; journey, 128–29; learning, 101–3; legends, 101; moralistic tales, 129–31; myths, 101; personal stories, 100; power of, 31; practice for, 102–3; read-alouds of, 98; reflection of, 149; riddles, 100; scary stories, 100; scenes of, 149; side coaches of, 149; situation segments of, 149; within stories, 129; tall tales, 101; types of, 99–101; word choices in, 102

story elements, 137–39

story map, 127

story structure, 126–27

The Storyteller's Beads (Kurtz), 99

storytelling, 99–103

Strega Nona (dePaola), 41

Stringbean's Trip to the Shining Sea (Williams, J. and Williams, V.), 129

Structuralism in Literature (Scholes), 122

structure: recognizing, 4–5; of texts, 4–5

students: comprehension of, 133; discussions for, 146–47; drawings of, 133; engaging, 187; grade levels of, 89; immersion of, 149; individual interests of, 89–90; inspiring of, 131; morals of, 131; opportunities of, 104; reaching all, 39, 86, 132, 183

subgenres: of fiction, 36–42; literary elements of, 37–38; of nonfiction, 54–56

Sugar Changed the World (Aronson and Budhos), 7–8

Sullivan, Robert, *162*

Summer of the Mariposas (McCall), 128–29

sustained silent reading. *See* SSR

The Tale of Despereaux (DiCamillo), 82

The Tale of Peter Rabbit (Potter), 3, 40–41

Tan, Shaun, *191*

Taylor, Mildred, 136

Teach a Donkey to Fish (Smith), 4

teachers: on authors, 93; on culture, 87, 89; recommendations by, 175; responsibilities of, 103–4; role of, 31. *See also* classrooms; Hernandez, Moises; students

TeachingBooks.net, 20

Teague, Mark, 42–43, 84, *85*

Teale, William, 50

techniques, 12

technology tip, 10, 20, 32, 56, 92, 94, 115, 180, 183

Temple, Frances, 128

text: craft of, 4–5; discussion of, 163–64; of *Freedom in Congo Square*, 67; in illustrations, 76–77; preparation for, 163; structure of, 4–5

themes: in actions, 133; challenges of, 132; exploration of, 131–34; of fiction, 35; in images, 133; inferences of, 35; questions of, 133; in statements, 132–33

time lines, 164

Titanic: Voices from the Disaster (Hopkinson), 51–52, 54

Too Tall Houses (Marino), 33

Tower, Cathy, 13

traditional literature, 177; categories of, 40; as fiction, 36–39

transmedia storytelling, 92

trickster tales: in fiction, 41; in literary units, 177

The Troll with No Heart in His Body and Other Tales of Trolls from Norway (Lunge-Larsen), 177

Trout, Bucksnort, 155–56

The True Story of the Three Little Pigs (Scieszka), 137, 173

Tubman, Harriet, 88

Turtle in Paradise (Holm), 124

twenty-first century, 2–6, 64–65

units. *See* literary units

value line, 147–48

Van Allsburg, Chris, 96

Vanderpool, Clare, 8, 113–14, 118, 129, 133

Vardell, Sylvia, 153, 188–91

video games, 88

visual elements, 45

Voices in the Park (Browne), 4, 96

Wally's Stories: Conversations in the Kindergarten (Paley), 12–13

Walt Whitman: Words for America (Kerley), 95

The War That Saved My Life (Bradley), 48
The Watsons Go to Birmingham—1963
    (Curtis), 3–4, 113–15
Watts, Franklin, 162
Weatherford, Carole Boston, 67–77, 69, 88
Wiesner, David, 50, 64
What Came from the Stars (Schmidt),
    41–42
What Do You Do with a Tail Like This?
    (Jenkins and Page), 81
When You Reach Me (Stead, R.), 6, 29
Where the Wild Things Are (Sendak), 5, 174
Who Is Malala Yousafzai? (Brown and
    Thompson), 163
Why Mosquitoes Buzz in People's Ears
    (Aardema), 101
The Widow's Broom (Van Allsburg), 96
Wiggins, Grant, 175, 190–91
Wiles, Deborah, 10, *10*, 64
Willem, Mo, 86
Williams, Anne, 17

Williams, Jennifer, 129
Williams, Vera, 129
Williams-Garcia, Rita, 116–18
Winnie-the-Pooh (Milne), 94
Wolf, Shelby, 122
The Wolf's Chicken Stew (Kasza), 87
Wonder (Palacio), 116–19, 122–23, 132
Wong, Janet, 153, 188–90
Woodson, Jacqueline, 29
Working Cotton (Williams, A.), 17

The Year of the Dog (Lin), 96, 97
Yep, Laurence, 192
Yokota, Junko, 50
Yolen, Jane, 173
You Read to Me, I'll Read to You (Hoberman),
    87

Z Is for Moose (Bingham), 43
zodiac symbols, 121–22. *See also* Souriau,
    Etienne

About the Authors

Miriam G. Martinez teaches reading and children's literature courses at the University of Texas at San Antonio. She is actively involved in the Children's Literature Assembly, the National Council of Teachers of English, the International Literacy Association, and the Literacy Research Association. Her research and publications focus on the nature of children's literary meaning making, children's responses to literature, and their understanding of various literary genres and formats. She also conducts content analyses of children's books.

Charles Temple teaches children's literature, storytelling, writing for children, and international education at Hobart and William Smith Colleges in upstate New York. He is active in the International Literacy Association, the National Storytelling Network, the Society of Children's Book Writers and Illustrators, and the Comparative and International Education Society. Besides works for children, he has coauthored many books in the literacy and children's literature fields. He promotes children's book development and teaching for critical thinking in many countries around the world, currently in Liberia, Sierra Leone, and Tanzania. He lives with his wife, Codruta, in Geneva, New York. They have five children, two grandchildren, and a spirited springer spaniel named Jackie.

Junko Yokota directs the Center for Teaching through Children's Books and is professor emeritus of National Louis University in Chicago. Her research focuses on visual narratives in picture books, multicultural and international literature, digital storytelling, and literacy instruction through quality literature. She has held research fellowships at the International Youth Library in Munich, the Prussian Heritage Foundation at the Staatsbibliothek in Berlin, and a Fulbright Fellowship at the University of Wrocław in Poland. She has served on numerous awards committees such as the Caldecott, Newbery, and Batchelder, and she has served on international juries such as Bologna, Nami, and the Hans Christian Andersen. She lives in Evanston, Illinois, with her husband, William Teale.